THE MAGICIAN'S DOUBTS

THE MAGICIAN'S DOUBTS

Nabokov and the Risks of Fiction

Michael Wood

PRINCETON UNIVERSITY PRESS
PRINCETON, NEW JERSEY

Published by Princeton University Press,
41 William Street, Princeton,
New Jersey 08540
Copyright © 1994 by Michael Wood

First published in the United Kingdom by Chatto & Windus Limited,
Random House, 20 Vauxhall Bridge Road,
London SW1V 2SA
Published in the United States of America by Princeton University
Press in 1995, by license with Random House UK

Library of Congress Cataloging-in-Publication Data
Wood, Michael, 1936–
The magician's doubts : Nabokov and the risks of
fiction / Michael Wood.
p. cm.
Includes bibliographical references and index.
ISBN 0-691-00632-6
1. Nabokov, Vladimir Vladimirovich, 1899–1977
—Criticism and interpretation. I. Title.
PS3527.A15Z96 1995
813'.54—dc20

Princeton University Press books are printed on acid-free paper
and meet the guidelines for permanence and durability of the
Committee on Production Guidelines for Book Longevity
of the Council on Library Resources

Printed in the United States of America
by Princeton Academic Press

3 5 7 9 10 8 6 4 2

for Gaby

Contents

Acknowledgements

My warm thanks to Malcolm Bradbury, Janice Price and Belinda Dearbergh for getting me started on this work; to Paul Barker, Brian Boyd, Hermione Lee, Luke Menand and Jonathan Steinberg for alert and sympathetic readings of pieces of it; and to Jenny Uglow for her enthusiasm and delicacy, and her understanding of the sort of book it wants to be.

My friends and colleagues and students at Exeter know I owe them more than I can say; but I should like others to know that too.

Preface:
Tricks of Loss

There was once a Russian writer, let's call him V, who was prodigiously gifted: learned, intelligent, observant, inventive. He wrote poems, plays and novels, but above all novels, and in the first part of his career he built up a considerable reputation in the limited but distinguished circles of those who could read him: Russians abroad, other non-Soviet readers of Russian. One such reader, herself a novelist, said V's book about a tormented chess genius was certainly the best novel of the emigration; later she said it was the best Russian novel of the century.

By the time he was 23, V had lost much of what anyone can lose: his country (renamed, repossessed), his father (murdered), most of his family (dispersed into various exiles). What he had, what he would always have, were style and memory, and the abiding love of (genitive and accusative) the woman he married three years later. He wrote an eloquent autobiography insisting on how little is lost, even in the midst of terrible losses; a long, brilliant novel about the possibility of happiness, the brightness and specificity of its detail, compared with the dark monotony of sorrow. It is not happy families that are all alike, as Tolstoy suggested; it is unhappy families.

V stayed in Berlin for some years, learning almost as little German as he later claimed he did; then briefly in Paris; then the United States, where he made a living by teaching the Russian language and Russian and European literature. A scandalous book brought him late and surprising fame and wealth, and he moved to a hotel in Switzerland, where he continued to write, enjoying both glory and privacy, and died at the age of 78, a man who told his son that he had accomplished what he wished in life and art.

This is a success story, and nothing should take its success away. It records courage and dignity, discreet concern for members of the family and for history's victims, and almost incredible amounts of hard, unseen labour – the more we learn about V's life, the more he seems to have devoted it to the scruples of his art, almost literally acting out the self-extinction T S Eliot preached (but couldn't practise) as the condition of artistic progress. The very lightness of V's novels conceals mountains of weighty preparation; the slightest

1

glance or joke often depends on hours of pedantry, summoned, worked through, and abolished, as if Ariel needed Prospero's books, but also needed to let them go. Or as if art were itself a morality, a form of cathedral sculpture demanding all the more care because it may well be seen only by God. V's letters are a wonderful lesson in this respect: his friends often miss his meaning, but he accepts their misses as an aspect of art's risk, a stance which must be a form of humility if it is not a form of arrogance. Only once, to an editor, does V explain at length an overlooked subtlety, and there is both pathos and a sense of futility in the explanation. If explanations are needed, someone has failed, either writer or reader, or perhaps both. Even success stories must skirt failure, fall into it at times.

And we can ask questions even about undeniable successes. Hard work and dignity, discretion in sorrow and an acceptance of good fortune, are all fine things, but they are also compatible with great pride and a mandarin indifference to much of what matters to other people. Even V's fortitude, his patience in his American obscurity, may be a sort of hauteur: of course they don't know who I am, but then who are they? Light novels *are* light novels, whatever weight lies behind them. At this point, our ideas of V begin to multiply. The man you admire seems to me too cautious, complacent even in his courage – it's easy to be brave when you offer life no hostages, or have given up on all but the tiniest number of chances of damage. The writer who so moves me can't really be the one you find so trivial, so self-regarding, so dedicated to tinkling and twinkling prose: must be another fellow with the same signature. We don't need to resolve these differences, and probably couldn't resolve them anyway. But they are worth exploring, and the point of this introductory fable is to suggest a story within V's story.

It is an obvious story, an open secret, but it may help us to re-describe V's performances, both in life and in art. It concerns language, and a loss which is neither denied nor accepted but painfully courted and dutifully embraced, as if it were death itself and also the only gate to a second life; loss reconstrued as discovery.

I call the story a fable because although the facts I mention belong to the life of a historical person, Vladimir Nabokov, and are as accurate as such facts can be, I am guessing about the mentality behind the facts, and I don't want to hide the guesswork. I call the man V not to deny his connection to the historical Nabokov, but to refuse too narrow and inflexible and immediate a connection, and to leave room for others. This V is my Nabokov, if you like; or one

2

of my Nabokovs; I'll call him Nabokov from now on. But I do also want to suggest that this life itself really is a sort of fable, as all achieved careers are: exemplary, purified, haunting. It is a writer's life, the life of a person who became, as he said, 'almost exclusively a writer'. His Swiss tombstone, with admirable accuracy and completeness, simply says *Vladimir Nabokov écrivain 1899-1977*.

Nabokov was born in St Petersburg and died in Montreux. The Russian novelist I mentioned is Nina Berberova, and the novel she regarded so highly was *The Defence*, 1930, one of ten novels Nabokov wrote in Russian while he was living in Berlin. His father was assassinated there in 1922 by right-wing Russian terrorists. The woman Vladimir Nabokov married, in 1925, was Véra Slonim; their only child, Dmitri, was born nine years later. Nabokov's autobiography, written in the United States – having fled from Russia to Germany in 1917, and from Germany to France in 1937, the Nabokovs found themselves fleeing from France in 1940 – is *Speak, Memory*, 1951. Nabokov taught at Wellesley, Harvard, Cornell, developing, as he put it, describing his weight as well as his status, from lean lecturer to full professor. In America he wrote the novels *Bend Sinister, Lolita* and *Pnin*, and worked on his translation of *Eugene Onegin*. After his retirement from Cornell in 1959 and his move to Switzerland in 1961, he completed *Pale Fire*, and wrote *Ada* (the long novel about the possibility of happiness), *Transparent Things* and *Look At The Harlequins*.

'Some day,' Nabokov told a friend, 'a sagacious professor will write about my absolutely tragic situation'. He was being whimsical, but more about the imagined professor's sagacity than about his own intensely felt plight. The 'situation' was the one created by his abandonment, soon after his arrival in America, of Russian as a language for the writing of fiction. He continued to speak Russian, and to write verse in Russian, but seems to have made a stern vow to himself about prose. He felt 'a terrible desire to write, and write in Russian,' he said to his wife in a letter, 'but it's impossible. I don't think that anyone who has not experienced these feelings can properly appreciate them, the torment, the tragedy.' *But it's impossible*. Part of the torment must have been the obscurity of the need for this horrible self-deprivation. The critic and biographer Andrew Field speaks of 'the intensity of pain which Nabokov experienced at the loss of his native language. He told me that it equalled in many respects and was a logical continuation of the pain he had experienced at the loss of Russia.' But Nabokov didn't *lose* his native language, he forswore the use of it for the purpose which most mattered to him. He became a phantom in his own prose, as if, he said, he had created the person who wrote in English but was not himself doing the writing. What Nabokov describes as a logical continuation of an earlier loss is, I think, a voluntary miming of that loss, an assumption of it as a kind of destiny. His vow was an acknowledgement of loss in the deepest, closest sense, the worst loss he could imagine for a writer, stylistic exile without end.

Before he left Europe, Nabokov had translated two of his Russian novels (*Laughter in the Dark* and *Despair*) into English, and in 1938-1939 had written a novel directly in English, *The Real Life of Sebastian Knight*, a remarkable work still severely underrated. He had known English since childhood, and had a degree from Cambridge. None of this amounts to a 'loss' of Russian, or seems to require it; and in letters Nabokov spoke casually of writing both in Russian and in English ('I have lain with my Russian muse after a long period of adultery'; 'I get more and more dissatisfied with my English. When I have finished [my book on Gogol], I shall take a three months' vacation with my ruddy robust Russian muse'). There is an element of bravado here, perhaps, and Nabokov said quite correctly that his 'private tragedy' was no one's business but his own. However, there is a rather complicated *double-entendre* at work, since Nabokov kept announcing the very tragedy he said was no one's business, and the tragedy itself was not quite where he said (and no doubt at the time believed) it was. This is one of the rare cases where Nabokov complains of his historical fate; and it is, symptomatically, a fate which seems almost entirely self-imposed.

Earlier Nabokov said he was 'too old to change Conradically'; later that he 'had to' give up his Russian, his 'natural idiom', his 'untrammeled, rich, and infinitely docile Russian tongue for a second-rate brand of English'. He compared his 'palatial Russian' to the 'narrow quarters' of his English, said the change was 'like moving from one darkened house to another on a starless night during a strike of candlemakers and torchbearers.' The houses are both dark, presumably, because Russian was already a language of exile, a language in shadow. The switch was 'exceedingly painful – like learning anew to handle things after losing seven or eight fingers in an explosion', although Nabokov also said he thought his Russian poems improved 'rather oddly in urgency and concentration' as a result of his abandonment of Russian prose. These images clearly tell an eloquent emotional truth even as they drastically simplify historical circumstance.

Certainly Nabokov 'had to' write in English if he wanted to

make some money and reach an audience other than that of émigrés, but why couldn't he write in Russian as well? He 'had to' give up Russian, it seems, not only in order to sell books in English but in order to write the English he wanted to write, to shake off the spectre of his Russian. He said in the same letter to his wife, rather oddly, that 'I myself don't fully register all the grief and bitterness of my situation'. The implication, clearly, is that a writer cannot, as a writer, have two languages, a view which makes Nabokov quite different from Samuel Beckett, for example, who wrote in French and English, and perhaps from most bi-lingual authors.

Much later, Nabokov translated his autobiography into Russian, and found himself 'after fifteen years of absence, wallowing in the bitter luxury of my Russian verbal might.' It was bitter, but it was luxury. Later still, translating his most famous novel into Russian, Nabokov spoke not of luxury, but of deprivation, a long-awaited linguistic springtime that had turned to autumn in his absence. His 'marvellous Russian language' had 'proved to be non-existent'. There are those who agree with this judgement, and those who disagree, and I can't judge at all. What matters, surely, is that Nabokov in the meantime had found, through his very loss, a fabulous, freaky, singing, acrobatic, unheard-of English which (probably) made even his most marvellous Russian seem poor, and therefore meant that the terrible decision of his early years in America had been right, that the second language could flower for him only at the cost of the first; had to become itself a new first language, a language to write in. Perhaps one cannot *love* two languages. Rising to the suggestion that his 'mastery of English almost rivals Joseph Conrad's', Nabokov protested: 'Conrad knew how to handle *readymade* English better than I; but I know better the other kind. He never sinks to the depths of my solecisms, but neither does he scale my verbal peaks.' The other kind: the kind you invent (one of Nabokov's favourite words) as a writer.

There is a passage in Nabokov's autobiography which constructs memory and understanding as a function of loss rather than as a redemption of it. Nabokov wonders whether he has missed something in his French governess: 'something ... that I could appreciate only after the things and beings that I had most loved in the security of my childhood had been turned to ashes or shot through the heart.' Nabokov could appreciate language itself only after he had made himself lose a language, and had found another in the ashes of his loss.

It is possible too – this is the heart and drift of my fable – that

Nabokov came to understand deprivation, marginality and help-lessness as well as he did through his abandonment of Russian as a literary language. He was a connoisseur of loss long before he went to America, of course, and a great denier of loss too, much attached to the idea of a world or a state of consciousness 'where nothing is lost'. But there does seem to be a sense in which neither his early losses nor his denials of them shook him or cost him as they might have – as they would have shaken or cost almost anyone else. He had retained, as Elizabeth Beaujour puts it in her book *Alien Tongues*, a 'profound sense of spiritual security, a knowledge of who and what he was that was totally independent of external status and of property . . .' This is what others, less kindly, call Nabokov's arrogance. We might also say the knowledge and the sense were dependent on Nabokov's *having had* external status and property in abundance, and a family pride which, thoroughly internalized, could insure him mentally against almost any kind of loss. *This* writer was too self-sufficient, too armoured against doubt to have written Nabokov's later novels, and this is the writer we meet in Nabokov's prefaces and classrooms and sundry truculent pronouncements about literature and life. The *other* writer, the one who gave up the literary language he had worked on and in for twenty years, and discovered thereby for the first time – at what level of intention I do not know – the intimate meanings of uncertainty, of exclusion, disarray, clumsiness and poverty, has a humanity the first writer lacks, or if you prefer, finds the humanity the first writer was so keen to hide.

Pleasure is not always innocent but it is usually honest, and a fairly reliable critical witness. The rather disconcerting pleasures of reading Nabokov are at the heart of this book, but the questions those pleasures raise reach beyond Nabokov into all kinds of corners of fiction and reading. They are old questions, but always in need of new asking. 'Curiosity,' a character remarks in *Bend Sinister*, 'is insubordination in its purest form.' Our subject, we might say, is Nabokov's restless and stylish insubordination; but also our own insubordination as readers, of Nabokov or anyone else – the weird mixture of loyalty and insurrection which constitutes any active response to a work of the imagination.

Nabokov's work, across a whole set of mannerisms and defences, indeed across its intermittent claims to be philosophical in a conventional, rather dated sense, is consistently philosophical in the way that much of the best contemporary fiction is: serious and playful, serious because playful. The questions raised often concern the role of irony and silence, and the nature and uses of fiction – fiction as estimate, hypothesis, framework, model, instance, experiment, downright lying. Nabokov's devious narratives thus turn into practical metaphors for this aspect of their business. They are not about philosophy in this sense, they are philosophy; not writing *on* topics, as Roland Barthes says in an autobiographical essay, just writing. This may seem to stretch or shift the notion of philosophy, and perhaps it does. I certainly don't want to claim the dignity of formal philosophy for Nabokov's novels or for what I have to say of them; or to topple fiction and philosophy into a single soup of speculation. But philosophy can be done (has been done) through riddles and fables and jokes as well as propositions, and criticism and philosophy probably need to get together here, and wherever meaning is plural and intricately determined by its situation. If novelists do this kind of philosophy they don't cease to be novelists and it isn't all they do. It is one of the grounds where they meet their readers.

Another ground, crucial in Nabokov but very hard to discuss, is the ethical. This is the realm of the unspeakable for Nabokov, but it is none the less (or for that very reason) everywhere implicit in his work. He is neither the aesthete that he himself and his early readers kept making out he was, nor the plodding moralist that recent criticism, with an audible sigh of relief, has wheeled on to the page. Moral questions, like epistemological ones, are put to work in his fiction. Nabokov doesn't write about them; he writes them.

I see the exploration of these moral and philosophical grounds as the work of commentary, but in a rather different spirit from Nabokov's long commentary on *Eugene Onegin*. His project there is to take us to a place and a time where we have never been, to offer historical notes on the clothes, food, manners, persons, language and the rest of another, lost world. The commentary that I have in mind is an intense, even intimate dialogue with provocative texts; a report on the adventure of reading. Like all adventures, it has its risks; among the things we shall almost certainly lose is our certainty. But to lose certainty is not to lose understanding or knowledge. What remains is a demonstrable richness in the texts themselves, not so much meaning as a set of possibilities of meaning, a syntactical or structural chance of what I shall call wisdom but would be happy to give a more modest name. Texts we care about will both resist and reward us; not necessarily in that order.

I have concentrated on Nabokov's works in English, but the Russian works, especially *The Defence* and *The Gift*, have also been much in my mind. 'We think not in words but in shadows of words,' Nabokov said, and the shadow of his Russian helps us with the shadow of his English. The absent language reminds us of the many absences in Nabokov's seemingly so complete and confident later prose. Nabokov was too elegant, too much the literary dandy, to let us see him groping, for words or anything else – he never gave interviews without advance notice of the questions, or without having carefully written out and rehearsed his answers, although he did implausibly fake spontaneity now and again. But doubt is what we find lurking in his apparent assurance, like death in Arcady. He is an unsettling writer as well as a funny one because he is deep where he looks shallow, moving when he seems flippant. He is still the conjuror he remembers being as a child. 'I loved doing simple tricks – turning water into wine, that kind of thing.' Simple tricks, but hard to follow.

I

Deaths of the Author

*'To write is not to engage in an easy
relationship with an average of all possible
readers, it is to engage in a difficult
relationship with our own language ...'*

Roland Barthes, *Criticism and Truth*

(i)

Vladimir Nabokov died on 2 July 1977. It was his last afternoon as
himself, as Auden said of the day of Yeats's death: 'he became his
admirers' – and his detractors and his publishers and anyone who
cares to take one of his books from a shelf. He became a memory;
disappeared into his name, rhyming with 'cough' and almost always
associated with *Lolita*, as in 'Don't Stand So Close to Me', 1986, the
murky popular song by The Police ('He starts to shake, he starts to
cough,/Just like the old man in/That famous book by Nabokov').

It is one of the mysteries of death that it should seem, in the case
of an artist or anyone with a public face, to make so little difference
to all but those close to the person. What has changed? There will
be no more books, tunes, painting, films, acts from that source. But
what if there weren't many, or any, such performances still to
come, what if the work's epilogue or aftermath had already started?
What if the work we have is already rich and deep, enough for a
lifetime? What more do we want? We shall not be able to meet the
person we probably should not have met anyway; we shall not
write the letters she/he might not have answered. Such deaths are
like the deaths of acquaintances we have not seen for ages, would
never have seen again. A scarcely perceptible shift in what was
already an absence.

But the deaths of figures whose work we care about do diminish
us, take away a piece of our world, even if we can't quite say how
our world is poorer. These persons were not persons for us, but

9

they were not mere reputations either. They were habits of affection, ways of looking and thinking; they altered, as Catherine Earnshaw says of her dreams, the colour of our mind. This life of theirs cannot be changed by their deaths; can be changed only by our death or involvement in some other form of mental wreckage. But there's the rub. The Argentinian writer Julio Cortázar has an intimate, unforgettable note on just this subject:

> After the age of fifty we begin to die little by little in the deaths of others ... Sometimes we no longer thought much about them, they'd remained behind in history ... In some way they were still there, but like paintings no longer viewed as in the beginning, poems that only vaguely scent our memory.
>
> Then – everyone has his beloved ghosts, his major interceders – the day arrives when the first of them horribly bursts out in the newspaper and radio scene. Maybe we'll take some time to realize that our death has begun on that day too; I knew it that night when in the middle of dinner someone indifferently alluded to a television news item that said Jean Cocteau had just died in Milly-la-Forêt ...
>
> The rest have followed along ... Louis Armstrong, Pablo Picasso, Igor Stravinsky, Duke Ellington, and last night, while I was coughing in a hospital in Havana, last night in a friend's voice that brought the rumour from the outside world to my bed, Charles Chaplin. I shall leave this hospital, I shall leave cured, that's for certain, but, for a sixth time, a little less alive.

I would suggest only that one can begin this process much earlier or quite a bit later than fifty. Similarly, for Roland Barthes the 'middle of our life' was not a generalised, arithmetical point – thirty-five, say – but the day we *feel* we are going to die ('this is not a natural feeling; what's natural is to believe oneself immortal'), as distinct from abstractly knowing this mortal fact. Time in this context is a matter not of the clock but of chance and temperament.

I start with these mementoes because I am about to talk about deaths which are largely fictional and metaphorical (real too in their own modes) and want to make sure I give physical death its due: propitiation, perhaps, and a mark of piety towards what is actually irreplaceable, untransferable in those lives now gone. Nabokov in particular teaches us about particulars, offers to define reality 'as a kind of gradual accumulation of information; and as specialization'. 'In art as in science there is no delight without the detail'. 'I guess it's your father under that oak, isn't it?' a character asks in *Ada*. 'No,' Ada answers crisply, 'it's an elm'. The man referred to is nominally her father, and the questioner has no reason to go beyond the nominal. The gist of the question is therefore right, and Ada is chiefly indulging her passionate pedantry of the specific. But it is good to know an elm is not an oak; it may even be practice for knowing when a father is not a father.

(ii)

Like the rest of us, authors die at least twice. Once physically, once notionally; when the heart stops and when forgetting begins. The lucky ones, the great ones, are those whose second death is decently, perhaps indefinitely postponed. But there is another death of the author, most famously chronicled by Roland Barthes in an essay of 1968 and modelled on the death of God. To die in this sense is to be unmasked as a fiction, as a figment of faith. 'Death' reveals that there has been no life, only a dream of life. The historical fact that both dreams – of God and author – have been real for so long and for so many people, and indeed are in several respects the same dream, is what makes the metaphor so powerful. This late lapse in critical or religious belief can only seem like a violent event, a death or murder rather than a defection or a discovery. For Nietzsche the 'immense event' of God's death is so sudden that even the murderers have not realized what they have done. The occurrence, Nietzsche says, is 'still on the way' to them, further off than the furthest stars.

The death of the author, similarly, has not caught on in publishing circles, and certainly it is tactless, when living writers are present, to insist on their absence. Even dead authors can be frisky, leaving letters, interviews, articles and autobiographical memoirs all over the place. But these persistences should not obscure the interest of Barthes' scenario. We can see the death of the author as a recent entry in a long series of modern metaphors for the difference that writing makes, a series that begins, or at least comes to emphatic consciousness, in Flaubert. 'No lyricism,' was his prescription for *Madame Bovary*, 'no reflections, personality of the author absent.' 'The artist must so arrange things that posterity will not believe he ever lived.' This not a death but an apparent abdication; a swerve or erasure. Flaubert was also interested in ostensible absence as a step to omnipotence or a proper hauteur, a form of rhetorical hygiene.

The author in his work must be like God in the universe: present

11

everywhere, and visible nowhere ... The effect, for the spectator, must be a kind of astonishment. 'How has that been done?' they must say, and they will feel crushed without knowing why.

Joyce's Stephen Dedalus fastidiously prolongs and parodies this view: 'The artist, like the God of the creation, remains within or behind or beyond or above his handiwork, invisible, refined out of existence, indifferent, paring his fingernails.'

But Flaubert and Joyce are talking strategy, considering ways of seeming to be absent, but only seeming. So was Mallarmé, when he said the 'pure work implies the elocutionary disappearance of the poet, who yields the initiative to the words ...' We are still a long way from Barthes, and from the echoing absences explored by Jacques Derrida in his work on difference and deferment and dissemination. T S Eliot too, the most famous and most strenuous of the apostles of impersonality, was talking strategy rather than theory, only his strategy was moral rather than technical, a school of abstinence.

> The progress of an artist is a continual self-sacrifice, a continual extinction of personality ... Poetry is not a turning loose of emotion, but an escape from emotion; it is not the expression of personality, but an escape from personality. But, of course, only those who have personality and emotions know what it means to want to escape from these things.

Impersonality, as becomes clear in the cautious middle of that last sentence ('know what it means to want to'), is a desperate dream, a sort of cleansing of the merely personal. It happens, by miracle or some extraordinary feat of asceticism (in *Macbeth* and *Coriolanus*, Eliot says, not in *Hamlet* or the *Sonnets*), but it doesn't happen often, and scarcely at all, Eliot's tone suggests, to us. It is an ethic for writers, not a description of writing.

The modern writers who do bring us close to Barthes and Derrida, and to the form of authorial death which mainly concerns me here, are Yeats and Proust. 'The poet,' Yeats said, 'is never the bundle of accident and incoherence that sits down to breakfast'. Proust said the same more generally for the writer: 'a book is the product of another self (*un autre moi*) than the one we display in our habits, in society, in our vices'. These are metaphors too, of course, but psychological and critical rather than technical or moral. They project second, writing personalities, like the ghostly twin a writer has in Henry James' story 'The Private Life', scribbling away in the man's room while the chap himself dines in society, chats, takes walks, plays billiards.

Effectively, such metaphors identify the writer with the text, with the labour rather than the labourer, and they declare the text's independence from its often messy origins. The text for Eliot is an achievement, an abnegation, it is where we see the (nearly) vanished author on the way out. For Yeats and Proust the text secedes, makes such struggles irrelevant or forgettable. It is where writers learn, retroactively, who they were *as writers*, what else they were apart from the persons having breakfast. In the material, historical world, the separation can hardly be so neat or dramatic, although the illustration is vivid and helpful. The author who suffers, is amused, has intentions, second thoughts, makes mistakes, patiently lines words up one after another, cannot actually be sacked or severed in this way – or not unless we allow a radical shift in our notion of what a ghost-writer is. Even the strictest of the American New Critics of the 1940s, pursuing what they called the intentional fallacy to its various lairs, acknowledge the historical author as a *cause* of a work's existence. Equally, a text cannot be reduced to or equated with an author's project, the weight of desire and need, the mere will to work, independent of effect and achievement. The question is not whether the metaphors are metaphors, but what force and application they have, how we are to use them or reject them.

Nabokov's practice in fiction aligns him with Flaubert and Joyce, but his work in criticism and translation bring him closer to Yeats and Proust. We are not, he says, to 'search for "real life" in the dead ends of art', where 'dead ends' is a compliment, a tribute, a perverse pointer to the finished object. 'In art, purpose and plan are nothing; only the result counts. We are concerned only with the structure of a published work'. 'Structure' is a word Nabokov often uses to mask and distance the questions we are looking at; a figure for the writtenness of writing. He distinguishes categorically, not between the person and the writer but between their precise shadows: two kinds of reader/commentator. 'As Pushkin's historian,' he says, he gloats over all the verses omitted from the final version of *Eugene Onegin*. 'As a fellow writer, I deplore the existence of many trivial scribblings, stillborn drafts, and vague variants that Pushkin should have destroyed.' The same person, Nabokov is suggesting, can be historian and judge, biographer and critic – and in this he is following the purest New Critical orthodoxy with regard to authorial intention – but he or she can't do both jobs at the same time. And we can't edit texts to suit our own sense of the author, 'republish a dead author's works in the form we *think* he might have wished them to appear and endure' (Nabokov's italics). In one sense this argument confirms the author's death as a creature apart from the work. But it also means that the text is where the author triumphantly revives.

Introducing his translation of *Eugene Onegin*, 1964, Nabokov proposes an august and strenuous ideal of readership: 'Unless these and other mechanisms and every other detail of the text are consciously assimilated, *Eugene Onegin* cannot be said to exist in the reader's mind.' Every other detail; consciously assimilated; cannot be said to exist. These despotic phrases call for a long commentary, and in one sense this book is such a commentary. For the moment it will be enough to note that the textual result is assumed to be active in all its parts and moments, to leave no residue, or slack; that Nabokov makes no allowance for an unconscious effect on the reader, of the kind that Eliot and William Empson, in all their criticism, take to be very important; and that for Nabokov there is only one kind of reader, only one kind of 'existence' for a text, or at least for this text. 'Pushkin' would be a name for what we are reading, for the achieved design, if *Eugene Onegin* were not the name we wanted; but the historical Pushkin doesn't appear at all in this formulation – he belongs only to his historian. When Nabokov speaks of Pushkin as a figure in his own poem, he is emphatically clear that the autobiographical effect is stylized, a literary effect not a confession. The author is ubiquitous and absent, as in Flaubert; a cancellation of accident, as in Yeats; and a demand for meticulous attention, as in most modern writing.

(iii)

It is possible to see the author as neither dead nor alive, neither a second self nor a textual performance, but as mere paper. Swift has a very good joke along these lines in *The Battle of the Books*. I have suggested that modern dreams of impersonality begin with Flaubert, but modernity, here as elsewhere, is not so much a fresh start as a jogged memory, new only because all second and later chances are new in their way. 'I must warn the reader,' Swift says in an ostensible note from the Bookseller,

to beware of applying to persons what is here meant only of books in the most literal sense. So, when Virgil is mentioned, we are not to understand the person of a famous poet called by that name, but only certain sheets of paper, bound up in leather, containing in print the works of the said poet, and so of the rest.

'The most literal sense' is exact and limited, since the books here have been physically fighting, waging the war of the Ancients and Moderns: 'the Books in St James's Library, looking upon themselves as parties principally concerned, took up the controversy, and came to a decisive battle . . .' But the poker-faced assertion illustrates an important usage. Sheets of paper *are* often what we mean by an author, and all we mean, or in many cases, can mean. The joke also glances at the life of books, their independent career in the world, their ability to stand up for themselves, cause trouble; and it also reminds us of our muddle, of our eagerness to leap from text to writer, to forget the works for the person, thereby courting a kind of death of the text, as if only the personal mattered to us. There is probably another, swirling level to the joke too, which suggests that being a book is a form of grandeur, and if Homer and the classics are 'only' books, that is precisely what an Ancient is; the Moderns haven't yet got beyond being persons.

It is also possible to get thoroughly bewildered about authors, tumble from text to intention without quite knowing what we are doing.

> Student explains that when reading a novel he likes to skip passages 'so as to get his own idea about the book and not be influenced by the author'.

This is a note discarded during the writing of *Pale Fire*; a marvellously funny thought, but I'm curious about our amusement, about possible divergences within it. If we share the joke, do we share it like a ride, all of us in the same car, or like a cake, each of us taking a different piece? Does our (my) amusement have the same shape as Nabokov's? Is it a joke, for example, about the self-evident silliness of the student's plan, and therefore of certain famous tenets of the New Criticism, of the 1940s and after? How could we not be influenced by the author? What is reading if not submitting to such influence, to whatever authority we find in the words, even if we do have to find it rather than passively receive it? Whose could it be if not the author's? The joke then is not on the student but on the teachers, a whole school of criticism, confused from the start, confused in its deepest assumptions. Of course the New Criticism in no sense recommended skipping passages. On the contrary: it was emphatically committed to the whole text, and thereby to the textual, implied author; saw no one else. It was the supposedly extraneous biographical author, the hazy inferences lurking in known names, which were to be excluded from consideration; mere intention or reputation. We might intend a masterpiece and achieve a flop; even Shakespeare can be seen to nod, if you don't know she's Shakespeare. Nabokov's joke would then be on a dim idea of reader liberation, a parody in advance of Barthes' dismissal of the Author ('The birth of the reader must be at the cost of [*doit se payer de*] the death of the Author').

Or is the joke about getting the wrong end of an interesting idea? The student would be right not to want to be influenced by the separable or sermonizing author, by an author's meaning pictured as somehow distinct from the text, behind the text; only ludicrously mistaken in thinking skipping would help. Skipping in fact, Barthes would say, might well increase the author's influence, leave the reader without defence against presuppositions and prejudices. Or it might abolish the author's and all other influence, scrap the very act of imaginative reading. The fault though would lie not with a school of criticism but with a loopy misunderstanding of an important principle. One wouldn't have to be a New Critic to feel this way. When the American critic Lionel Trilling said in 1947 that *Hamlet* is 'not merely the product of Shakespeare's thought, it is the very instrument of his thought', and that 'if meaning is intention, Shakespeare did not intend . . . anything less than *Hamlet*', he was perhaps expressing precisely the idea the student mangled. The student's wish not to be influenced by the (textual) author is incoherent, merely comical; but it may be a muddled version of an attractive desire not to be bullied by teachers or gossip or duty; to attend (only not enough) to the text; to see reading as a form of creation.

Beyond these two interpretations there is a faint, offbeat comedy in the very wording of the student's thought, in the notion of a reader's being *influenced* by an author: it's too much and too little, a mixture of boast and tautology, as if we were to say we were influenced by our education. The author is not dead here but somehow both mislaid and inflated, and if we put the two jokes together, Swift's and Nabokov's, we get an interesting composite image of a genuine difficulty about sheets of paper and the persons

16

we find or fail to find in them. Reading is a material act, a retracing of a moment of writing, the author's influence is inescapable: we don't make a move without him or her. But the sheets of paper are also currency, forms of social behaviour, and their reach and effect will often go beyond anything we can call influence. Once words are in motion they cannot be revoked and won't always mean what we thought they meant, or wanted them to mean. Anyone who has ever quarrelled knows this; let alone anyone who has ever written, even a letter or a shopping list.

(iv)

Vladimir Nabokov can't have been much of a bundle of accident and incoherence even at breakfast, and he certainly endorsed Yeats' view of the artist as 'something intended, complete'. He appears to have treated much of his life as art in this sense, not out of a desire to deceive or hide but out of discretion and a belief that style begins at home. His privacy itself seems poised, a work of discipline. Even moments of horror come across as virtually unruffled. The night his father was assassinated in Berlin in 1922 Nabokov remembers as 'something *outside life*, monstrously slow, like those mathematical puzzles that torment us in feverish half-sleep'. This is an entry in a diary, not meant for publication. The torment must have been terrible, must have remained terrible, but this private language already holds it at bay, subordinates it to an imagery of distance and unreality. Nabokov's 'coldness' in novels and interviews is among other things a continuing act of courage, a refusal to be bullied by the rages and accidents of history, or by the possible pity of others. His fictional character Pnin, a comic Russian exile who is everything Nabokov was not, teaches himself 'never to remember' a girl he loved and who later died in Buchenwald, 'because, if one were quite sincere with oneself, no conscience, and hence no consciousness, could be expected to subsist in a world where such things as Mira's death were possible.' Nabokov always remembered such events, but his writing construed them obliquely, as a form of duelling with history: his art was an answer to what Pnin couldn't bear to think of.

There is therefore something comic in the recent attempts of Nabokov's son and others to redeem the writer for conventional kindness; the death of the author scored for muzak. Dmitri Nabokov is amazed that this lovable fellow could ever have been perceived as 'austere, cold, somehow inhuman', and John Updike, who should know better, says 'And, really, what a basically reasonable and decent man'. I don't doubt for a minute that Nabokov was reasonable and decent, and as kindly as the next great writer – kindlier than many, surely. But that isn't why we read him, and he himself spent a lifetime building an austere, cold and unreachable public persona, as immune as could possibly be from such soggy apologies. In a letter of 1954 he remarks that what others see as an '"unpleasant" quality' in a particular chapter of *Pnin* is actually 'a special trait of my work in general'. He doesn't mean his work *is* unpleasant, only that it doesn't shy from unpleasantness, perhaps even that it specializes in unpleasant matters; and by implication that being 'basically reasonable and decent', while charming for one's friends and family, can hardly be a serious part of the artist's business.

Nabokov insisted that 'the best part of a writer's biography is not the record of his adventures but the story of his style'. The biography is still paramount in this claim. The author is not dead or intending to die, he is seeking a perpetual controlling share in the interest his work arouses. But who would be the subject of this biography? The old, dead author after all? Is there an alternative? What are all the names littered about the above paragraphs if not the names of authors? Do 'style' and 'adventures', in spite of what Yeats and Proust say, simply belong to the same person? What does it mean to say they do or they don't? Is Nabokov, in these pages, in the title of this book, an implied historical person or the name of a performance, certain sheets of paper? How many Nabokovs are there, or how many do we need? We could ask these questions about any writer, of course, and probably should. About Marguerite Duras, for example, or Italo Calvino; about Milan Kundera or Jean Rhys. We shall get different answers in different cases, feel the need variously to narrow or widen the gap between author and text. But we can't make the gap go away, and in each case we shall get a whole deck of answers. The deck is what's interesting, I think. It gives us choices, and it may clear our heads about what it is we are choosing. If the death of the Author really is the birth of the reader, then the birth of the reader is the start of a whole family of (lowercase) authors. That is one way of saying what reading is.

(v)

To write is not to be absent but to become absent; to be someone and then go away, leaving traces. 'Writing', Barthes says, 'is the destruction of every voice, of every origin.' Well, writing is stealthier than this; it doesn't destroy, even at its most dramatic it only discreetly ruins our various dreams of immediacy, converts them to fragments, vestiges, questions. It replaces or rejects voice, abandons origin and moves on, it shakes off all secure, firmly guaranteed connection to its beginnings. It has to do this, can do no other; that is what writing is. It is important to see how simple, even pedestrian this idea can be. To speak of death or destruction is to express an amazement that we should still keep stumbling over it. All metaphorical absences are preceded, when we write, by the most literal absence possible. We can't be there when our friends read the message saying 'Back in a minute'. Or if we are there, the message is cancelled, not only untrue, but unwritten – unwritten, undone (as distinct from not done). Literary texts differ from this message in all kinds of ways, but resemble it in this crucial respect. Indeed the message is already literary in this sense: it needs reading, it can be misread or hesitated over. This is one of the things Jacques Derrida means by his intricate evocation of absence, and the idea is none the less deep and difficult for being so familiar. 'Every piece of writing is in essence a testament' (*Tout graphème est d'essence testamentaire*). Derrida's 'essence' seems a bit hazy, but I would settle for the memorable metonymy. The text, any text, is a will, we are present at its reading. The will, as every nineteenth century novelist knew, is where the dead are most alive; a functional autobiography, immortality secured in the quarrels of others.

Authors can be, and routinely are, constructed and reconstructed, but construction is different from revelation or assumption. We know (we hope) what we are doing, the process can be inspected, and the breaking of the orthodoxy of the *automatic* link between presumed writer and interpreted text will have served its purpose. Barthes himself writes of the possible, perhaps inevitable resurrection of the author, a dusty but not unattractive *revenant* among the glittering new techniques. The author is dead as an institution, he says (still no doubt prematurely) in *The Pleasure of the Text*, 1973, although as a person he is merely 'dispossessed'. 'But in the text, in a certain way, *I desire* the author: I need his image (*sa figure*), as he needs mine.' If we think of authors as desired and reconstructed, we are reminding ourselves of their human history, avoiding the familiar and tempting thought that they are just 'there', like mountains or weather, fallen from the hand of God.

Michel Foucault writes of an 'author function', which is a way of

classifying certain practices of language. Letters, contracts, anonymous texts, for instance, have persons who sign and write them, but
not 'authors'; what we need to understand are the 'rules of construction' for what we call an author, how we arrive at such an idea,
and what use we make of it. Foucault reverts interestingly to St
Jerome's four criteria for establishing authorship in an age when
several writers might use the same (traditional) name. They are:
consistency of value (is this work good enough to be regarded as
written by Brother William?); conceptual or theoretical coherence
(does it accord with our general sense of Brother William's doc-
trine?); stylistic unity (do we recognize Brother William's
characteristic vocabulary and turns of phrase?); historical moment
(does this work refer to people or events we know to belong to a
time later than that of Brother William's death?). It is easy to see
how these criteria can be adapted for a variety of texts, and how
strongly they are still in force. As Foucault wryly says, 'modern literary criticism ... scarcely defines the author otherwise'.

Now an author in St Jerome's sense plainly is some sort of 'construction': we (or our culture or our history) have put the pieces
together, they could have been assembled differently – and in fact
often are. But we have not made or just found the pieces. They were
left for us to find, and they were put together when we got to them.
We are perhaps the city planners here, or the demolition experts,
but we are not the architects. Or not the first or only architects. We
can of course ignore the first architect, or dismiss the very idea of
such a figure, and build a whole city of our own out of the dis-
assembled stones. This is what Barthes seems to invite us to do, and
what all kinds of readers do anyway, whether this is what they intend or not. But Barthes only seems to invite this. What he wants is
to rob the first architect (Author or God) of His undivided theological authority and get to know the firm's partners on more
democratic terms.

The author cannot do without the reader, but the reverse is also
true – however shadowy and marginal the author's role may seem
to have become. When Barthes says it 'will always be impossible', *à
tout jamais impossible*, to know who speaks in a Balzac text, he
means impossible to know in an old-fashioned, metaphysical sense:
to know for sure and in only one way. On a more modest view, it is
possible to name quite precisely the voices we hear in a Balzac text,
and Barthes himself, in *S/Z*, 1970, spends a lot of time doing just
that. There is no reason why these voices, in their sheer plurality,
should not *be* 'Balzac'; indeed it is hard to see how they could not

be. We can have as many Balzacs as we like; what we cannot really want is the entire absence of any sort of Balzac, and Barthes, in spite of his polemical flourishes, is not asking us to want it. If there is no imputable direction to a text, no chance of an encounter with a mind other than ours, we cannot *read*, we can only make private mental doodles on the script in front of us. Even when we assume a mind in a text, we can of course read wrongly; and we can get lost. But if there is no imaginable mind in question, no set of needs or specifiable context, we can't even read wrongly. Or: we might be able to read in a very modest, functional sense, to unscramble a basic meaning – say the meaning of the phrase 'Back in a minute' – but not be able to act on it, or take the meaning any further. If we didn't know what time it was, or who had left the message, or where 'back' was, there would be very little we could do with the words, in spite of our knowing quite clearly what they meant. Our ordinary use of 'reading' covers both of these rather different activities: being able to spell out and pronounce the name Humbert Humbert, for instance, and being able and willing to imagine him, as he cries out to us to do.

We can return, I think, to the flutter of questions I asked earlier. What would it mean to write the story of a writer's style rather than the record of a writer's adventures? Whose story would this be? What does it mean to separate, for whatever reason, the person and the writer, or as Eliot lugubriously puts it, 'the man who suffers and the mind which creates'? Who is Nabokov, and how many Nabokovs do we need?

Style in most cases is going to be an act, a perceived public performance. So the subject of a biography even in Nabokov's sense would be the writer we create from our reading of the texts, a critical fiction although not (we hope) a falsehood. More precisely, the writing subject is a critical fiction erratically haunted by our guesses at the character of the person behind the performance; guesses we may welcome as insights or deplore as methodological muddle, but which we can hardly resist anyway. Even the most austere New Critics have moments when they must believe that the cautiously constructed 'Nabokov' or 'Marvell' or 'Dickinson' just *is* Nabokov, or Marvell, or Dickinson, the person behind all the masks. The very notion of the mask implies a face. The metaphor of the second self is an attempt to take us away from all this, to bury the writing self in mystery, and leave us only with the words. I think this is laudable if you're not a conventional biographer, and might be an interesting place to start even if you were; and this is a book about

Nabokov's words and how they are arranged. But I also think we have to be prepared for the ghosts, for the unruliness of the mystery. No lively self will stay buried merely for our critical or conceptual comfort, and there will be times when even the most divided or hypothetical of writers will look undeniably solid and whole.

So how many Nabokovs? Four or five, perhaps, but that's being economical. The man is several persons, and the writer perhaps even more. I have used the name Nabokov to mean a number of quite different things, but I haven't lingered or agonized over this, and I think the context usually makes the meaning clear. Where it doesn't, I have stopped to say what I mean, but it may help if I describe what I take to be the four major or most frequent meanings of the name. They are:

1)   the historical person whose life has been impeccably told by his biographer Brian Boyd, and whom I glance at occasionally here, but who is not my principal subject.

2)   a set (also historical) of attitudes, prejudices, habits, remarks, performances which is highly visible, highly stylized, and which I find dull and narrow, and having almost nothing to do with the writing I admire: Nabokov the mandarin.

3)   a (real) person I guess at but who keeps himself pretty well hidden: he is not only tender and observant but also diffident, even scared, worried about almost everything the mandarin so airily dismisses. I would think this person was a sentimental invention of my own if Nabokov's texts were not demonstrably so full of him, and if I had any reason to invent him. Given the choice I would prefer another Nabokov in his place – someone less predictably the obverse of the haughty public presence. This diffident, doubting person is the one I think of most often as the author in Barthes' later sense: the textual revenant rather than the face on the dustjacket.

4)   identifiable habits of writing and narrating: mannered, intricate, alliterative, allusive, perverse, hilarious, lyrical, sombre, nostalgic, kindly, frivolous, passionate, cruel, cold, stupid, magical, precise, philosophical and unforgettable. Particular clusters of these characteristics are what we identify as Nabokov the author in Swift's sense, the performance on the sheets of paper.

All of these meanings keep shifting, of course, particularly the last set, but I have tried throughout the book to mark out and explore a specific distinction which I have found helpful, and which may also be useful to readers. It is the distinction between style and signature.

One meaning of signature, according to the *Oxford English Dictionary*, is 'a distinctive mark, a peculiarity in form or colouring etc on a plant or other natural object formerly supposed to be an indication of its qualities, especially for medical purposes'. This is a sense Ben Jonson seems to be using metaphorically when he evokes the signature of the stars ('You shall be/Principall Secretarie to the Starres:/Know all their signatures'). But the idea of a signature on a note or cheque is relevant too. It is how we recognize and verify the identity of writers; other things about them too. A literary signature would then be the visible shorthand for a literary person; a style would be a more complex but still legible trace of that person's interaction with the world. Writers usually have more signature than style, I think. Signature is their habit and their practice, their mark; style is something more secretive, more thoroughly dispersed among the words, a reflection of luck or grace, or of a moment when signature overcomes or forgets itself.

Much of Nabokov's work is strikingly signed, immediately identifiable as his. This work is intelligent and amusing, but often elegantly impatient, anxious to cut off questions which threaten to become too messy or difficult. We can't mistake it for anyone else's, but we can't always admire it. And then there is richer and more subtle work which is not signed in this sense, which doesn't have the distinctive mark or name in its words. But it is Nabokov's, and I think more intimately so than work which more obviously evokes him, or our image of him, or his image of himself. No one else could have written it; if it is not at once unmistakable, it is at length irreplaceable, untransferable. While we could parody Nabokov's signature, although not easily, since most of us don't have anything like the necessary linguistic agility, his style is beyond any parody we could imagine, let alone produce.

It's not that style is always or simply better than signature. The signature may be wonderful and the style quite modest. But the style will always be stealthier, and in Nabokov's case the style is intricate and haunting and powerful, while the signature can be dazzling to the point of weakness. So I think the distinction does have a certain critical and theoretical force – it is, if you like, an amalgamation and resplitting of St Jerome's first and third criteria for authorship, the notions of value and of stylistic unity – and sparingly and flexibly used, it may help us to understand the shape and behaviour and force of language, Nabokov's or anyone else's. I don't wish to beat the distinction into the ground, to suggest that we need a manic classifying spree, turning every piece of writing into style or signature, as if there were no other territory, or no combinations or crossovers were possible. Obviously what is signature for one reader could well be style for another. That wouldn't matter as long as we could talk about our decisions. What does matter is that style and signature seem to engage us differently, to involve a different relationship between textual author and consenting reader. Style is more impersonal in Eliot's and Flaubert's sense: we think about the writing before we think about who wrote it.

Here is a famous, strongly signed passage from *Lolita*:

> The front hall was graced with door chimes, a white-eyed wooden thingamabob of commercial Mexican origin, and that banal darling of the arty middle class, van Gogh's 'Arlésienne'. A door ajar to the right afforded a glimpse of a living-room, with some more Mexican trash in a corner cabinet and a striped sofa along the wall. There was a staircase at the end of the hallway, and as I stood mopping my brow (only now did I realize how hot it had been out of doors) and staring, to stare at something, at an old grey tennis ball that lay on an oak chest, there came from the upper landing the contralto voice of Mrs Haze, who leaning over the banisters inquired melodiously, 'Is that Monsieur Humbert?' A bit of cigarette ash dropped from there in addition. Presently, the lady herself – sandals, maroon slacks, yellow silk blouse, squarish face, in that order – came down the steps, her index finger still tapping upon her cigarette.
>
> I think I had better describe her right away, to get it over with. The poor lady was in her middle thirties, she had a shiny forehead, plucked eyebrows and quite simple but not unattractive features of a type that may be defined as a weak solution of Marlene Dietrich.

The writer here, within the fiction, is the snooty and devious Humbert Humbert, but that kind of indirection is also part of Nabokov's signature. Humbert's eye is observant but weary; both he and Nabokov enjoy the play of different linguistic registers ('graced', 'thingumabob', 'afforded a glimpse', 'Mexican trash'), and both are dedicated to the meticulous control of images and timing. Nothing left to chance here, and no space for mistakes. It's not just that we see Charlotte Haze through Humbert's seeing her, we see her in sections, in a sardonic reconstruction of his first view. The 'weak solution' is a brilliant and dismissive metaphor, since it manages to turn both Charlotte and Marlene Dietrich into chemical concoctions.

Here's another famous passage from the same book, equally strongly signed, I think, but more sentimental:

> What I heard was but the melody of children at play, nothing but that, and so limpid was the air that within this vapour of blended voices, majestic and minute, remote and magically near, frank and divinely enigmatic – one could hear now and then, as if released, an almost articulate spurt of vivid laughter, or the crack of a bat or the clatter of a toy wagon, but it was all really too far for the eye to distinguish any movement in the lightly etched streets. I stood listening to that musical vibration from my lofty slope, to those flashes of separate cries with a kind of demure murmur for background, and then I knew that the hopelessly poignant thing was not Lolita's absence from my side, but the absence of her voice from that concord.

The flashes of cries are evocative, and the noises of the valley are beautifully exact, but the soft-spoken, Edwardian diction of the passage (melody, vapour, limpid air, magically, divinely, demure murmur, and the sickly concord) suggests two minds, Humbert's and Nabokov's, trying hard for a tone to which they are not accustomed: Humbert because he is seeking, sincerely or not, to sound contrite, Nabokov because he is allowing the moralist in himself to have one of his rare canters in the open. This elegant, slightly over-beautified language is Nabokov's signature when he takes a break from irony; as if in compensation, sardonic control gives way to a maudlin recommendation.

A little earlier in the book, Humbert drives to Clare Quilty's house to kill him. He finds the place, and decides to return in the morning.

> Gently I rolled back to town, in that old faithful car of mine which was serenely, almost cheerfully working for me. My Lolita! There was still a three-year-old bobby pin of hers in the depths of the glove compartment. There was still that stream of pale moths siphoned out of the night by my headlights. Dark barns still propped themselves up here and there by the roadside. People were still going to the movies. While searching for night lodgings, I passed a drive-in. In a selenian glow, truly mystical in its contrast with the moonless and massive night, on a gigantic screen slanting away among dark

drowsy fields, a thin phantom raised a gun, both he and his arm reduced to tremulous dishwater by the oblique angle of that receding
world – and the next moment a row of trees shut off the gestic-
ulation.

There is a great deal of Nabokov's signature here: the alliteration,
the invocation of Lolita, the implicit parallel between the movie and
Humbert's projected murder of Quilty. 'Selenian' and 'mystical'
are reminders of Humbert's fussy learning. But there is also something I want to call style in this passage. Overall, it is the desolate,
terminal effect of the completed image; in detail, the effect's chief
ingredients, in so far as I can identify them, are the recurring word
'still', with its delicate suggestion of solipsistic surprise that the
world could go on when Humbert and Lolita were separated; the
barns which prop themselves up; the astonishing but not fanciful
'siphoned' and 'dishwater'; the slant of the screen and its relation to
the moving car; the double meaning of the thinness of the phantom
raising a gun; and the peculiar helplessness of the word 'gestic-
ulation', a sadly latinate miming of the plight of those reduced to
mere gesture. The passage is clearly Nabokov's, and a wonderful
piece of writing; but it is not, if I am right, as visibly and typically
Nabokov's as the others.

For a last example of style, I'd like to turn to 'Signs and
Symbols', 1948, a story I consider in a later chapter. This is a work
which is rich in style and signature, and in style and signature together. Here is a passage of what I am calling style. An old couple
are on their way to visit their mentally ill son on his birthday,
taking him a present:

That Friday everything went wrong. The underground train lost its
life current between two stations, and for a quarter of an hour one
could hear nothing but the dutiful beating of one's heart and the rustling of the newspapers. The bus they had to take next kept them
waiting for ages; and when it did come, it was crammed with garrulous school children. It was raining hard as they walked up the
brown path leading to the sanitarium. There they waited again; and
instead of their boy shuffling into the room as he usually did (his
poor face blotched with acne, ill-shaven, sullen, and confused), a
nurse they knew, and did not care for, appeared at last and brightly
explained that he had again attempted to take his life. He was all
right, she said, but a visit might disturb him. The place was so
miserably understaffed, and things got mislaid or mixed up so easily,

that they decided not to leave their present in the office but to bring
it to him next time they came.

I can't see anything here that looks like Nabokov's signature; yet I
can't think of another writer who could have managed the casual,
brilliant and quietly angry complexities of the fifth sentence in this
paragraph. The old couple have to wait 'again', and the boy has
'again attempted to take his life' – this second 'again' is the first hint
we have that the son is dangerous to himself, and suddenly illumi-
nates and expands our sense of the parents' sorrow. The 'bright'
explanation of the nurse makes her either heartless or unable to be
brisk and compassionate at the same time, and helps us to understand why the old couple don't care for her – no doubt they have
had bright explanations from her in the past. This is all discreet and
strong, but the most dazzling, half-concealed effect in the passage is
the conjuring up on the page of the son who doesn't appear at the
hospital, with his acne and his shuffle and his confusion. We see the
person the parents are unable to see; see with the eyes of their waiting minds. We are not disappointed as they are, but we come close
to their disappointment, and their continuing sadness, through our
own glimpse of the boy. *Instead* of their sullen boy, they get the
nurse and her explanation, her news of worse than sullenness. This
is style because it does so many things at once, and isn't signature.
It works largely through syntax and small words, and is so subtle
that it reflects not a meticulous control of a fictional world but a
disciplined vulnerability to the shocks of a historical one. Of
course, the control and the vulnerability are related to each other,
the first presumably an answer to the second. When the answer is
difficult, scarcely manageable, only style will allow the writer to
continue to write, and may produce some of his or her most powerful work. When the answer is too easily had, the writing
accumulates excesses of signature.

(vi)

Some deaths of the author are mere slips or illusions. Nabokov
appears on a published photograph in the 1930s, but is identified as
Jacques Audiberti. Rectification, or resurrection, is relatively easy.
However, when Nabokov writes of *Conclusive Evidence* (the first
title in America of the book called *Speak, Memory* in England and
later in both countries; in Russia and France the book was called

Other Shores), he glosses the phrase as meaning 'conclusive evidence of my having existed'. Why should such evidence be needed, conclusive or not? Nabokov doesn't doubt his own sense of his existence, but he clearly feels he needs to prove his past to others, since his earlier life, his spectacular loss of family, home and two refuges in exile, must seem unreal to them, a fancy, a legend. The evidence for this past's reality is the fondness and specificity of the text itself, the gleam and shimmer of the writing: conclusive. But the near-death of the author's old self, his rescue at the hands of memory and patience, are alarming brushes with the brutal violence of history, reminders of the appalling variety of ways in which lives can be lost. The murder of an author, even a metaphorical murder, is quite different from a composed theoretical death.

2

Lost Souls:
The Real Life of Sebastian Knight

> *the martyr*
> *Catches his death in a little flutter*
> *Of plain arrows. A grotesque situation,*
> *But priceless . . .*

Geoffrey Hill, 'Of Commerce and Society'

(i)

Nabokov's first novel in English, written in Paris in 1938-1939, when he thought he might work in England but didn't know he would move to the United States, is a work about authorship and loss; about a dead author and what remains of him. Its very title – *The Real Life of Sebastian Knight* – looks like a trap, a joke on all those who are rash enough to believe they know what it means.

It is easy to be too confident about the real; easier still, in our century, to be too sceptical. The real is what we cannot not know, Henry James said. In practice, the real (what we call the real) is often what we care about or just take for granted: the true, the authentic, the characteristic, the vital, the irresistible, or what we suppose or want to be (some of) those things. In *The Real Life of Sebastian Knight*, Nabokov routinely uses the word 'real' and its relatives to mean: not false or sham ('She possessed . . . that real sense of beauty which . . .'), typical ('a real healthy Britisher'), valid or intelligible ('Is there anything real or possible in the contrast between . . .'), not disguised ('who Madame Lecerf really was'). The real can be a matter of perspective – 'bookkeeping or bookselling looks singularly unreal in the starlight' – and rather less routinely, Nabokov uses the word to suggest the metaphysical, what we can know only through some alien or improbable mode of cognition. 'Something real' is what a man on the edge of death might learn:

29

Now he had caught something real, which had nothing to do with any of the thoughts or feelings, or experiences he might have had in the kindergarten of life . . .

Nothing to do with what we mostly call reality. The metaphor of catching the real echoes a usage earlier in the book, where the metaphysical becomes the metalinguistic:

I felt immensely sorry for him and longed to say something real, something with wings and a heart, but the birds I wanted settled on my shoulders and head only later when I was alone and not in need of words.

It is quietly surprising, and entirely in keeping with Nabokov's thought and style, that the birds do land, even if too late and beyond language. They are among the reasons why we shouldn't be too sceptical about reality.

These usages, though, could be found in almost anyone's repertoire. The real is a banality and a longing. It is what we hold in our hands, often without knowing it, and what always escapes us; what is there and what can't be there; what we would miss if we lost it, what we miss and dream we have lost. The title of *The Real Life of Sebastian Knight*, therefore, is not so much simple or mock-simple, deep or complex, as ordinary and mysterious, mysterious in the way the ordinary often is. Sebastian himself finds 'a poetic solace in the obvious and the ordinary which for some reason or other I had overlooked in the course of my life'. This is encouraging, but no doubt you have to lose the obvious and the ordinary pretty thoroughly before you can find them again in quite this way.

The real life of Sebastian Knight is at times the straightforward object of the narrator's hope, his 'desire to see the real man behind the author'; at other times it is Sebastian's books (he is 'laughingly alive in five volumes'), at others still it is the act of writing, the tussle with language:

Perhaps we shall be nearer the truth in supposing that . . . his mind was a turmoil of words and fancies, uncomplete [sic] fancies and insufficient words, but already he knew that this and only this was the reality of his life.

The narrator's 'this and only this', of course, is itself a brave, forlorn attempt to get the insufficient and unmanageable word 'reality' to stand still. 'Real' belongs, as the philosopher J. L. Austin says, to the family of adjustable terms by which we seek to 'meet the innumerable and unforeseeable demands of the world upon language'. It also buries these demands, makes them seem irrelevant or already dealt with, even as it (more or less) meets them.

The problem proliferates in Nabokov, banality and longing chasing each other. Perhaps a real life is not an existence, however solid and undeniable, but the best or most memorable moments of an existence, instants of exaltation or insight, times when the self is most itself: real life rather than mere living. In *The Eye*, 1930, Nabokov's narrator glosses what is real for him as 'oppressive and tender, provoking excitement and torment, possessed of blinding possibilities of happiness, with tears, with a warm wind'. Or – we now approach one of the most subtle and urgent suggestions of *The Real Life of Sebastian Knight* – what is real is the life we lead when we lose ourselves, when we abandon or are driven from the rational fiction of our identity; when we fall in love, for example, and especially when we fall deeply, hopelessly, brutally, stupidly in love.

There is one last possibility: that the real life of Sebastian Knight, as of anyone who has succumbed to what the narrator calls 'the strange habit of human death', is just the life we shall never see again, the life that was once secret and is now lost. Biography in this sense is not a quest for truth but a refusal of death. The refusal is vain in the literal sense, since nothing will bring these persons back, and desperate in all kinds of other senses; but it has its moments of near-miracle. Beyond all easy spiritualisms, the dead do speak, they counsel us through memory, through our late but often luminous understanding of what they would have said. The doubt and the pathos, and much of what is so moving in *The Real Life of Sebastian Knight*, are in the fact that the luminous, here as elsewhere, carries no guarantees: it may be luminous or it may be just dazzle. If we were certain either way, things would be easier. Or rather, we *are* certain each way, but on different occasions. It's just that no occasion certifies or simplifies the next.

The real for Nabokov is always refracted. There are no bare facts, as he puts it in his book on Gogol. The inevitable refraction is a disappointment to our dream of an uncomplicated, unmediated truth, an easily accessible real life, but there is no opposition between reality and refraction. The real is not less real

31

because it is refracted, that is the way it comes to us. 'It is as if a painter said: look, here I'm going to show you not the painting of a landscape, but the painting of different ways of painting a certain landscape, and I trust their harmonious fusion will disclose the landscape as I intend you to see it'. Paintings of ways of painting are not at odds with painted things; the landscape doesn't vanish, it (finally, possibly) gets disclosed. This analogy is the narrator's way of evoking the effect of Sebastian Knight's first novel, the preciously titled *The Prismatic Bezel*. But his own narrative method is much the same. A voice rings out across a rainy afternoon in Cambridge, offering to tell the narrator 'the real story of Sebastian Knight's college years'. The voice is a fantasy, sounding only in the narrator's head, yet he interprets it not as an illusion but as a potential parallel to fact, what didn't happen but might have, 'the echo of some possible truth, a timely reminder'. The real story is not simply given, but it is not abandoned as a chimera. We attend to the telling, and to the telling of different ways of telling. 'Remember that what you are told is really threefold: shaped by the teller, reshaped by the listener, concealed from both by the dead man of the tale.'

The dead man is an early instance of Roland Barthes' author, displaced and resurrected by Nabokov's phrasing. The corpse is both absent and active, pictured as continuing to conceal what the others shape and reshape.

(ii)

Sebastian Knight was born in St Petersburg in December 1899 – or in our January 1900 if the narrator is using the Old Calendar. He escaped from Russia during the Revolution, studied English litera-ture at Cambridge, stayed in England, wrote novels and short stories, acquired a modest fame – fame enough for his secretary Mr Goodman to think there was some mileage in a quick, bland, generalizing book about him. He died early in 1936, of a heart condition which had also killed his mother, 'a rather rare variety of angina pectoris, called by some doctors "Lehmann's disease".' His novels were *The Prismatic Bezel*, 1924, *Success*, 1925-7, the autobiographical *Lost Property*, begun in 1929, and *The Doubtful Asphodel*, 1935 – the dates are those of writing, since our narrator doesn't always give us dates of publication, and on one occasion contradicts himself when he does. Sebastian Knight also wrote three short stories, 'The Funny Mountain', 'Albinos in Black' and

'The Back of the Moon', 1927-1929, later collected in a volume taking its title from the first story.

The narrator thinks Sebastian is 'a great writer', 'one of the most remarkable writers of his time'; but the novel doesn't require us to agree. On the evidence – Sebastian is plentifully quoted, most of his titles seem to have a tinge of parody in them – he is a melancholy, intelligent, funny, tricky, writer hampered by his whimsy and his dandyism, his habit of converting all feeling into elegance. A travesty of Nabokov himself perhaps, or a picture of the writer Nabokov sometimes thought he might be. Better still, a picture of the writer many critics thought and still think Nabokov is. Late in the novel a 'fairly well-read' Englishman says he likes Sebastian Knight's books 'in a way', although 'the author seemed to him a terrible snob, intellectually, at least'.

> Knight seemed to him to be constantly playing some game of his own invention, without telling his partners its rules. He said he preferred books that made one think, and Knight's books didn't, – they left you puzzled and cross.

The narrator rather defensively says he doesn't know whether a novel of Sebastian's makes one think, and doesn't care if it doesn't. 'I like it for it's own sake. I like its manners'. This is loyal, but confirms rather than alters our critical impression. Sebastian has many of Nabokov's gifts, but not all of them. He might have written 'The Vane Sisters', for example, or *The Eye*; but not 'Signs and Symbols' or *The Defence*. He is the character Henry James thought could not be created: the (successful) author who is more interesting as a person than as a writer, more compelling when he is not working than when he is. Or to put that another way, the book he is in is deeper and funnier than any book he could write.

The comedy is delicate here, since the suggestion I have just made stands the ostensible theme of *The Real Life of Sebastian Knight* on its head. Our narrator is sure of his own ineptness as a writer, his manifest inferiority to Sebastian. He is Sebastian's half-brother. His and Sebastian's father married again a year after Sebastian's mother left him; died as a result of a duel when the boys were fourteen and seven respectively. The children grew up together in St Petersburg, although they were not close, in part because of the difference in age, in part because of Sebastian's rather austere temperament, friendly, courteous but cool. The narrator rather touchingly recalls his 'wistful' boyhood attempts to get Sebastian to notice him, to abandon his 'constant aloofness'; and the book he is writing is among other things part of his continuing attempt to reach Sebastian, even as a shade or a memory. 'I dare say', the narrator remarks of Sebastian, 'he mistrusted too strongly the commonplace of eternity to believe . . . in his own ghost', but the narrator himself doesn't mistrust it at all, eagerly imagines Sebastian 'trying to be helpful' from beyond the grave, peering over the narrator's shoulder as he writes, and possibly amused by this humble book. The boys fled Russia with their (step) mother via Finland in 1918. After Sebastian's move to England, the half-brothers met only a few times, although Sebastian wrote to the narrator (in Russian) just before he died, and the narrator raced across France to arrive (too late) at his deathbed. It is this encounter in a hospital, of which more later, which appears to have started the narrator on his book, on this book.

We never learn the narrator's name(s), only the initial of his first name, and it is not easy to know what to make of this discretion. 'Oh, hullo, V.,' Sebastian says when he meets the narrator in Paris. The punctuation perhaps suggests that Sebastian literally uses the initial as a friendly nickname, but the rest of the text suggests otherwise. Sebastian says 'Oh, hullo, Victor, or Vassily, or Vladimir, or Vissarion', and the narrator retains only the initial, as if he inhabited one of those cautious nineteenth-century novels, where the names of persons and places, and the terminal figures of dates, disappear into dashes and hints. 'I named myself too,' he says when he meets a man called Silbermann, but the only name we hear is Silbermann's. Mr Goodman is described as trying to pronounce 'our simple Russian name', that is, the narrator's and Sebastian's, but the name is not given. Late in the book the narrator identifies himself to a nurse, but not to us. 'My name is [I mentioned my name]'.

Why is V being so discreet about himself? There doesn't seem to be any dark secret or particular reason why his first or family names should not be known, entirely leaving aside the fact that he is a fictional character anyway. He is anxious not to obtrude, and his anxiety is what makes him so obtrusive. 'As the reader may have noticed, I have tried to put into this book as little of my own self as possible.' We are to notice how unnoticeable he is being. 'Let me repeat here that I am loth to trouble these pages with any kind of matter relating personally to me . . .' Why repeat it? What the performance with the name suggests is not that the name matters (or doesn't matter), but that invisibility matters, that V wants very much to feel that he is outside Sebastian's story, an onlooker, not a part of it. By the end of the novel his invisibility is in shreds, even if his name still eludes us. We know as much about him as we do about Sebastian, if not more; and he knows that in several (but not all) serious senses, he *is* Sebastian.

V claims at first to be quite different from Sebastian, but also mysteriously close to him. The claim is so beautifully balanced that we can't know whether we are dealing with an insight or a fond delusion.

> Once I happened to see two brothers, tennis champions, matched against one another; their strokes were totally different, and one of the two was far, far better than the other; but the general rhythm of their motions as they swept all over the court was exactly the same, so that had it been possible to draft both systems two identical designs would have appeared.

He and Sebastian have 'some kind of common rhythm', V suggests; so that 'when I imagined actions of his which I heard of only after his death, I knew for certain that in such or such a case I should have acted just as he had.' Not that V claims to have Sebastian's 'genius', or 'riches of the mind', or 'facets of talent'.

> The difference between his power of expression and mine is comparable to that which exists between a Bechstein piano and a baby's rattle. I would never have let him see the least sentence of this book lest he should wince at the way I manage my miserable English.

We may notice a curious gap between the baby's rattle and the implied boast in both brothers being tennis champions, even if one, like Sidney Carton's imagined rest in *A Tale of Two Cities* is 'far, far better'. But let's say V is right. Sebastian is in another league. The common rhythm remains, and V's curious decision to write his book about Sebastian in English. This is not an obvious move: V is entirely Russian, he doesn't have an English mother, hasn't been to Cambridge, and in exile he has always lived in Paris. In this case, it's not that V would have acted as Sebastian did, it's that he is acting as Sebastian did, trailing him from one language to another, miming a life as well as seeking to reconstruct it.

V is writing two books; or rather, like Humbert Humbert, sets out to write one book and lapses into another. He is planning a biography of Sebastian, gathering material for it; tells people about it when he interviews them. But he is still 'longing' to start on it, 'about to begin' when more than halfway through the book we are reading. He may still write his biography, but I think we must suspect that he has in fact done something different, and stealthier: turned the story of his unwritten book into the book itself, a painting of the ways of painting which delicately discloses the landscape. He talks in his second chapter of 'having interrupted my second chapter': the 'interruption' is actually the chapter's conclusion, its last three pages. V's account of his quest for Sebastian *is* his evocation of Sebastian. We see Sebastian, if we see him at all, in the narrated search, not in a final finding; a refraction. The projected biography is complete before we know it, before it even ostensibly starts.

This is an elegant strategy, and faithful to Nabokov's notion of reality; but the book (V's, Nabokov's) would be a little tame if it did no more than illustrate its own theory. V and Sebastian are in different leagues, I want to suggest, because although V lacks Sebastian's experience, ingenuity and weary charm, he manages to orchestrate, in the story of his miming and missing and finding of Sebastian, a work which complements and deepens Sebastian's own, a memoir which borrows the modes of fiction, and complicates their relation to various orders of reality. Or: Sebastian wrote his novels and short stories, but V has written Sebastian. V is not to be identified with Nabokov, of course. The one is a character in a novel, a man tangled in the fictional relations he depicts, haunted by a brother who has preceded him; the other is the novelist, inhabits another space entirely, has invented both V and his brother for reasons of his own. It becomes clear, however, once we pay attention to V's repeated mentions of 'this book', the one we are reading, called, like Nabokov's, *The Real Life of Sebastian Knight*, that his text is necessarily identical with Nabokov's, word for word, rather as Pierre Menard's version of *Don Quixote* repeats but does not simply duplicate that of Cervantes. V and Nabokov may have different ideas about many matters, but their timing is the same.

(iii)

Sebastian Knight is an English writer, a man who seems to have abandoned the language of his father and his childhood. Both boys learned English when they were small, and Sebastian wrote verse in English. Once Sebastian was at Cambridge, he 'spoke Russian gingerly', V says, 'lapsing into English as soon as the conversation drew out to anything longer than a couple of sentences'. V reports with some relish that Sebastian's English, however fluent and idiomatic it became, 'was decidedly that of a foreigner', since he rolled r's, misplaced stresses and 'made queer mistakes'. Just like Humbert Humbert and (in some respects) Vladimir Nabokov.

The crucial detail, however, which V reports but does not comment on, is that Sebastian's English is not only his mother's tongue but implicitly represents an engagement with his mother's absence, an act of mourning. He keeps his teenage poems in a drawer, along with 'the photograph of a sister of one of his schoolmates; some gold coins; and a small muslin bag of violet sweets. The poems were written in English.' We learn more about the girl, Natasha Rosanov, later in the book; the gold coins are there, I take it, to create a little note of randomness, an effect not of the real but of the unarranged. What matters, though, is the juxtaposition of the sweets and the poems in the drawer, of the sweets and the English language in V's prose. Sebastian's mother gave him the sweets when she last saw him, some eight years before. The child hasn't eaten them or lost them; he has grown up and kept them; they are what he has of her. They, and her language. She is delicately, metonymically connected to the very fact of his being a writer, and the young Sebastian, for good measure, signs his poems with 'a little black chess-knight drawn in ink'. This is an intimation of the chess theme to be found everywhere in the novel, but it is also a way of naming his mother without words, and when Sebastian moves to England he takes her name as his own. Virginia Knight is thus inscribed in whatever real life Sebastian Knight has; and he dies her death by inheriting her heart disease.

Sebastian's mother is described as 'a strange woman, a restless reckless being'.

> She was fond of my father after a fashion, a fitful fashion to say the least, and when one day it occurred to her that she might be in love with another . . . she left husband and child as suddenly as a raindrop starts to slide tipwards down a syringa leaf . . . I do not like to dwell in mind upon that day in a Paris hotel, with Sebastian, aged about four, poorly attended by a puzzled nurse, and my father locked up in his room . . .

V is reconstructing this moment from what his own mother has told him, and his language, beautifully precise at this point, registers haunting ambiguities. 'When *one day* it *occurred* to her that she *might* be . . .' Almost every item in that little chain suggests an unbearable lightness, a sense of desire and/or loyalty so flimsy that anything could blow it off course. Yet the image of the raindrop on the syringa leaf, carrying just the same denotative meanings, has an entirely different tone: grace and innocence enter what remains an act of abandonment. Just the same ambiguities are present when Virginia reappears, some four years later, and V's mother takes Sebastian to a St Petersburg hotel to see her. Virginia is associated with the romance of travel, and Sebastian is said to have inherited from her a 'passion for sleeping-cars and Great European Express Trains'. She kisses her son, and bursts into tears, 'as if Sebastian's warm tender temple was the very source and satiety of her sorrow'. Source and satiety: the strange, touching suggestion is not only that sorrow arises and is appeased in the same place, the same person, but that sorrow can have a satiety, that it is an appetite and can be satisfied. Virginia then chatters nervously to V's mother, and gives Sebastian the bag of sweets, 'a small parcel of sugar-coated violets'. 'This was all', V says, 'and next year she died.'

'Sebastian could never forget his mother,' V remarks a little later, but it's not entirely clear that he understands how his half-brother's grieving memory works. He speaks of 'morbid glamour', 'remembered charm', 'soft radiance', but makes Sebastian's relation to his vanished mother seem entirely passive, a youthful disability. That is not the relation the poems and hoarded sweets and the assumption of her name and language suggest, and when Sebastian, in his book *Lost Property*, speaks of visiting the place where his mother died, he says he remembers the name of the pension as 'Les Violettes'. If this *is* where she died, the echo of the violet sweets is a natty Nabokov effect, a touch of literary dandyism, and a glance at life's grim little jokes and coincidences. But if Sebastian has named the pension himself, lent it the colour and identity of his treasured token, then a curious self-mocking yearning is at work – self-mocking because Sebastian is about to tell us that the pension *and* the town are the wrong place, that his mother didn't die anywhere near there. The mockery enhances the yearning, because the metaphor of desire remains even in the error, especially in the error: Sebastian's mother would have died, should have died in a place that echoes her gift to him, she would have died in relation to him, to his last sight of her; died, *for* him perhaps, he would always have been in her story, as she is always in the language of his.

But Sebastian has not abandoned the language of his father, only removed himself from it. Nabokov makes things difficult for us here by allowing such Russianizing zeal to V, such eagerness to reclaim Sebastian for his homeland.

> I know, I know as definitely as I know we had the same father, I know Sebastian's Russian was better and more natural to him than his English. I quite believe that by not speaking Russian for five years he may have forced himself into thinking he had forgotten it. But a language is a live physical thing which cannot be so easily dismissed. It should moreover be remembered that five years before his first book – that is, at the time he left Russia – his English was as thin as mine . . .

We would wonder about the knowledge of anyone who stutteringly used the word 'know' four times before he got to the predicate of his sentence, and in Nabokov such behaviour is a sure sign of shaky ground. V is also forgetting for the moment that Sebastian had an English mother, so that however 'thin' his language was, it would have a quite different emotional resonance from V's own.

But V's insistence doesn't have to mean he is completely wrong; it may mean only that he is anxious. He is certainly saying something that matters about the contribution of language to the texture of a life. We cannot know how Sebastian feels about his Russian; we know only that late in his life he fell in love with a Russian woman, and spoke and wrote to her in Russian, and that curious confusions arose as a result. In one sense the confusions were always there, so that even V's best evidence points two ways.

He quotes Sebastian as writing 'that one of the purest emotions is that of the banished man pining after the land of his birth', but the idea seems literary rather than confessional, and is followed by an evocation of a quotation-soaked olde Englande hardly to be confused with any sort of Russia: 'the blue remembered hills and the happy highways, the hedge with its unofficial rose and the field with its rabbits, the distant spire and the near bluebell . . .' It becomes clear that Sebastian is deliberately over-tinting this image, and that if he admires the emotion in question, he has no time for the writing it induces in him: 'because I have an innate distrust of what I feel easy to express, no sentimental wanderer will ever be allowed to land on the rock of my unfriendly prose'. So V may be right to speak of the 'somewhat artificial' character of Sebastian's passion for his mother's land rather than his motherland, but cannot plausibly show, as he anxiously wishes to, that Sebastian had 'real affection' for Russia. Sebastian as a man and as a writer built artifice and distance all around him. What attracts him in the idea of exile, perhaps, is not the pining for the lost country but the purity of the loss. V almost tells us as much when, rather like Charles Kinbote in *Pale Fire* attributing his own national nostalgia (or fantasy) to a writer he admires, he imagines Sebastian sitting on a fence in the Cambridge countryside and thinking of 'some misty sunset beyond a black Russian fir-wood', only to add 'oh, how much I would give for such a memory coming to him!'

It is true, though, that Sebastian remains caught between two languages: not all is wishful in V's vision. Sebastian's complex cultural situation is figured in the two bundles of letters, both from women, one English and one Russian, which V discovers in Sebastian's flat when he goes through his effects after his death. Sebastian has requested that the bundles be destroyed, and V destroys them, wryly remarking that he is 'sorry to say the better man won'. He recognizes the English Clare Bishop's handwriting in one set, sees nothing of the other letters except a few words which flare up 'in full radiance' as the paper burns.

> The words I had seen were Russian words, part of a Russian sentence, – quite insignificant in themselves, really (not that I might have expected from the flame of chance the slick intent of a novelist's plot). The literal English translation would be 'thy manner always to find' . . . – and it was not the sense that struck me, but the mere fact of its being in my language.

Whenever Nabokov mentions chance we probably need to wonder what he is up to, but the game here seems to be a kind of double bluff: the words *are* less significant than the language they are in. What matters to V is that Sebastian loved a Russian woman, as if the very fact represented a return to Russia.

Similarly, what seems to V most important about Sebastian's last letter to him is its language. As we have just seen, and he now repeats, he regards Sebastian's Russian as 'purer and richer than his English ever was', and he patiently transliterates what he regards as all the key words.

I am, as you see, in Paris, and presumably shall be stuck [*zasstria-noo*] here for some time. If you can come, come; if you can't, I shall not be offended; but it might be perhaps better if you came. I am fed up [*osskomina*] with a number of tortuous things and especially with the patterns of my shed snake-skins [*vypolziny*] so that now I find a poetic solace in the obvious and the ordinary which for some reason or other I had overlooked in the course of my life.

The letter is addressed to V but didn't start out that way: 'This letter was begun almost a week ago, and up to the word "life" it had been destined [*prednaznachalos*] to quite a different person'. The person, presumably, is Sebastian's mysterious Russian mistress. It is significant, of course, that the first three sentences of a letter to one (Russian) person can stand unchanged as the first three sentences of a letter to another; that a former mistress and a scarcely known half-brother should indifferently, as they say in French, be the recipients of a confidence about the 'obvious and the ordinary'. Sebastian's diffidence, his desperate attempt at the offhand, means that not even in misery and the shadow of death can he become less remote. The language of feeling is so alien to this subtle novelist that we can't tell from his tone whether he is talking to his mistress or his relative. More striking still, the point where V's and Nabokov's metaphors appear to meet, is the simple fact of Sebastian's lonely return to a language which is no longer his but conflates so many concerns of his life, since it is the language of his dead father, of his own early years, and of his last love. V is the virtually accidental audience for this crowded communication, fraught with the weariness and sadness and fear it cannot name. Sebastian turns to him 'as a shy guest in a strange house will talk at unusual length to the near relative with whom he came to the party. So forgive me if I bore you [*dokoochayou*], but somehow I don't much like those bare branches and twigs which I see from my window'. V is all Sebastian has; or rather, he is his one real non-literary reader, the person to whom he can write non-fiction in the language of his lost life.

(iv)

'Now the lives of the characters shine forth with a real and human significance ... A new plot, a new drama utterly unconnected with the opening of the story ... seems to struggle for existence and break into light'. This is V's account of developments in *The*

Prismatic Bezel, but it also announces, with a faint and likeable sentimentality ('real and human'), a shift in V's own work, his arrival at what he calls 'the crucial point of Sebastian's sentimental life'. *The Real Life of Sebastian Knight* is two books in yet another sense than the one I suggested earlier (V's and Nabokov's). The first nine chapters (out of twenty) are engaging and lightweight, a little flat at times, a little fussy. There are moments of lucid and delicate writing (the brilliant sketch of a sunlit, wintry St Petersburg, the haunted evocation of Sebastian's empty flat in London). Sebastian's life and friendships are pleasantly drawn, the problems of biography addressed; but it all seems rather gently literary, very low key. In the tenth chapter Sebastian's first two novels are described in some detail; and in the following chapter, a new and stronger novel begins.

This novel concerns, not Sebastian's life and writings but his unhappy love and his death, along with V's quest for Sebastian's elusive mistress, and his race to be at Sebastian's bedside. Sebastian, already ill, and having consulted a heart specialist, becomes cranky and bad-tempered, meets a Russian woman at a spa in Alsace, behaves very strangely on his return, then abandons England and his English mistress, the affectionate, modest, intuitive Clare Bishop. Shortly after Sebastian's death some six years later, Clare herself dies in childbirth, the child also dying.

In V's narrative, Clare's death comes right at the beginning of his eleventh chapter, as if announcing the new novel's dark music in a throwaway. 'She had seemed to be such a normal and healthy young woman, how was it that she bled to death next to an empty cradle?' Well, how was it? Such questions in fiction cannot be innocent or rhetorical as they are in life. Death in a novel, whatever the characters feel about it, is a piece of the novel's language, a sign planted and picked up. We can ask why V places the death of Clare where he does, but we need also to ask, rather more grimly, why Nabokov has her die at all, what the death-sign says.

First, and most generally, it says that death itself for Nabokov, as I shall argue more fully in a later chapter, is a graceless, pointless interruption of life, a form of surprise, never natural. His work is full of sudden diseases, suicides, duels, murders, and the pattern in *The Real Life of Sebastian Knight* is very similar to the pattern in *Lolita*: a hero/writer dies of his heart, a woman/girl dies in childbirth. Unnecessary death, let's say, is a freakish and cruel event, and also the way of the world. Or: all deaths are unnecessary. Second, the suggestion is that Clare's death is a part of

Sebastian's, an extension or fallout from it; she can live without him, but not beyond him. Third, we may think that her love for Sebastian has shortened her life, magically contaminated it. And fourth, that both V and Nabokov need Clare's death at this point in the novel because it jumps the gun, so to speak, ends Clare's life *and* her role in the book, frees Sebastian and the reader for his second, miserable affair. Clare is the end of Sebastian's happiness.

V cannot understand what Sebastian saw in the supposedly worthless Russian woman who tormented him. This is partly because V is almost as distressed by the thought of Sebastian's irrational behaviour as by the thought of Sebastian's sorrows, and partly because he is trying to keep sexual motives out of his book altogether. He is content to think of Sebastian and Clare together because he can picture them as neutered accomplices, almost siblings, exempt from desire as they are exempt from unreason:

> She entered his life without knocking, as one might step into the wrong room because of its vague resemblance to one's own. She stayed there forgetting the way out and quietly getting used to the strange creatures she found there ... They must have had a glorious time together, those two.

Sounding more and more like his hysterical descendant Kinbote, V complains of the 'hissing vulgarity' of the word sex, 'the "ks, ks" catcall at the end', and says he 'cannot help doubting whether there is any real idea behind the word'.

> Indeed, I believe that granting 'sex' a special situation when tackling a human problem, or worse still, letting the 'sexual idea', if such a thing exists, pervade and 'explain' all the rest is a grave error of reasoning.

We need to go slowly here, because the full context shows Nabokov at his devious best, making and unmaking a polemical point, and orchestrating doubts just where he seems to be dismissing them. V refuses to discuss Sebastian's and Clare's sex life, because he does not believe a sexual dissatisfaction, even if there was one, would account for Sebastian's strange behaviour and his leaving Clare. This seems entirely plausible, and our faith in V is enhanced by the fact that he has already found a fine metaphor for Clare's place in Sebastian's sentimental education: 'she had ... dallied at some pleasant sunlit corner of Sebastian's life, where Sebastian himself had not paused'. Sebastian's life is about to go dark, and Clare's own swiftly evoked death, as we have just seen, is a narrative announcement of the darkness.

Of course we are invited to smile at V's prudery, but otherwise he seems to be saying pretty much what Nabokov himself says in many of his anti-Freudian excursions. The 'sexual idea' is a dim abstraction, and even if it were livelier could hardly explain 'all the rest', whatever that is. The difficulty here, and the stealthy joke, is that V knows, as Sebastian doesn't, that sex is about to play an essential role in Sebastian's life: within a paragraph he is on his way to Blauberg, in Alsace, where he will meet the Russian woman who makes him so unhappy. In *Lost Property*, Sebastian has a fictional character speak of 'this other passion' but not as 'a comedy of the flesh' contrasted to a 'pure love': 'All is flesh and all is purity'. This seems to be a manner of saying that love may be happy or doomed but will be sexual either way. V quotes the passage as illuminating the mood of Sebastian's shift from Clare to the Russian woman, but then doggedly refuses to see what it says. What V wants to do, apparently, is to cancel out not only Sebastian's sexual relations with Clare but also, in advance, his presumably more turbulent sexual relations with his later love. So V is right to say sex is not an explanation for human events, and probably right to think there is often no 'real idea behind the word'. But he is wrong to believe sex can be banished as a force in human events, and nervously, fearfully wrong to believe there is *never* a real idea behind the word. We know he is wrong because of our own experience and because of what Sebastian tells us; and because V almost repeats in his own person the very error he fails to understand in his half-brother.

Faithful to the strategy of painting the ways of painting, V tells us everything we are going to learn about Sebastian's Russian love through V's account of his own pursuit of her. He fails to get a list of names from Sebastian's Alsatian hotel, and wonders whether he can write the book without the woman: 'A book with a blind spot. An unfinished picture, – uncoloured limbs of the martyr with the arrows in his side'. But of course without the woman, neither V nor we can really see the arrows. A chance acquaintance – a sort of Hitchcockian appearance of the relenting author, perhaps – procures the hotel list for V, and he narrows it down to four possibles. They turn out to be: a Russian Jewish woman in Berlin, entirely charming but not at all suited to the role of the vamp; an unthinkable elderly Russian woman in Paris, with orange hair and a moustache; and two other Russian women in Paris, whom V hears a lot about but has difficulty in meeting, Mme de Rechnoy and Helene von Graun. To be precise, he never sees Helene von Graun, but (probably) meets Mme de Rechnoy, although he doesn't recognize her because she has changed her name and he thinks she is French: she is the Mme Lecerf who is almost certainly Sebastian's unkind mistress, and who may or may not resemble Sebastian's mother.

Vladimir Alexandrov sees a connection between mistress and mother in the terms in which they are described to us, and in their both wearing black. Virginia Knight is 'a slim, slightly angular woman, with a small quivering face under a huge black hat'; Mme Lecerf is 'a small, slight, pale-faced young woman with smooth black hair ... her black dress was high at the neck, and she used a long black cigarette holder'. I agree the evocations are similar, but I think that the similarity is faint, and that its faintness is as important as its presence. We are in uncertain territory here; in the territory of uncertainty. More significant is V's noting that Mme Lecerf is said to have 'violet dark eyelids', thus repeating the theme of the violet sweets and the pension called Les Violettes, but it's still not clear what we are to make of the clue. Does Sebastian's shaky heart imagine it has found his mother's ghost at last? Are we looking at a real clue or only at one of these elegant lures that tease our appetite for meaning? If the women are to be linked, do we think of their lightness and charm, the raindrop on the leaf, or their moral frailty and the pain they cause? Could we *not* connect the women, since Sebastian in his unlucky passion seems to be pursuing not so much his mother's fading presence as her old absence, her habits of infidelity? Has he fallen in love with his own, and his father's unhappiness? 'Sebastian could never forget his mother, nor could he forget that his father had died for her'.

V hears about the shallow Mme de Rechnoy from her ex-husband: 'you may find her in any cheap novel, she's a type, a type. And she loved inventing some rare illness and going to some famous kurort, and ...' V thinks he may have solved his problem, but worries about the 'plausible, too plausible trail'. Isn't the image 'a trifle too obvious'? 'The whimsical wanton who ruins a foolish man's life ... The more I thought of it, the less possible it seemed.' He is talking himself out of it, but does he want a grander love for Sebastian, or a nicer one? Does he want not to be in a novel, or only not in a cheap one? When V finally meets Mme Lecerf, he is taken with the 'delightful old-world suavity in her

45

crystal clear French'. 'A nice quiet, quietly moving person', he
says of her, although a little later he is stuffily bothered by her
'French sense of humour in connection with connubial matters'.
He thinks Mme Lecerf's accent is Parisian, but imagines there is
something 'very Russian' about the 'soft curve of the cheek and
the upward dart of the ghostly eyebrow'. He is already falling for
her, talks of 'her dark velvety eyes', 'her queer velvety eyes', and
gradually confesses that he finds her 'quite attractive', 'after all
quite a pretty young woman' and finally 'decidedly a pretty
woman'. He thinks Sebastian's ghost may be amused by his saying
'that for a moment I thought of making love to that woman'. He
toys with a plan of returning to her house at night, pretending he
has forgotten a book. At this point he discovers who (he thinks)
she is, devises a little test which establishes that she is Russian
after all, and departs.

'There seemed to be a slight family likeness', V muses at the
start of the chapter where all this unravels, 'between Nina Rechnoy and Helene von Graun', – that is between Nina Rechnoy,
and the woman whom Mme Lecerf, presumably lending her friend
her own story, describes to him as Helene von Graun. 'Between
the two there was not much to choose, Nina was shallow and
glamorous, Helene cunning and hard; both were flighty; neither
was much to my taste...' That Mme Lecerf should prove so
much to his taste, and that she should quite probably be the person in both of these portraits, confounds all of V's clichés, his
bland claims about female types and the sort of woman Sebastian
could or could not have loved. The confounding of the clichés is
the point, and for this purpose Mme Lecerf doesn't have to be
Mme de Rechnoy, or indeed Sebastian's lover at all; the possibility
that she could be is enough. V's incipient feelings for Mme Lecerf
entirely ruin his pompous judgements, and more important, show
us in miniature precisely how Sebastian, or anyone, could fall in
love with a charming and mischievous woman.

The strongest argument for Mme Lecerf's actually having been
Sebastian's mistress is that she evokes a man who sounds exactly
like Sebastian, capable of 'some long and obscure speech about the
form of an ashtray or the colour of time'. She is still speaking in
the third person, pretending to describe her friend's affair, and she
says nothing about the man's nationality or name or particular
habits.

You see, I don't know who the man was, but I gathered he was a

difficult sort of man. She says she liked his looks and his hands and
his manner of talking, and she thought it would be rather good fun
to have him make love to her – because, you see, he looked so very
intellectual, and it is always entertaining to see that kind of refined,
distant, – brainy fellow suddenly go on all fours and wag his tail.
What's the matter now, *cher Monsieur*?

V is clearly very distraught at this picture, but it gets worse.

He got positively wicked when he found out that he was falling in
love with Helene ... He told her bitterly that she was cheap and
vain, then he kissed her to make sure that she was not a porcelain
figure. Well, she wasn't. And presently he found out that he could
not live without her, and presently she found out that she had had
quite enough of hearing him talk of his dreams, and the dreams in
his dreams, and the dreams in the dreams of his dreams. Mind you,
I do not condemn either. Perhaps both were right and perhaps
neither, – but, you see, my friend was not quite the ordinary
woman he thought she was – oh, she was something quite different,
and she knew a bit more about life and death and people than he
thought he knew.

The friend in the story finally tells the man who may be Sebastian
that she doesn't want to see him any more, and V says he has 'no
more doubts' about the truth of the story and the identity of the
couple, 'though the picture of Sebastian was atrocious, – but then,
too, I had got it secondhand'.

If reality is refraction, we cannot do better than secondhand,
and V's quest for the real woman in Sebastian's later life is like a
later fictional quest for Flaubert's real parrot. It is not that the
woman can't be found; it is that even found, she will hardly be
recognized. 'There are many kinds of love and many kinds of sorrow', Mme Lecerf says, resisting the suggestion that her friend (or
she herself) was necessarily sorry or not sorry to hear the news of
Sebastian's death. 'Why ought we to assume that she loved him
enough to be upset by his dying? Or perhaps she did love him,
but held special views about death which excluded hysterics?
What do we know of such matters?' Neither the speaker nor the
imagined person is the ordinary woman Sebastian thought his mistress was. But then perhaps ordinariness doesn't exist, except in a
simplifying projection. Julia Kristeva in her book on strangers
suggests that an attention just to the faces of other people ought to
reveal to us 'the non-existence of banality in human beings'.

Sebastian's return to what he calls the obvious and the ordinary is a move in the right direction, an abandonment of the rather self-congratulating cultivation of the extraordinary that marked his earlier life, at least as V saw it ('it was simply his becoming aware that the rhythm of his inner being was so much richer than that of other souls . . . Even then . . . he knew that his slightest thought or sensation had always at least one more dimension than those of his neighbours'). But he still had one discovery to make, fell short of a last finding: that the ordinary itself is not quite what it seems.

We cannot put a single person together out of the various images of Sebastian's mistress, and our failure is our lesson. We learn from it not that there is no truth or merely that truth is multiple but that refractions are always worth looking at again, that the reality of persons may be glimpsed in the very moment we seem to miss them, perhaps in the very manner of our misses.

(v)

Falling unhappily in love with a possibly flighty Russian woman, Sebastian enacts several stories at once, scrambling psychoanalytic variants into what looks like an elaborate riddle. His love is a *retour au pays natal*, and a return to his first language; it repeats his father's helpless emotional experience with a foreigner, or (to him) a semi-foreigner. Sebastian's heart condition, and his sense of his own mortality, must be precipitating factors too; as if unhappiness might defeat death, or had to be experienced before death made even misery irrelevant.

But the *pays natal*, although the motherland, is not the land of the mother. Abandoning her language, and the language of his art, Sebastian finds his mother again in the behaviour of the woman he loves. He goes home, it seems, only to lose home; to discover that home itself is a form of loss.

Kristeva suggests that Sebastian 'falls victim to a veritable regression', but what happens to him is more like a cancellation of return. Or a travesty of return, which V tries nobly to read as the real thing. Kristeva keeps her account straight by multiplying mothers. Sebastian simply slides from one to the other. His English is the language of his 'almost unknown mother, the dead language of a dead mother'. But then he 'attempted the return journey to the language of his Russian childhood which was that of his second mother'. This is helpful because it reminds us that language is the issue, that love and fidelity in this novel are always

coloured by questions of linguistic allegiance, *are* questions of linguistic allegiance. When Sebastian says the only real number is
One ('And love, apparently, is the best exponent of this singular-
ity'), he must include language under his dispensation. To have
two languages would be to have none.

But then Kristeva's sense of the psychoanalytic paradigm as
answer to a problem, rather than another version of the riddle
itself, causes her to miss the contradictory nature of the evidence
offered by Sebastian's case. The case certainly has a psychoanalytic
shape and tilt, but it is constructed as an intricate impossibility, a
crossing of narrative wires, and functions chiefly as a metaphor for
a crisis rather than as a reading of a character's, or anyone's mind.
Sebastian's 'second mother' is not really marked as a mother at all
in the symbolic economy of this book, so he has only one. But
then this one, the first and only one, divides and recombines
alarmingly, speaks two languages but has only one morality,
becomes home and exile, comfort and temptation, violet sweets
and violet eyelids. She is herself the crisis. Sebastian mourns for
her, as Kristeva's strangers and melancholics mostly mourn for
their mothers. But his mourning, always severely displaced, is
finally taken from him, or he throws it away; the love of his life
feels like a parody. He loses his mother, and then he loses his loss,
her dead language dies. He looks for old differences, and finds
only the same.

We cannot identify Nabokov with Sebastian, or with V. Or
rather, we should perhaps identify him with both, and then leave
him some space to spare. But we can hardly ignore the fact that
the novel we are reading displays an English title and a Russian-
looking author's name, with no sign of a translator in sight. Even
the purest of New Critics would have to make something of these
signs. And the faintest biographical curiosity will tell us that the
book was written in English by a Russian who had learned his
second language in much the same way that Sebastian learned his:
in childhood in St Petersburg, and as a student at Cambridge.
Sebastian went on to become an English writer; Nabokov was
about to become one, or at least a writer in English. But what
does this mean for our reading of the novel?

A little later, arrived in America, Nabokov would complain bitterly about the difficulty and sorrow of having to give up his
Russian. Like Sebastian, he seems to have believed that the only
real number was One, and that, as I have already suggested, one
cannot *love* two languages. Love them, that is, as a writer must

love the instrument of his or her art. But we can go a little further. Nabokov seems actually to have experienced all major linguistic shifts as forms of infidelity, so that *The Real Life of Sebastian Knight* was a betrayal as well as a triumph, an offence committed not against the Russian language, but against *his* Russian language, the one he had worked on for twenty years or more. Similarly, his returns to Russian, once he had dedicated himself to English as his language for fiction, were acts of adultery, carefully rationed sessions of escape from his new consort. To Edmund Wilson he writes jokingly, and pretty tastelessly, of 'sneaking visits' and sporadic 'intercourse' with his Russian muse, and we could perhaps simply ignore these remarks, if we were not held by the intense equation between language and unhappy love in *The Real Life of Sebastian Knight*. Sebastian is not sleeping around, he is losing his soul and his peace.

Sebastian, I think, is a portrait of Nabokov's fear, an image of the reason Nabokov could not return to Russian for important work for such a long time; not even (until 1954) for his autobiography. There is superstition in such abstinence, of course, but there is also an understanding that language, like love and like death, alters us and affirms us, clings to us and explores us; that it involves the irrevocable, and makes us who we are.

(vi)

Mistakes – ones which are only mistakes and ones which are blunderings into insight – are absolutely central to *The Real Life of Sebastian Knight*, and it is important that they should always look like comic mistakes. That is the form unlikely understandings must take when they appear in the world of likeliness. Walter Benjamin, the critic Robert Alter suggests, seems to have meant something like this when he spoke of the 'comic aspects of Jewish theology', in Kafka. 'The encounter between Creator and creature' Alter says, must seem absurd if it is authentic, an 'irruption of the transcendent into the paltry realm of the human'; and absurd in a different way if it is faked or dreamed, if there is no Creator to be encountered. Both absurdities haunt Nabokov's work, although they are lighter in colour and in weight than in Kafka, and the Creator is almost always the novelist in disguise. They are often transposed into dream-coherences, no longer properly absurdities at all but still vulnerable to mockery and doubt. Comedy here tends to serve belief rather than undo it; but scepticism in turn controls the genre.

Sebastian's mother died in 'the little town of Roquebrune', some years after leaving her Russian husband and her then four-year-old son. Much later Sebastian, finding himself in the south of France – there is a Roquebrune close to Monaco – remembers the name of the place, and even of the pension where the death occurred, although as we have seen he may have shaped this second name to his artistic and emotional needs. He visits the house, tries to see it as his mother saw it, even seems to glimpse her, 'a dim slight figure in a large hat', mounting some steps in the garden. Later still, in London, he mentions his excursion to a cousin, who casually corrects the image, returns the ghost to limbo: 'Oh, but it was the other Roquebrune, the one in the Var.'

We are at liberty to suspect Sebastian made the whole story up, or at least tilted it to show its special flicker of ghastly comedy. Even so, the most important aspect of the mistake would still be the pattern it proposes, which is echoed twice later in the novel. First (in narrative time), V finds the woman he is looking for without knowing he has found her; he is in the right Roquebrune, so to speak, without recognizing the name or the place. Later in the book, racing to reach Sebastian's hospital in France, he sits for a while in the next room from his dying half-brother, listening to the faint sounds of his sleep, seeming to understand deep mysteries through this close, silent communion. 'That gentle breathing was telling me more of Sebastian than I had ever known before.' The gentle breathing is not Sebastian's, though. A nurse he talks to tells V he has been in the wrong room. The night porter, impatient, sleepy and French, had confused two English names, Knight and Kegan. Sebastian died the day before, and was in any case using his Russian name. The other Roquebrune.

Sebastian perhaps saw such mistakes as mockeries of desire, characteristic figures of human disappointment. But V refuses to be disappointed, determinedly realigns his Roquebrune.

> So I did not see Sebastian after all, or at least I did not see him alive. But those few minutes I spent listening to what I thought was his breathing changed my life as completely as it would have been changed, had Sebastian spoken to me . . .

The thought is both absurd and compelling, a revelation and the burlesque of a revelation. It's not that the wrong dying man will do as well as the right one, or that any dying man will do. It's that the error itself was a feat of generous imagination, a promise of connection, a willingness to learn whatever love teaches, and a reminder of the deep and often grotesque indirection of oracles. They don't speak, as Heraclitus said, they give signs. The dying Sebastian himself could only have done the same, and couldn't have offered the same lesson of ridicule and humility.

What V learns is remarkably similar to certain suggestions in the fiction of Jorge Luis Borges, whom Nabokov cannot have read at this time: 'that the soul is but a manner of being – not a constant state – that any soul may be yours, if you find and follow its undulations . . . Thus – I am Sebastian Knight'. He is 'impersonating' Sebastian, that is, 'acting Sebastian', he is Sebastian-as-performance, Sebastian-as-metaphor, his text is Sebastian, the book we have read is Sebastian Knight's *real* real life. But then V cannot stop the act:

> for, try as I may, I cannot get out of my part: Sebastian's mask clings to my face, the likeness will not be washed off. I am Sebastian, or Sebastian is I, or perhaps we both are someone whom neither of us knows.

This is tricky stuff for a self-confessed dull fellow. *Part, mask* and *likeness* prolong the very distinction these sentences deny. V is Sebastian in that Sebastian has become inescapable, he will never again untangle Sebastian from his life; a haunting. But Sebastian is only a role that has stuck to him; he does not possess Sebastian's past or memory or 'real life', and has quite different gifts. The impersonation of Sebastian keeps Sebastian faintly alive but insists even more visibly on his death.

This novel's deepest mood is what Nabokov elsewhere calls that of the preterist: a longing for lost treasures, tastes, languages, countries, loved ones, a hope that they may be magically stored somewhere because they *cannot* have vanished, simply gone like smoke. Sebastian's book *Lost Property* is among other things 'a summing up, a counting of the things and souls lost on the way' – there is a faint but painful ambiguity in the notion of lost souls. V speaks, a touch sentimentally and self-interestedly, of 'little things which will wander away and perish' if he can't collect them in his book; finds it 'hard to believe that the warmth, the tenderness, the beauty' of Sebastian's relationship with Clare Bishop 'has not been gathered, and is not treasured somewhere, somehow, by some immortal witness of mortal life'. It's hard to believe because we don't want to believe it, not because we can't believe it or it doesn't seem true. Loss is not denied in these perspectives, indeed in one sense it is all there is; but the imagination refuses what the heart knows, and refuses on ethical grounds. Accepting loss when one must is not the same as believing loss to be acceptable. The fragility of this distinction means we need both irony and faith to sustain it, and a willingness to laugh when pathos turns to posturing. This is one of the (many) reasons why comic mistakes are important.

There are hints that V *is* Sebastian in another sense; that he has made him up. He speaks of 'all these books that I knew as well as if I had written them myself', perhaps because he has written them, or at least imagined them, and when Sebastian's name is spelled with a v in a telegram – 'a transcription of its Russian spelling' – the narrator recognizes his own initial and 'for some reason unknown' goes into the bathroom and stands in front of the mirror for a moment. 'For some reason' is unusually clumsy and therefore probably a signal, like the awkward prose at the end of 'The Vane Sisters'. Of course, no signal at all is needed if the suggestion is merely that V identifies strongly with Sebastian – that's been clear all along – or even that he no longer knows how to separate himself from the object of his quest. The letter and the mirror seem more awkward, more forceful than this. Has V invented Sebastian, is Sebastian a fantasy, the fiction's fiction? The discovery V appears to make on the novel's last page – 'I am Sebastian Knight' – would then function as a double bluff. The man who is Sebastian confesses to impersonating him, rather as Guy Burgess, a Russian spy, used jovially to confess to being a Russian spy. The v would represent, on the plane of accident or overdetermined narrative, the near-collapse or threat of collapse of the two selves into one; the tilt of the dream self back into the daily one.

I don't believe these hints quite add up to a reading, but they do invite us to take the notion of fiction one stage further still. V as author of Sebastian and his life and friends, V as novelist within the novel, would be quite a different figure from V the panting, baffled biographer; but he could not be the solution to a riddle, and he wouldn't, as author, be any less fictional than he is as narrator. Or any more, or less, fictional than Sebastian Knight. This is the condition the narrator's last sentence glances at: 'perhaps we both are someone whom neither of us knows'.

'Perhaps' registers V's suspicion that he may be authored as well as author, as all fictional and other creatures are if there is a God. But for us, of course, there is no 'perhaps'. V and Sebastian just are someone whom neither of them know, or could know; they are Nabokov, in whatever way or ways fictional characters 'are' their authors. And this really, unequivocally is Sebastian Knight's real life, the only life he has, as a character made of words, inhabiting this book. We must be careful with our interpretation of 'only', though. Sebastian Knight is fiction several times over: Nabokov's, ours, V's, that of several other characters in the novel, perhaps his own. But fiction in this sense is not opposed to reality, it is a construction and construal of it. The last sentence of the novel doesn't, as Nabokov himself may have felt, and as many binary-minded critics have certainly thought, release us into 'mere' fiction, a world that turns out to have been 'only' a book. It points precisely to the precarious but possibly continuing life of whatever has been thoroughly, painfully or ecstatically imagined. Sebastian Knight, a haunted and haunting figure of loss and (undeniable, endlessly denied) absence, was born in language in Paris in 1938, and moves me close to tears now, in Devon, in 1994 – and has moved many others between those dates, and will move many others for a long time to come. That is a far from negligible form of real life.

The Real Life of Sebastian Knight, usually taken as one of the thinnest of Nabokov's novels, *is* slender and delicate, but appealing for just those reasons, a small monument to the fragility of hope and loyalty. It touches us across its tricks, because of its tricks – its tricks are images of our eagerness to deceive ourselves. If it is not a great masterpiece it may be something more precious: like Ford's *The Good Soldier* rather than Tolstoy's *War and Peace*; or like Debussy's string quartet, for which, if I had to, I would give away all Beethoven.

3

The Cruelty of Chance:
Bend Sinister, 'Signs and Symbols',
'The Vane Sisters'

*No, wait a minute. Each mortal in the room
must, momentarily, have died. But just as
the fledgling artists put their own faces on
their canvases, so they had perished in their
own particular ways.*

Jean Stafford, 'The Philosophy Lesson'

(i)

Nabokov regularly told his readers there were no symbols in his
work, and in one rather limited sense this is true, or nearly true.
More precisely, what we have in Nabokov's work, as elsewhere in
life, is a choice of symbolisms. We *make* some structures of meaning literal in relation to others; the end of the tether may be a literal
or a figurative place. Nabokov's critical comments are often both
haughty and too tidy, swishes of mandarin mischief, but they are
also worth attending to. Lent a little patience, they can reveal dis-
criminations they appear to ignore or rush past: a distinction, for
instance, between grounded, contextual symbols (which he calls
metaphors) and the sort of shopping list symbol hunters frequently
have.

'The notion of symbol itself has always been abhorrent to me',
Nabokov writes in a review of W W Rowe's *Nabokov's Deceptive
World*, 1971. 'The symbolism racket in schools attracts computer-
ized minds but destroys plain intelligence as well as poetical sense.'
However, Nabokov goes on to make clear that for him the opposite
of the symbolic is not the literal but the specific and the concrete,
which includes metaphor. If we see only free-floating symbols in a
text (alias 'labels' or 'pointers'), delayed action devices 'supposedly

planted by an idiotically sly novelist', we shall miss the whole intricate, organic show, with its 'live fragments of specific
description, rudiments of metaphor, and echoes of creative emotion'. 'The fatal flaw in Mr Rowe's treatment of recurrent words . . .
is his regarding them as abstractions.' When words and images return in his work, Nabokov says, they return in different contexts
and therefore with different meanings, colours and effects. He
doesn't step into the same scene twice.

What is interesting here is Nabokov's simplification of his art,
and what hides in the simplification. The 'live fragments' and
'creative emotion' are themselves broadly and rather unimagina-
tively symbolic, part of a highly generalized, conventional
mythology, embodying assumptions about art and nature, about
art *as* nature, which Nabokov himself elsewhere vehemently
attacks. Nabokov does use symbols, even in his own sense of
symbol; in his story 'Signs and Symbols', for example. At a
moment of human distress he lays a damaged bird on the street: 'A
few feet away, under a swaying and dripping tree, a tiny half-dead
unfledged bird was helplessly twitching in a puddle'. The image is
specific enough in its detail, and the swaying and dripping tree is
clearly visualized; but the bird (tiny, unfledged, helpless) comes
straight from a ready-made lexicon, a sort of Hollywood handbook
of metonymy. It may, however, prove Nabokov's critical point,
since we can use his own argument about abstraction to see how the
image seems both loose and overloaded, a shortcut, too easy a claim
on our sympathy. Further, Nabokov does of course step into the
same scene twice, and more than twice; steps again and again into
several favourite scenes. He is right to suggest the scenes are never
exactly the same; wrong if he is saying they are entirely different,
can't be connected or compared. But is this what he is saying? It
seems so:

> the sound of a bath being filled, say, in the world of *Laughter in the
> Dark*, is as different from the limes rustling in the rain of *Speak,
> Memory* as the Garden of Delights in *Ada* is from the lawns in *Lol-
> ita*.

Just how different *is* that, though? Hugely different, is the unmistakable implication; and the context certainly suggests that only a
fool could confuse or generalize such moments under the undif-
ferentiated headings of 'water' or 'garden'. But Rowe wasn't doing
that anyway, and Nabokov's language, in spite of its scornful,

polemical drive, leaves the question of resemblance curiously open. Seeing this is part of what I mean by lending him our patience. But what is he up to?

He is, I think, trying to make important distinctions in a language and a tone which are too stuffy for the job; and he is trying to bury the fact that he *is* the idiotically sly novelist he mocks, as well as a much more interesting one. A first distinction not only concerns reading in and out of context but raises the question of what a context is; a second signals the difference between critical thinking, however subtle, and the implied, enacted, multifarious thought of a work of art. The burial of the idiot is stranger, part of a clash between Nabokov's writing practice and his image of himself; or of a clash between different practices. He regularly plants labels and pointers; leaves clues and plays games. He invites the very reader he despises, often alienates other readers, and makes the pleasure of still other readers a mystery to themselves – this book is among other things an attempt to map certain regions of that mystery. The puzzle element of Nabokov's fiction strikes me as the least compelling aspect of it, but it isn't dull or empty, and I don't think it is separable from the rest. What is extraordinarily compelling is the question of how the sly idiot, the haughty mandarin and the great, doubting magician get along together. Particularly when they meet up with, or actually become, as Nabokov did in the years immediately after the Second World War, the theorist of pain.

(ii)

'So suddenly did his guards disappear that, had he been a character in fiction, he might well have wondered whether the strange doings and so on had not been some evil vision and so forth.' He is a character in fiction, he does wonder; but the strange doings don't go away, or cause less pain, or become less evil. A few minutes pass, and are described by the narrator as they must seem to this character. They are very long minutes, they seem like years, and are evoked with a coolness and a confidence which make the hyperbole seem almost literal, a matter of mere observation: 'Four years elapsed. Then disjointed parts of a century. Odds and ends of torn time. Say, twenty-two years in all'.

Time is stretched and torn, the guards vanish like shadows because the mind of this character is being subjected to tortures which are incompatible with what we like to think are the ordinary processes of clocks and the world. He is Adam Krug, protagonist of

Nabokov's *Bend Sinister* 1947, a distinguished philosopher in an imaginary European country which has recently undergone a revolution. His wife has been ill and has died; the new regime, headed by an unlovely former schoolmate of Krug's, wants his support, which he refuses, in spite of pressure put upon him and his friends. The regime arrests Krug and his eight-year-old son, and separates them. Krug has no hesitation in lending his support once his son is at risk, and immediately says so. Several horrible things now happen.

A child is brought in, 'a thin frightened boy of twelve or thirteen'. His head is 'newly bandaged', hurt in some unknown but presumably clumsy and ugly act of violence for which the following grotesque excuse is offered: 'nobody was to blame, they said, he had slipped on a highly polished floor and hit his forehead against a model of Stevenson's [*sic*] engine in the Children's Museum'. This image is worth pausing over because of its crazy ingenuity – Nabokov's villains are often stupid but they share their author's concern for details – and because of the compassion which must creep into our reconstruction of the action behind the excuse. Children do slip on polished floors, they do hit their heads, Stephenson's Rocket, for a certain generation, was what (male) children were supposed to dream of. But this very generality, the murmur of the stereotype, shows us what is wrong. These notions concern children, not this child. He might have slipped in the Museum but he was probably beaten in a cell. Stephenson's Rocket represents an eerie attempt to evoke a conventional childhood and to borrow its innocent violence for an entirely different universe. In any case this unfortunate child is the wrong age and the wrong boy: he is Arvid Krug, son of Professor Martin Krug, not David Krug son of Professor Adam Krug. Near enough, one might think, for a brutal regime dedicated to the abolition of difference. But even the officials are embarrassed by this mistake, and there is more blundering under way.

David, it seems, has been taken to the wrong building. He was supposed to have gone to 'the best State Rest House' but has instead been delivered to a location even an icy official hesitates in describing, 'a kind of – well, Institute for Abnormal Children'. We learn of what happens in this place – it is not exactly an Institute for Abnormal Children – and Krug is finally shown a ragged amateurish film in which David appears. This is the last time Krug sees him alive, a small boy in overcoat and slippers, gazing out from the screen, meeting his father's desperate eyes, but unable to recognize them or any help or comfort, because he is only a photographed figure and cannot see beyond the flat world which contains him. He is alive because he moves, because he was alive when the film was taken; but also dead, as Barthes says photographed people always are, already a memory, since an 'accident' has occurred. Soon after this Krug is shown the dead boy lying in the infirmary, his face gruesomely prettified, his body hidden, a vision of harm turned into a kind of sickly art.

> The murdered child had a crimson and gold turban around its head; its face was skilfully painted and powdered: a mauve blanket, exquisitely smooth, came up to its chin.

Its head, its face, its chin. This is not David, it is a statue in Kitsch; all our horror rushes back to the live boy in his last moments, to the ghastly breaking and bruising now covered up by paint and powder, turban and blanket. As so often in Nabokov, we have to imagine the worst; to use the specifics he gives us to divine the ones he withholds.

Let us return to what we see before Krug sees the film. The whole sequence is masterly, and could I think have been written by no one but Nabokov. This is style rather than signature, and we need to see how delicate and oblique and powerful the style is: it works through indirection, horror, anger, grim and hilarious burlesque and an intimate if parodic understanding of what was soon to be called the banality of evil. Nabokov said the 'main theme' of the novel was 'the beating of Krug's loving heart, the torture an intense tenderness is subjected to – and it is for the sake of the pages about David and his father that the book was written and should be read'. Critics have been unusually reluctant to follow the author in this case, and have concentrated on the philosophy and the politics of the novel. I think the philosophy is interesting, although not in obvious ways. The politics are surely trivial, not because the questions they address don't matter or because Nabokov is a mere aesthete, but because his overtly political formulations are always too broad and easy, have none of the interest and intricacy of a fully imagined political world. I'm inclined to go even further than Nabokov with regard to this book. It is some pages about David and his father, specifically the father's imagining of David's pain and fear, which lift this novel from the brilliant but rather brittle and excessively fussy realm in which it appeared to be stuck. The American philosopher Richard Rorty says 'the death of a child is

Nabokov's standard example of ultimate pain', and we can refine this suggestion further: the pain of a child is Nabokov's dominant image of moral horror, even more unbearable than a child's death, and an emblem of everything that threatens to wreck whatever meaning and coherence life may seem to have. More specifically still, we can say that the suffering of the innocent is what unsettles all comforts for Nabokov, endlessly torments conscience and consciousness – I am thinking of the reported death of Pnin's friend Mira Beloshkin in Buchenwald, but also of the exclusion and suicide of Lucette in *Ada*, a title which among other things evokes the idea of hell. The child in *Bend Sinister* and elsewhere is both an immediate victim and the delegate of other innocents. The child's pain – our awareness of the child's pain – is where our moral world ends.

Krug learns about the atrocious mistake regarding David from one Crystalsen, 'Second Secretary of the Council of Elders', and initially identified only as possessing a 'red face, blue eyes, tall starched collar'. They are walking towards a police car which will take them to the place where David is being kept. The passage begins in innocuous-seeming indirect speech, but very soon modulates into other modes, particularly, abruptly, that of a direct address from the speaker which registers Krug's distraught responses without actually reporting them. Even when Krug hits Crystalsen we are told not about the blow but about Crystalsen's activities with his handkerchief.

> It was quite clear that something had gone dreadfully wrong; the child had been taken to a kind of – well, Institute for Abnormal Children – instead of the best State Rest House, as had been arranged. You are hurting my wrist, sir. Unfortunately, the director of the Institute had understood, as who would not, that the child delivered to him was one of the so-called 'Orphans', now and then used to serve as a 'release-instrument' for the benefit of the most interesting inmates with a so-called 'criminal' record (rape, murder, wanton destruction of State property etc). The theory – and we are not here to discuss its worth, and you shall pay for my cuff if you tear it – was that if once a week the really difficult patients could enjoy the possibility of venting in full their repressed yearnings (the exaggerated urge to hurt, to destroy, etc) upon some little human creature of no value to the community, then, by degrees, the evil in them would be allowed to escape, would be, so to speak, 'effundated', and eventually they would become good citizens.

The smooth flow of Crystalsen's patter is reflected in the reported speech – 'unfortunately', 'as who would not' – but he also relays what must be the language and point of view of the authors and students of the 'theory' – they are the ones who speak of 'the most interesting inmates' and 'the really difficult patients'; enact government policy about what is 'evil', and what is and is not of 'value to the community'. They are also quoted (by Crystalsen) and spoofed (by Nabokov) as their vocabulary proceeds from the technical ('release-instrument') to the ludicrous ('effundated'). Deeper still in this textual trap, the language gives other games away: 'benefit', 'enjoy', 'yearnings', the implication that rape and murder are only 'so-called' crimes, that the urge to hurt and destroy is not a problem as long as it's not 'exaggerated' – all this suggests the real sadism entangled in the travesty of social theory. 'Wanton destruction of State property' seems to be a rather different sort of offence: probably just as much fun as rape and murder but more reprehensible, perhaps not even 'so-called' at all but the real thing, because socially so much more undesirable. The offhand 'now and then', almost hidden in the movement of the prose, adds its own little touch of horror.

We may sense that Crystalsen is enjoying himself, that he knows that this conversation is Krug's inferno, the ideal torment, that the idea of David caught up in such activities is worse than anything Krug has imagined. The bland abstraction of the theory functions as a kind of insolence, trivial in itself, but helping to degrade the very notion of suffering. It is at this moment that Krug hits Crystalsen.

> The experiment might be criticized, of course, but that was not the point (Crystalsen carefully wiped the blood from his mouth and offered his none too clean handkerchief to Krug – to wipe Krug's knuckles; Krug refused; they entered the car; several soldiers joined them). Well, the enclosure where the 'release games' took place was so situated that the director from his window and the other doctors and research workers, male and female (Doktor Amalia von Wytwyl, for instance, one of the most fascinating personalities you have ever met, an aristocrat, you would enjoy meeting her under happier circumstances, sure you would) from other *gemütlich* points of vantage, could watch the proceedings and take notes.

'Well' mimes the storyteller settling back into his stride, getting on with the good old tale. Is this man mad, or merely diabolical? Crystalsen *is* enjoying himself, surely, in spite of his bloody mouth, perhaps now because of his bloody mouth. The atmosphere has changed slightly though, with the 'Doktor' and the ghastly *gemüt-lich* and the cheery Americanism of 'sure you would': this is sadism as a cosy social occasion, as if it were both homely and fashionable, as if there were intimate links between certain strata in Germany and a certain heartiness in America. Nabokov's story 'Conversation Piece 1945' pursues just this connection.

> A nurse led the 'orphan' down the marble steps. The enclosure was a beautiful expanse of turf, and the whole place, especially in summer, looked extremely attractive, reminding one of those open-air theatres that were so dear to the Greeks. The 'orphan' or 'little person' was left alone and allowed to roam all over the enclosure. One of the photographs showed him lying disconsolately on his stomach and uprooting a bit of turf with listless fingers (the nurse reappeared on the garden steps and clapped her hands to make him stop. He stopped). After a while the patients or 'inmates' (eight all told) were let into the enclosure. At first, they kept at a distance, eyeing the 'little person'. It was interesting to observe how the 'gang' spirit gradually asserted itself. They had been rough lawless unorganized individuals, but now something was binding them, the community spirit (positive) was conquering the individual whims (negative); for the first time in their lives they were *organized* ... [Nabokov's, or Crystalsen's, italics]

We move into a mode of writing Nabokov has borrowed from Joyce, and uses extensively in this novel: the deadpan parody of a highly conventional prose, in this case that of something like a genteel travel brochure ('attractive', 'so dear', 'reminding one', 'especially in the summer'). The photograph by contrast seems unadorned, unaltered: the child is disconsolate but distressingly obedient. It's as if Crystalsen had discovered a new mode of torture, the plain punch – or had forgotten for an instant the mythology he represents. The child is still anonymous, not yet David, and perhaps not David at all; although for Krug's anguish of course he can be only David, David is all children at this moment. The language then returns to its monstrous sociology: 'It was interesting to observe...' What is observed is ostensibly how individuals form a group, in effect how a handful of psychopaths become a miniature mob.

> Doktor von Wytwyl used to say that this was a wonderful moment: one felt that, as she quaintly put it, 'something was really happening', or in technical language: the 'ego', he goes 'ouf' (out) and the

pure 'egg' (common extract of egos) 'remains'. And then the fun began. One of the patients (a 'representative' or 'potential leader'), a heavy handsome boy of seventeen went up to the 'little person' and sat down beside him on the turf and said 'open your mouth'. The 'little person' did what he was told and with unerring precision the youth spat a pebble into the child's open mouth. (This was a wee bit against the rules, because generally speaking, all missiles, instruments, arms and so forth were forbidden).

The jokes are not very funny here, neither the cliché offered as quaintness nor the antics with eggs and egos, and the psychologist target is too easy: a sitting doctor. But Nabokov is delaying and distracting us. We are suffering with Krug but unable to get at our suffering, forced to attend to this litter of nonsense strewn in our path. A new note of coyness enters the prose ('fun', 'a wee bit against the rules'), as if the thugs were just mischievous, lovable fellows, and there is of course an anti-climax in the spitting of the pebble into the child's mouth. This is ugly and frightening, but we have been girding ourselves for worse. There is worse, much worse, we are not allowed to linger in our faint relief, and what is worse is what is *not* forbidden, the joyous point of the whole exercise, now revealed not only as sadistic, but as gloatingly dedicated to the idea of its own perfection, to the well-oiled rhetoric which is able to make mutilation and murder sound like therapy.

Sometimes the 'squeezing game' started at once after the 'spitting' game but in other cases the development from harmless pinching and poking or mild sexual investigations to limb tearing, bone breaking, deoculation, etc. took a considerable time. Deaths were of course unavoidable, but quite often the 'little person' was afterwards patched up and gamely made to return to the fray. Next Sunday, dear, you will play with the big boys again. A patched up 'little person' provided an especially satisfactory 'release'.

The smug mock-regret about the 'unavoidable' deaths is particularly unpleasant, as is the teacherly direct speech ('Next Sunday, dear ...'), but the 'mild sexual investigations' are scarier, and 'deoculation' is all the more chilling because it takes a moment for the non-Latinist to work it out. All this is part of what I mean by Nabokov's indirection. The last sentence is nastiest of all, deep into sophisticated sadism, where one enjoys not only the hurt of others but their damage, hurt on top of damage, and we may remember that for much of her novel Lolita feels like a patched up little person, Humbert especially relishing sex with her, for instance, when she has a fever. Nabokov closes this sequence by reminding us of its ultimate, intimate location: 'Now we take all this, press it into a small ball, and fit it into the centre of Krug's brain where it gently expands'. It is the expansion of this ball, I suggest, which drives Krug mad, and not, as Nabokov says, his own pity for his invented creature. Or rather, this pity is another name for the madness, and has the same result. It is not possible to imagine such tortures and stay sane; although poor Krug does, alas, stay sane long enough to see the movie.

There are, I think, two chief ethical implications in this horribly haunting episode and the grisly linguistic performances that constitute it; implications which are present in most of Nabokov's later work. One, relatively facile and slightly snobbish, is that tyrants and thugs have no taste, that evil is a form of vulgarity. This may be true in some ultimate spiritual sense, but I doubt it, and it doesn't look as if it's true in any world we are likely to inhabit. Evil is if anything more stylish than good, and to think of it as vulgar is mainly a way of refusing to contemplate its attractions – and of making its occasional, fortunate vulgarity seem more important than it is. The banality of evil is a different matter, but at times Nabokov seems to mask his understanding of it in an aesthete's shudder.

The other implication is very powerful, and very difficult to follow out, because it takes us beyond words. It is that evil is literally unspeakable; that all speech about it incurs and legitimizes a conversation that should never have taken place – as if we were to discuss the pros and cons of Hitler's racial policy, or of torturing little children. If we need to debate these things, if we *can* debate these things, we are already morally lost, adrift in a limbo of ethical abstraction. Thus it is morally obtuse to think that *Lolita* is an immoral book; but even more obtuse to think it is a book with a produceable, paraphrasable moral. A German student appears briefly in *Speak, Memory*, a 'well-bred, quiet, bespectacled' fellow whose 'hobby' is capital punishment, that is, watching it and taking pictures of it. It is as much a feature of Nabokov's ethics as it is of his style that this psychopathic interest should be described as the harmless pursuit of a 'young collector' who although he has 'attended a few passable hangings in the Balkans and a well-advertised although rather bleak and mechanical *guillotinade* ... on the Boulevard Arago', has so far not been lucky enough to 'see something really good'. He expects 'great things' from a beheading in

Regensburg, but is severely disappointed. It's true that Nabokov goes on to imagine the collector's good fortune during the Hitler period, so we can't really miss his moral point. But the point is chiefly made in the language he uses for the young man's earnest enthusiasm, the imitation of German sincerity; the enormity lurks in the gaps of this idiom.

What Nabokov's fiction offers us, among all its high jinks and genuine lightness of heart, is a range of images and narratives of brutality and horror, instances rather than propositions or arguments. The Holocaust itself, I suggest, is figured in Nabokov as a recurring massacre or mutilation of the innocent; it is what cannot be borne, let alone performed, except by moral monsters; what cannot be spoken of, except by the monsters' witting or unwitting allies. But it is also what *must* be borne, because it is what there is, and culture and the mind are not entirely helpless. And whereof we cannot speak, as Wittgenstein didn't quite say, we can make pictures and stories, relays of signs and symbols.

We need to see this possibility in order to take Rorty's important reading of Nabokov's morality where it seems to lead but doesn't quite go. Rorty ascribes to Nabokov 'an inability to put up with the thought of intense pain', so that he 'does not attempt to portray Krug's pain. More than that, he refuses to countenance the reality of a pain that great'. This is pretty startling, in the light of what we have just read. It's true that Nabokov doesn't *portray* Krug's pain if by 'portray' we mean literally describe or articulate, in the sense in which Wittgenstein was using the notion of speaking about things: naming them, discussing them, making sense of them. It's true too that Nabokov does finally 'save' Krug from his 'senseless agony' (Nabokov's phrase) by letting him know he's in a novel. But what strikes us, surely, is the drastic demand Nabokov has made on our imagination, and the terrible lateness of his act of rescue. How much more pain did we want? How much more could we take? 'Refuses to countenance the reality of a pain that great' seems particularly odd, since this pain precisely is at the heart of Nabokov's sense of history and his response to it in fiction. But perhaps Rorty is just going a little too fast; or I am. 'Refuses to countenance' must mean refuses to endorse rather than refuses to acknowledge. As I suggested in my previous chapter, there is a delicate but considerable difference between accepting loss when we have to, and judging loss to be acceptable. The same goes, perhaps even more emphatically, for the facts of pain.

65

(iii)

Nabokov published 'Signs and Symbols' in 1948. He referred to it as his story about the old Jewish couple. We don't learn directly from the work itself that the people are Jewish. The husband's brother is called Isaac, the woman has a Rebecca among her social memories, a nervous Aunt Rosa is killed by 'the Germans', 'together with all the people she had worried about'. Perhaps these hints are conclusive enough. We know the couple are immigrants in America, that they have left behind a dark and turbulent European history; that Isaac, nicknamed 'the Prince', has done well in the New World; that they speak Russian, that their English is not good. They live in a big unnamed American city. Their son, born late in the marriage and now about twenty, is in a mental hospital, 'incurably deranged in his mind'. The couple set out to visit him, taking a birthday present, a basket of ten assorted jams in little jars. They are not allowed to see him, because, they are told, he has 'again attempted to take his life'. The couple return home with their present, consider the possibility of removing their son from the hospital, having him to live with them. This is all that happens in the story. Or all but one haunting thing, which gives the work its eerie resonance, picks up and prolongs its implications, carries it beyond observation and tenderness into dizzying regions of fear and speculation.

'Signs and Symbols' was a story, Nabokov said, with an 'inside' as well as an outside, a secret figure in the carpet: 'a second (main) story is woven into, or placed behind, the superficial semitransparent one.' This makes the work sound more like a riddle than it probably is; and Nabokov's jostling metaphors (inside, woven, behind, surface, transparency) are perhaps misleading in other ways. In fact, the very multiplication of metaphors – Nabokov, writing in 1951 to Katharine White, an editor at the *New Yorker* who has refused a story of his, is being unusually explanatory – may be an indication of the difficulty of saying just what is going on. What seems to me most striking about the story is its immense shadowy background of pain and frightening possibility; not its secret but its silence. It is full of things not said, fuller than Nabokov's writing often seems; and it may help us to see what's not said elsewhere; to see that even such a talkative, explicit writer has his silences, that his silences may be larger, more eloquent, than we reckoned.

The old couple's son has been diagnosed as suffering from something called 'referential mania' – which sounds like a literary disease, even like a lot of literature. Reference become mania: an unsympathetic definition of realism. The mania might be the reader's too: what Nabokov calls 'the fatal error of looking for so-called "real life" in novels'; trying to 'reconcile the fiction of facts with the facts of fiction'. Other forms of reference would be possible, of course, and a non-manic reading might find 'some correspondence' between life and fiction, or trace the way 'pain, for instance, or dreams, or madness, or such things as kindness, mercy, justice . . . are transmuted into art'. It's not 'life' that Nabokov resists as a category, it's 'real life', the life that claims comfortably to know it's real. In his bibliographical note to *Nabokov's Dozen*, 1958, for example, he is happy enough to speak of remembered life and even actual facts without apology or any sense of difficulty. 'Real life', though, appears as a sort of nasty smell, held at bay in a wince of quotation marks.

But the young man's case is more complicated, more clinical. And his affliction is virtually all we know of him in the story; apart from a face blotched with acne and a shuffling walk, he is his mania.

In these very rare cases the patient imagines that everything around him is a veiled reference to his personality and existence. He excludes real people from the conspiracy – because he considers himself to be so much more intelligent than other men. Phenomenal nature shadows him wherever he goes. Clouds in the staring sky transmit to one another, by means of slow signs, incredibly detailed information regarding him. His inmost thoughts are discussed at nightfall, in manual alphabet, by darkly gesticulating trees. Pebbles or stains or sun flecks form patterns representing in some awful way messages he must intercept. Everything is a cipher and of everything he is the theme . . . He must always be on his guard and devote every minute and module of his life to the decoding of the undulation of things. The very air he exhales is indexed and filed away.

We recognize the scenery, if not the condition. This is the animated landscape of romantic poetry, but experienced as paranoia. Clouds, trees, air (the passage continues with mentions of plains, mountains and firs) all speak, as in so many poems, but don't speak *to the person*. It's as if a whole region were whispering behind Wordsworth's back, and whispering about him. The absence of other people makes this seem very different from other types of paranoia; but paranoia is what it is, since it deals in secrecy and conspiracy, and finds them absolutely everywhere: 'everything around him', 'wherever he goes', 'incredibly detailed', 'inmost thoughts', 'always', 'every minute'. In his *Gogol*, 1944, Nabokov associated this condition, and indeed this story ('I shall have occasion to speak in quite a different book of a lunatic who constantly felt that all the parts of the landscape and movements of inanimate objects were a complex code of allusion to his own being, so that the whole universe seemed to him to be conversing about him by means of signs') with Gogol's 'morbid view' of a world he took to be 'alive with dark stratagems and incalculable dangers'. Nothing escapes the projected design, which Nabokov also calls 'a dense tangle of logically interacting illusions'.

The phrase 'in some awful way' is both an apparent slackness in the writing and a sort of reprieve from the meticulous, totalizing madness: the vagueness at least leaves something to our imagination. That a seeming weakness of style should look like a faint bid for sanity is not incidental in Nabokov's world, and I shall return to this troubling impression. The logical interaction of the illusions is important too, and dictionary definitions of paranoia are very revealing. 'Mental disorder,' the *Oxford English Dictionary* says, 'with delusions of grandeur, persecution etc; abnormal tendency to suspect and mistrust others'. There are bothersome implications here. Is there a normal tendency to suspect and mistrust others?

Etymologically (I learn from the *Oxford Companion to the Mind* – a splendid book, even if the title sounds as if it might have been invented by Nabokov) paranoia means 'being out of one's mind', and apart from its clinical definition, 'has slipped into general use to refer to enhanced suspiciousness'. Only 'slipped'? A paranoid question. 'Enhanced' is rather like 'abnormal', since it seems to assume a going rate of suspicion, a steady state prior to enhancement. Clinically, paranoia is

> the name given to one type of functional psychosis ... in which the patient holds a coherent, internally consistent, delusional system of beliefs, centring round the conviction that he (or, more rarely, she) is a person of great importance and is on that account being persecuted, despised, and rejected.

More rarely, she. A great deal of history is compacted into that bracket: what if you don't (have not been allowed to) feel important enough to have delusions of importance? The *Companion* goes on to point out that people who are not mentally ill also may have traits associated with paranoia (if they are, for example, 'opinionated, touchy, and have an idea of their own importance which the rest of the world does not endorse') and that 'paranoiac delusions bear a disconcerting, embarrassing resemblance to the beliefs held and propagated by founders of religions, by political leaders, and by some artists . . .'

There is really too much to comment on here. Let's stay with the delusion of importance, and the ideas of coherence and internal consistency. What is both frightening and philosophically interesting about such a conjunction is the weird, dangerous meeting of flexibility and rigour: a necessary looseness in the concept of importance is grounded and exploited by the logical tightness of the illusion itself. How important are we? Who is to say? What sort of sense of our own importance would be delusional? This is like asking what level of distrust would be normal, and the test can only be empirical and local, external to the person, since the (coherent, consistent) delusion will be ingenious and entirely plausible in its specialized rationality, ready to bend any evidence at all to its own purpose. Prejudice, in this sense, works in exactly the same way as paranoia; or prejudice is a form of paranoia. Of course you don't see the Jews (or the Catholics or the Templars or the Arabs) at their fiendish work of running the world, their invisibility is an aspect of their power. It wouldn't be a real conspiracy if we could see it in action. But then, what sort of empirical test do we apply? The famous crazy cases are easy enough to spot. If I think I am Napoleon, or that my actions have the consequences of those of Napoleon, the delusion is clear: almost any piece of my life will serve as a test. But suppose I get the sense of my own importance slightly but disastrously wrong, find myself only just but unmistakably over the edge into paranoia. Where was the edge, what marked it? I'm not suggesting there isn't an edge, or that we couldn't recognize it practically; only that seeing the edge could be a delicate affair, and that we live, perhaps necessarily, among relatively unquestioned hierarchies and pools of opinion: agreements about what matters, what is reasonable, what is sane. Communities work in this way, but a community will feel like a conspiracy if it's against you.

And it may be against you. These matters are historical as well as psychological. Whole social groups, even whole nations, have gone crazy, taking their craziness as a norm; and to point to this craziness has been to become abnormally suspicious and mistrustful, as when one imagines the French army or the British police might forge evidence. The point is that enhanced suspiciousness may be horribly wrong, an isolating, suicidal mania; and it may be horribly right, a desperate diagnosis of a culturally improbable truth. There

69

is no mistaking which is the case of the young man in Nabokov's story. But the possibility of the other case connects him to us, and to his parents and their history, and permits the central reflection of the story, the mother's meditation on the 'waves of pain' that constitute the world for her family. The young man is said to be 'totally inaccessible to normal minds', but there are doubts lurking even in the terrible security of that exclusion. He is painfully separate from us, but also painfully like us; inaccessible but not beyond our imagination; other but not an alien.

'After all,' his mother thinks, 'living did mean accepting the loss of one joy after another, not even joys in her case – mere possibilities of improvement'.

> She thought of the endless waves of pain that for some reason or other she and her husband had to endure; of the invisible giants hurting her boy in some unimaginable fashion; of the incalculable amount of tenderness contained in the world; of the fate of this tenderness, which is either crushed, or wasted, or transformed into madness; of neglected children humming to themselves in unswept corners; of beautiful weeds that cannot hide from the farmer and helplessly have to watch the shadow of his simian stoop leave mangled flowers in its wake, as the monstrous darkness approaches.

The old woman's thoughts have Nabokov's signature, although not his strictest style. They are a little too discursive, too dependent on merely sketched verbal gestures ('endless', 'for some reason or other', 'unimaginable', 'incalculable' – these words and phrases suggest not a relaxation, like 'in some awful way', but a determined Conradian bid for mystery) and the weeds seem sentimentalized (do they need to be 'beautiful' to catch our sympathy, would they do any better if the farmer was an elegant aesthete, or an ape who didn't stoop?). But the overall effect of the passage is strong, and there are fine touches of precision. The children hum rather than merely stand or crouch; the corners are as neglected as their occupants. The passage moves meticulously from pain to tenderness to neglect to vulnerability and helplessness, a specific train of ideas. The woman may be thinking of her own tenderness in relation to her son, wasted because unrecognized, or of a tenderness in the young man which has now been turned to madness, and the tenderness may or may not carry over directly into the images of children and flowers, but her concentration on the 'fate' of tenderness is clear. She has become her tenderness in the way her son has become his mania. The monstrous darkness collects the mystery earlier only gestured towards. It is death, the shape of the approaching farmer; it is the end and perhaps the origin of pain; it is madness and history, what consumes the son and what killed Aunt Rosa.

We don't have to be paranoid to worry about the destruction of tenderness. But to think of giants is to take up fancifully, as in a fairy-tale, a relative of the son's delusion; and to think of tenderness as undergoing a special fate, as somehow particularly placed in the sights of pain and brutality is mildly to suffer from referential mania in respect of tenderness. The dark monsters, historical and psychological, presumably don't care about tenderness or anything else, they are not subtle or human enough to target what we cherish. But if tenderness is what we choose to highlight in the world, if it is what we are, and if we believe, as many don't, that there is a large amount (an incalculable amount) of tenderness on offer, then it must seem as if tenderness is specially marked out for crushing and wasting and madness, and the hyperbole will not seem a hyperbole at all. On this wavelength sanity meets insanity, although we don't have to confuse them. The Nazis destroy tenderness in the way the clouds and trees silently talk about the young man: the vision is irresistible from the sufferer's end. But then we find here a desolate empirical test. The Nazis did destroy tenderness, among countless other things. We cannot know whether the clouds and trees are talking about us, and chances are they would have other things in mind, if they had minds. Referential mania is also romantic in Henry James' sense, since it focuses on things 'we never can directly know', 'things that can reach us only through the beautiful circuit and subterfuge of our thought and our desire'. Or, we might add, through the (often equally beautiful) circuit and subterfuge of our terror. We have to see it as madness until we can get it in some fashion, however hyperbolic or metaphorical, to join the real ('the things we cannot possibly *not* know, sooner or later, in one way or another').

What happens, though, when we know the reality but cannot quite believe it, because the fantastic alternative is too appealing, or contains too much of the truth of our emotions? When referential mania both joins the real and stands apart from it? This is where 'Signs and Symbols' ends, and I need now to mention the one other thing that happens in the story. It is quite simple. The telephone rings. The time is past midnight, 'an unusual hour' for a telephone call to the old couple's flat.

It is a wrong number, the girl on the line wants to speak to some unknown person called Charlie. The old woman, whose English is better than the old man's, explains the mistake. The telephone rings again. It is the same girl, and the old woman explains again, in greater detail: 'You have the incorrect number. I will tell you what you are doing: you are turning the letter O instead of the zero.' The couple were awake anyway, drinking tea, discussing the future of their son. The old man rather childishly concentrates on the jam jars, the present they have taken to the hospital and brought back. He reads off the names of the different varieties. These are the last two sentences of the story. 'His clumsy moist lips spelled out their eloquent labels: apricot, grape, beech plum, quince. He had got to crab apple, when the telephone rang again.'

I don't want to bury this discreet moment under commentary. I should like us to listen to Nabokov's silence rather than invade it. But what do we imagine is happening when the telephone rings for the third time? I hear common sense (the old couple's, mine, no doubt Nabokov's) telling me that it is the same wrong number again, the girl who wants Charlie. I can't know this for sure, though, unless someone picks up the telephone, and no one ever will. This fictional telephone can no more be picked up than Hamlet can be resurrected. Equally, of course, it will keep ringing for as long as anyone reads the story. What other voices say to me is: this time it's the hospital, bad news, something has happened to the son. Or: it is the wrong number, but it's meant for the old couple all the same, some malign force, friend of giants and farmers, is using this mistaken girl to torture them. It is because the call might be from the hospital that the very wrongness of the number seems cruel. Could the old couple *not* think this, *not* feel persecuted at their midnight tea? Can we *not* feel this on their behalf? In this context, even the slight suspicion of a conspiracy becomes a form of pain. Do we, perhaps for the first time, wonder whether there is something hereditary about referential mania, dormant but always possible in a later generation? Or do we think referential mania must be intuitively correct after all, the only way we can possibly account for the brutal, ingenious, so-called accidents of the world? The strength of this story is that what seems to be the 'right' reading, the banal, accidental wrong number, is simultaneously the sanest and the hardest to settle for. We have been set up, by the account of the young man's mania and his mother's investment in tenderness, to believe in pain but not in accidents. This belief is reinforced, of course, by the fact that the endlessly ringing telephone is not, cannot be, a textual accident, since it is where Nabokov deliberately ends his story. Referential mania is one of the ways in which we find an author in a text. Like all manias, it can go too far, but perhaps nothing less than mania will even get us started on the quest.

Nabokov is mildly doing here what he extravagantly does elsewhere. At the level of represented life in the fiction there is a question, which pits, let us say, the possible craziness of a person against the possible craziness of the world, and pits against both the merely random, the realm of chance. We are suspended here, with the characters. On the level of the writing, however, the question is answered, chance is abolished. The doubt *in* the story, so to speak, is cancelled *by* the story. If the couple could know they were figures in a fiction, they would know they were being tormented by Nabokov, author of the ominous third telephone call, and indeed of the other calls, and of the couple and their unhappy son. Adam Krug, as we have seen, acquires just this knowledge, but at the expense of his sanity and his textual life. We have also seen that V, in *The Real Life of Sebastian Knight*, has an inkling of this knowledge, but it is only an inkling, and only in the last words of his novel. There is a similar moment at the end of *Invitation to a Beheading*, where Cincinnatus C, in the midst of his own execution, steps away from the simulacrum which has been his reality, and moves towards 'beings akin to him'. Beings, we may imagine, like his author, or like the readers of the text he is in; or like the characters in *another* novel, where human difference is not punishable by death.

In 'Signs and Symbols', the fictional levels are separate, the second easily forgotten; but they can be seen to comment on each other. In the story, there is the frightened interpretation of chance, the difficulty of believing that chance is what it is; in the writing both an absence of chance and a carefully orchestrated interest in chance, a confirmation of our difficulty. This world *is* organized by a malign or at least mischievous agency, someone *is* whispering about these people behind their backs. For a comparable playing of narrative against character, we can look at the story 'That in Aleppo once', also written in English after Nabokov left Europe, and published a little earlier, in 1943. It takes the form of a letter addressed to someone called V, a writer, who is specifically asked not to mention Aleppo in his title when he turns this story into fiction. The allusion is to Othello, who having killed his wife, is about to kill himself and recalls his stabbing, in Aleppo, of a Turk who struck a Venetian and insulted Venice. V not only mentions Aleppo, he quotes the pleading request not to: 'It may all end in

Aleppo if I am not careful. Spare me, V.: you would load your dice with an unbearable implication if you took that for a title.' Similarly, the character meets a doctor at the end of his tale, 'although if you write it, you had better not make him a doctor, as that kind of thing has been overdone'. The doctor remains a doctor; overdone. A throw of the dice will never abolish chance, as the title of a poem by Mallarmé says, and loaded dice can never do better than simulate chance, and confess their simulation. It is in this sense that a stylistic weakness may seem like a liberation, a momentary escape from the overbearing design. These texts are metaphors for a world which is ordered but unsympathetic, run by a heavy-handed deity whom paranoia would rightly suspect of wanting to trash what is most precious to us, or at least wanting to tease us with that very suspicion. This is not the way the world is, for Nabokov or for us; but it is the way it may feel to us, must feel to many; and it is the way it is for Nabokov's characters. They inhabit our temptations and our fears; our thought and our desire.

Is this Nabokov's second story, his 'inside'? Well, I've done more than tell that story, but I don't believe I have really left it for a moment. Nabokov's plan must be simpler and more elegant than my chasing after it. My guess is that his second story concerns whatever connection we make between the telephone call and the young man's madness. In the first story there is unhappiness and separation, pain visited upon the innocent, and what characterizes the young man is his difference, his inaccessibility to 'normal minds'. In the second story, the young man's world invades ours; his clouds and trees become our telephone, and a new pain, the pain of a new uncertainty, is visited upon the innocent and the guilty alike. Nabokov asks us not whether there is a difference between the stories, but how secure the difference is.

(iv)

A child is tortured and killed; the father goes mad. A child is mad; the parents are beset by his unhappiness, and learn that the large persecutions of history have intimate and tiny echoes everywhere. But there are kindlier paranoias, and what is unspeakable is not always a horror. 'Signs and Symbols' has a twin among Nabokov's stories – the story Katharine White rejected for the *New Yorker*. It is called 'The Vane Sisters', and was written in 1951, although not published until 1959.

The narrator is French, and teaches French literature at a girls' college in New England. He hears of the death of his estranged friend Cynthia Vane and is afraid of being haunted by her, but also disappointed when her spirit seems to send no message, however oblique. In fact, both Cynthia and her sister Sybil, also dead, have written themselves into his prose, in the form of an acrostic in the last paragraph, indicating both their continuing presence and the nature of their intervention in his life. He has a dream that 'somehow was full of Cynthia' but remained curiously vague. Waking, he 'rereads' his dream, but cannot find what he feels 'must be there':

> I could isolate, consciously, little. Everything seemed blurred, yellow-clouded, yielding nothing tangible. Her inept acrostics, maudlin evasions, theopathies – every recollection formed ripples of mysterious meaning. Everything seemed yellowly blurred, illusive, lost.

Although he can't see them, both Cynthia and Sybil are inside his language, possessing his initial letters, which read: Icicles by Cynthia, meter from me Sybil. These discreet alphabetical ghosts are claiming that even before the narrator heard of Cynthia's death he was subject to their influence, since certain features of the visual world around him were arranged by them, marked by their style: the 'brilliant icicles' he was looking at one Sunday afternoon, the long shadow of a parking meter, reddened by the light of a restaurant sign. The girls know his tastes, his pleasure in aestheticized sensations. He is like a Symbolist poet on a spree, delighting in a day which he calls 'part jewel, part mud'. The narrator appears to notice nothing except his sensations, neither the Vane signature in these particular arrangements nor the verbal message lurking in his own writing. Indeed, as we have seen, the acrostic occurs in the very sentences in which he asserts there has been nothing to notice. But he does say, with the fussy precision which characterizes him (which at this point signals the ghosts' mischievous skill in parodying him), that he could isolate little 'consciously' – leaving room for an unconscious apprehension of the haunting.

Nabokov muted his views of this story over time. To Katharine White in 1951 he was confident, unapologetic and wounded ('I am really quite depressed by the whole business. The financial side is an entirely separate trouble. But what matters most is the fact that people whom I so much like and admire have completely failed me as *readers* in the present case' – Nabokov's italics). In 1959 he seemed happy enough to see the story merely as a puzzle and a challenge, and to congratulate *Encounter* readers who had cracked the code. 'My difficulty was to smuggle in the acrostic without the narrator's being aware that it was there, inspired to him by the phantoms. Nothing of this kind has ever been attempted by any author . . .' Except perhaps by the authors of chess problems. In 1974, Nabokov suggested that 'this particular trick can be tried only once in a thousand years of fiction,' and was, perhaps sincerely, willing to allow a doubt of its success: 'Whether it has come off is another question.'

The trick comes off, I think, but at the expense of the story. There is in 'The Vane Sisters' a delicate parable about mania and possession which is very hard to see for the sheer glitter of the riddle. The work as a whole is too bright or too dull, something we get or don't get, all jewel or all mud. Katharine White rather sniffily replied to Nabokov's letter by saying that they had certainly missed the acrostic ('that being rather out of the *New Yorker*'s line'), but nevertheless felt they had understood 'at least the general purpose of your story'. The problem, White continued, was that the characters themselves, 'these Vane girls', didn't arouse the emotions as the Jewish couple did in 'Signs and Symbols', and so were not 'worthy of their web', the elaborate style spun around them. Leaving aside the shudder we may share with Nabokov about the idea of a 'general purpose' for a story, we can agree about the thinness of the characters, although I would then want to add that the thinness is part of their charm, since their wispy unfocused passage through life is what is so moving about them, their one real claim on our interest. The 'inside' of the work, the structural pattern it shares with 'Signs and Symbols', is not thin at all, just folded away. The acrostic, we may feel, is merely the 'idiotically sly' novelist's way of pointing to what's hidden.

Nabokov's 'inner scheme', which he was so disappointed that White had missed, was 'the coincidence of Cynthia's spirit with the atmosphere of the beginning of the story' – that is, Cynthia's haunting of the story before we know who she is or that she is dead. Such haunting justifies and exemplifies Cynthia's scatty 'theory of intervenient auras', which is at the heart of the work and represents referential mania with regard to the afterlife. There is 'nothing particularly new' about Cynthia's 'private creed', the narrator dismissively remarks. It is merely a 'tame metaphysics', involving 'a fairly conventional hereafter, a silent solarium of immortal souls . . . whose main recreation consisted of periodical hoverings over the dear quick'. Cynthia's spiritualist sessions, also conventional, are described in comic, pathetic detail, 'little farces' where the shades of Wilde and Tolstoy and others are supposed to report obscurely on their former lives. Wilde's 'rapid garbled French' and the 'great crash' with which Tolstoy announces himself suggest if not authenticity at least a decent familiarity with the literary dead, but the narrator, however much we may dislike his tone, doesn't seem to be missing anything much at this point. Well, he may have missed a Wildean connection in the fact that the names Sybil and Vane come from *The Portrait of Dorian Gray*, but it's not at all clear what this subterranean allusion is meant to do.

The engaging and original feature of Cynthia's belief concerns not the presence or personality of the spirits, but their practice, the nature of their interventions, their mode of signalling to the living. Even the rationalist narrator finds this feature 'interesting' and 'ingenious', although he still adds that some of Cynthia's 'Jamesian meanderings' in this direction have 'exasperated my French mind'.

> For a few hours, or for several days in a row, and sometimes recurrently, in an irregular series, for months and years, anything that happened to Cynthia, after a given person had died, would be, she said, in the manner and mood of that person. The event might be extraordinary, changing the course of one's life; or it might be a string of minute incidents just sufficiently clear to stand out in relief against one's usual day and then shading off into still vaguer trivia as the aura gradually faded. The influence might be good or bad; the main thing was that its source could be identified. It was like walking through a person's soul, she said.

Cynthia recognizes the activity of a kindly spirit when she wins a vacuum cleaner in a lottery; of a spiteful one when her soup boils over. She sees Sybil's shade as organizing a series of minor events (the death of two trees, a building project, workmen who dig up the sidewalk) which encourage her to sell their old Boston house and move to New York. 'Sybil's personality, she said, had a rainbow edge as if a little out of focus'. In death as in life. An earlier phrase which seemed merely whimsical, pleasantly superstitious, or even perhaps entirely metaphorical – 'Cynthia had a feeling that her dead sister was not altogether pleased with her' – turns out to require the most literal reading possible.

Cynthia interprets the world around her as if it were (partially) written by the dead, as if events were an intermittent script. The narrator raises certain rather fanciful objections to such a scheme.

What happens when you can't recognize the writer, when the soul is too dim or dull or impersonal to be identified: 'there are anonymous letters and Christmas presents which anybody might send'. What if a 'usual day' means not the absence of a specific aura but a mixture of many auras? What about God? What if the spirits don't get on with each other, and the days of the living become a mere warfare of auras? Cynthia however is 'more voluble than explicit', unperturbed by such resistance, 'above generalities as she was beyond logic'.

'The Vane Sisters' would not be a Nabokov story if Cynthia's appealing theory were not backed by its parody, a clumsy, scarcely defensible twin. Ignorant of her own delicacy, indiscriminate in her enthusiasm for portents, Cynthia has been helping a Coleridgean librarian called Porlock to hunt for fatidical misprints in old books, annunciations of Hitler, for example, in a misspelling of hither. The librarian is more purely a connoisseur than Cynthia, since he is not interested in the actual prediction but only in the semblance of sense, 'the freak itself, the chance that mimics choice, the flaw that looks like a flower', as the narrator puts it with proto-Humbertian alliteration. The hither/Hitler example strikes the narrator as 'statistically insane', although he himself later, fighting insomnia, finds the name Taft written (twice) acrostically in Shakespeare's sonnets. I should add that checking this discovery I found one of the sonnets (Number 14) seeming to start on the acrostical naming of Nabokov. NABO, it went: 'Not from the stars do I my judgement pluck,/ And yet methinks I have astronomy;/But not to tell of good or evil luck,/Of plagues, of deaths, or seasons' quality'. Fortunately, the rest of the acrostic was entirely scrambled [NPOBBAAIOT], and I was sane again. The librarian's mania is chiefly there, of course, to give us a hint about games with letters, but his interest in 'the freak itself' looks forward to John Shade's acceptance, in *Pale Fire*, of texture rather than text. The way we feel about the improbable, even the statistically insane, may have to do with the lightness or heaviness of our interpretation of it, the tone rather than the truth of the claims we make.

There are of course other objections to the theory of auras, arguments that the narrator has ignored, that Nabokov presumably wants us to pursue *because* the narrator has ignored them, although this way yet another form of referential mania beckons. How are we to tell an aura from an accident, an intervention of the dead from a piece of mere circumstance which recalls the dead? If we don't believe the dead act in this or any way among the quick, how do we feel about Cynthia's theory? Curiously, I think scepticism may make us more sympathetic to it, more able to see its attraction, than we might be if we simply accepted it, or endorsed the narrator's condescending mockery. The theory's interest, surely, is double. First, the ghosts express themselves through ordinary events, they do not require a special track or apparatus. Their presence is therefore empirically indistinguishable from their absence, a matter of interpretation not of irresistible miracle. The work of the ghosts resembles that of the Company in Borges' story 'The Babylon Lottery' where a massive organization of chance is finally seen to be equivalent to unorganized chance on its own. Or it resembles the disease of the world sketched out in Pynchon's *V*, whose subtle symptoms blended in with the events of history, 'no different one by one but altogether – fatal'. Except that Cynthia's ghosts seem kindlier, less sinister, at worst a little mean. Second, the theory, whether accepted or not, responds very strongly to a need not to let go of the dead, indeed actually preserves them. It is a form of animated, externalized memory; a mode of resurrection. If there are ghosts, what matters is the 'manner and mood' of the inscription they make; if there are none, what matters is the brilliant authority of the imagination, the way it both respects and reworks the given world; finds hidden wonders in it without ruffling its surface.

Of course, there are ghosts in the story, it doesn't end in doubt. The telephone is answered, so to speak, even if the narrator doesn't answer it himself. In this and in many ways, 'The Vane Sisters' is different from 'Signs and Symbols'. However, it adds its own illumination to the question of mania, and complements our understanding of the earlier work. In both stories the world speaks a secret language, but only to the insane or those who believe in ghosts. The strongest, scariest appeal of this theme lies not in the language or what it says, or even in the question of its existence, but in the intuition of what it would feel like to be in the presence of such speech. In this respect, to read the last paragraph of 'The Vane Sisters' merely as a riddle is worse than missing the riddle altogether. If we can clear our heads of all the talk about acrostics – but is this possible, was this ever possible, hasn't the story itself set us up too firmly, even before we looked at the letters or Nabokov's note? – we may feel this prose is too strange and awkward to mean merely what it grammatically or semantically says. It would seem then not symbolic but cryptic, taken over, possessed not only by another person but by another system of signification. This, I suggest, might be an ideal reading of the story, if we could manage it.

We could miss the acrostic, fail to identify the ghost, but our sense of strangeness would be unshakeable, something reason could neither dispel nor resolve. We would experience the haunting, even if we couldn't see what haunted us. The mildness of the occasion, its distance from the terrors of 'Signs and Symbols', would either remove all question of paranoia or make us rethink paranoia, re-locate it perhaps, deprived of its demons, among the symmetries and reflections of everyday life.

Well, not entirely deprived of its demons, even then. Cynthia has died of a heart attack, it seems ('Say, I never thought there was any-thing wrong with Cynthia Vane's heart', the narrator's informant says); but Sybil committed suicide, desperate because she had been abandoned by D, an instructor with whom she was having an affair. Her last note, constructed with the dizzying, shallow cleverness which makes Nabokov so tiresome at times even to his admirers, says, 'Death was not better than D minus, but definitely better than Life minus D'. However, the context in which Sybil writes these words, and the words which precede them, are a good deal more in-teresting, less distracting.

Sybil arrives to take a French literature examination, which the narrator is invigilating. She is wearing high heels, carrying a suit-case, shrugs off her fur coat, asks when her grade will be available, sits the examination. The next day the narrator starts to mark the students' work in alphabetical order, although the books of Valev-sky and Vane have somehow been misplaced and come up prematurely. Cynthia would say Sybil's ghost was already quietly at work. Sybil's examination is written with pencils of different shades and strengths and sharpness, coloured by lipstick where she has sucked the point. It is, the narrator says, 'even poorer than I had expected', but bears 'all the signs of a kind of desperate conscien-tiousness, with underscores, transposes, unnecessary footnotes, as if she were intent upon rounding up things in the most respectable manner possible.' She is. Sybil ends her examination by borrowing a fountain pen and writing:

> *Cette examain est finie ainsi que ma vie. Adieu, jeunes filles!* Please, *Monsieur le Professeur*, contact *ma soeur* and tell her that Death was not better than . . .

The narrator takes the exam book to Cynthia, who even in her sad-ness is proud of the use Sybil managed to make of the academic occasion, and pleased by the narrator's pedantic pointing out of her sister's 'grammatical mistakes' – this too would be part of Sybil's inventive personality, her 'rainbow edge'. However, there aren't any grammatical mistakes in Sybil's note. There is an inspired misspelling, with grammar brought into line to match: *cette examain est finie* instead of *cet examen est fini*. What is over is Sybil's life and the movement of her hand, or what used to be her hand; her handwriting; this examination of her hand and her writing.

Nabokov's notebooks, as described by Brian Boyd, offer an unusual insight into the process of creation here, but don't really settle the question of intention, since the identifiable aim ends just before the most interesting verbal things happen. Nabokov had heard of a (male) student at Northwestern University who had committed suicide after taking a French examination, writing in French after the last question, 'I am going to God. Life does not offer me much'. Nabokov invites himself in his notes to 'adopt' this boy, and have him 'make some pathetic mistake in that last sentence'. He adds, 'Change it, of course . . . Probe, brood.' The next day Nabokov decided the suicide should be that of a young woman, and chose as her 'pathetic mistake' an error of gender, 'cette examen et celle de ma vie', this examination and that of my life. 'No English speaking person can master genders', Nabokov says rather grandly. But the mistake is pathetic only if we are ourselves frantic pedants – would the suicide have been more graceful if the grammar had been right? What is remarkable here, what moves the story from signature to style, is what is not in the notebook, the substitution of *examain* for *examen*. The unhappy Sybil momentarily becomes a cousin of Lewis Carroll and Joyce; and Nabokov.

The narrator has unwittingly prepared us for just this reading, for the painful pun he seems completely to miss, by saying Sybil's work 'displayed her usual combination of several demon hands'. It is, I think, the best and the deepest joke in the story, and again the notebooks get us only halfway there. Nabokov grumbles about the 'chaotic hell of handwritings' in his students' examinations, an image which has the same general meaning as the most obvious contextual sense of the phrase in the story. But a demon hand is more active than a hell of handwritings, and the old-fashioned 'hand' for script cannot *not* mean an ordinary hand as well. In effect, these demon hands reach everywhere into the fiction. One such hand is that of death, already propelling Sybil to the end of her examination and her life; another is that of Sybil herself, who from beyond death seems to have insinuated just this metaphor into the narrator's language. Demon hands generally evoke the mode of the sisters' presence in the story, as they write parts of the visual text, gesture through chosen letters of the prose. And a demon hand in this fiction must suggest an extensive, eerie connection between writing and possession, the vulnerability of any text to other uses of the alphabet. Paranoia, in such a perspective, may be tamed but can't be banished or entirely released from suspicion. The magician and the idiot continue their conversation; the mandarin and the theorist of pain murmuring their contributions.

4
The World Without Us:
Speak, Memory

*Is history not simply that time when we
were not born? I could read my nonexistence
in the clothes my mother had worn before I
can remember her.*

Roland Barthes, *Camera Lucida*

(i)

'I confess I do not believe in time,' Nabokov says in *Speak,
Memory*. The remark is grand, lordly, perhaps a little fatuous.
Time, we might say, doesn't care whether we believe in it or not,
doesn't depend on our belief. But of course Nabokov doesn't mean
he doesn't believe in time's existence or passage, he means he
doesn't believe in its sovereignty or absolute dominion. Time can
be eluded, cheated, even temporarily abolished, and since Nabokov
has just done this quite spectacularly in the pages we read before we
come upon this sentence, he is entitled to a bit of bravura.

He continues, though, 'I like to fold my magic carpet, after use,
in such a way as to superimpose one part of the pattern upon another.' 'After use' is elegant and discreet. The mind has its magic
carpets, it can travel in time, even against time, if not entirely away
from it. But Nabokov is not taking us with him on his flight, or
even, in this image, describing his flight for us, only doing what
seems a distressingly modest and belated trick, an arrangement of
the grounded carpet to create a sad illusion. The imagery may confess to more trickery, less flight, than Nabokov entirely wants it to,
and it doesn't really correspond to what happens in the text, to
what the trick looks like when it works. The passage we have just
read actually felt like a flight in time, a magical journey. A boy in
Russia in 1910 strays into a marsh looking for butterflies and,

83

delighted with his finds, eager for more, crosses this strange territory to emerge in the mountains of Colorado, continents collapsing together in the excitement of the chase. It's odd to be told we were only looking at an artful bit of carpet folding. What feels magical in the boy's adventure in the marsh is that *the boy himself* emerges in America, since as far as the prose tells us it's still 1910, no time has passed, the implied Nabokov has not grown up, as the historical Nabokov did before he hunted for butterflies in Colorado in 1947. The insistence on the created pattern in the text, the late folding, remembers the very fact the writing itself so beautifully elides, and the voice saying it doesn't believe in time is harshly and awkwardly caught betweeen time's brilliant but momentary abolition and its imminent and inevitable return.

The dominant posture in *Speak, Memory* is not disbelief in time and not simple submission to it. Nor is it, although Nabokov himself makes a number of rhetorical waves in this direction, a rebellion against time, an assault on the 'walls of time' or the 'prison of time.' It is an intricate engagement with what Nabokov, echoing Proust, calls 'time itself', and anticipating his own fictional character Van Veen, calls the 'texture of time'. One of the few attractions of Cambridge, England for the stylishly disaffected young Nabokov is 'a residual something that many a solemn alumnus has tried to define'. Nabokov continues, a no less solemn alumnus himself, 'I see this basic property as the constant awareness one had of an untrammeled extension of time . . . Nothing one looked at was shut off in terms of time, everything was a natural opening into it.' Into it, we note, not out of it; and into lots of it. 'Untrammeled' is the rather unusual word Nabokov also uses for what he thinks of as his freedom of movement within the Russian language as opposed to English. The would-be rebel against time, time's disbeliever, speaks even in his opening pages of time as 'a radiant and mobile medium.' Time is not only brutal passage and decay, it is also a form of awareness, and what Nabokov calls 'the birth of sentient life' is the birth of a consciousness that knows itself to be temporal. He associates the development of the mind itself with the very constraints it longs to deny: 'the beginning of reflexive consciousness in the brain of our remotest ancestor must surely have coincided with the dawning of the sense of time.' A little myth of origins. The remotest ancestor is figurative and hyperbolic, but the argument is immediate: we start to think when we think about time.

The curious, elegant, perhaps not fully intentional echoes in Nabokov's prose of the opening of Dickens' *Great Expectations* reinforce this argument in interesting ways. In Dickens' novel the orphan Philip Pirrip stands in a graveyard and learns who he is by a contemplation of the names of his dead parents and siblings, and by being terrified by a man later revealed to be the convict Magwitch.

> My first most vivid and broad impression of the identity of things, seems to me to have been gained on a memorable raw afternoon towards evening. At such a time I found out for certain, that this bleak place overgrown with nettles was the churchyard; and that Philip Pirrip, later of this parish, and also Georgiana wife of the above, were dead and buried; and that Alexander, Bartholomew, Abraham, Tobias, and Roger, infant children of the aforesaid, were also dead and buried; and that the dark flat wilderness beyond the churchyard, intersected with dykes and mounds and gates, with scattered cattle feeding on it, was the marshes; and that the low leaden line beyond, was the river; and that the distant savage lair from which the wind was rushing, was the sea; and that the small bundle of shivers growing afraid of it all and beginning to cry, was Pip.
> 'Hold your noise!' cried a terrible voice, as a man started up from among the graves at the side of the church porch.

Identity is a knowledge of death and geography and a fear which magically seems to find a fearsome object, as if Pip's growing afraid and crying had conjured Magwitch out of the marshes.

For the unorphaned Nabokov – for the infant Nabokov as the adult writer chooses to picture him – identity is an awareness of his own and his parents' age, and a ceremonial occasion, his father's birthday: 'the inner knowledge that I was I and that my parents were my parents ... was directly associated with my discovering their age in relation to mine.' The four-year-old child, the child who discovers he is four, is 'plunged abruptly' into time as into 'shining seawater':

> At that instant, I became acutely aware that the twenty-five-year-old being, in soft white and pink, holding my left hand, was my mother, and that the thirty-three-year-old being, in hard white and gold, holding my right hand, was my father.

The hard white and gold is the Horse Guards uniform, and Nabokov notes that his father had completed his military training long before this day in 1903, 'so I suppose he had ... put on the trappings of his old regiment as a festive joke'.

To a joke, then, I owe my first gleam of complete consciousness –

which again has recapitulatory implications, since the first creatures on earth to become aware of time were also the first creatures to smile.

There is a certain amount of pain and frustration, even anxiety, in that smile – 'for several years afterward I remained keenly interested in the age of my parents and kept myself informed about it, like a nervous passenger asking the time in order to check a new watch' – but there is excitement and delight too. Nabokov describes his father as 'an authority on Dickens', and it is touching, and makes one think again about the intentionality of the connection, that Nabokov's next allusion to *Great Expectations* should be connected with his father's death, simultaneously evoked and postponed. The father is to fight a duel, the boy is horribly afraid for him, the duel is cancelled. The writer can't revisit his relief at this moment without recalling his agony at another, when his father did die, in 1922, not in a duel but in a botched assassination attempt, caught in a line of fire intended for someone else. 'But no shadow was cast by that future event upon the bright stairs of our St Petersburg house.' No shadow is cast, but the stairs are dark with its absence; the future event lies in waiting. This is like Pip's seeing, in the last words of *Great Expectations*, 'no shadow' of another parting from Estella. He sees no shadow because there is none, and will be none, is the hopeful implication; or he doesn't see the shadow that has not yet arrived, but will. The second meaning can't be got rid of: the mere naming of the shadow, even in the form of a denial, ensures its persistence. Death, like time, like parting, can be averted but not forgotten; it haunts even the happiest occasions of its avoidance.

This haunting is the chief structural effect of *Speak, Memory*, and death and time themselves begin to look like masks for something that Nabokov and memory are reluctant to name: loss. Nabokov's habitual (overt) stance is that of memory's proud agent and possessor. Nothing is lost, the past is not a foreign country. Then was then and *is also* now:

> I see again my schoolroom in Vyra, the blue roses of the wallpaper, the open window. Its reflection fills the oval mirror above the leathern couch where my uncle sits, gloating over a tattered book. A sense of security, of well-being, of summer warmth pervades my memory. The mirror brims with brightness; a bumblebee has

entered the room and bumps against the ceiling. Everything is as it should be, nothing will ever change, nobody will die.

There are no Proustian intermittences of time or the heart here. Nabokov will have no truck with involuntary memory, or indeed with anything involuntary. Memory is an act of will, and of the will at its most determined and lucid and courageous. Nabokov writes of the 'almost pathological keenness of [his] retrospective faculty', and thinks it may run in the family. It certainly evokes and focuses on the family:

> the bright mental image (as, for instance, the face of a beloved parent long dead) conjured up by a wing-stroke of the will; *that* is one of the bravest movements a human spirit can make.

Nabokov hates sleep, a form of 'mental torture' which is also a 'nightly betrayal of reason, humanity, genius', and in his dreams his dead loved ones 'always appear silent, bothered, strangely depressed, quite unlike their dear, bright selves'. Another anti-Proustian argument for deliberate consciousness: the very reality of these persons in the memory depends on the will's image of them.

> It is certainly not then – not in dreams – but when one is wide awake, at moments of robust joy and achievement, on the highest terrace of consciousness, that mortality has a chance to peer beyond its own limits, from the mast, from the past and its castle tower. And although nothing much can be seen through the mist, there is some-how the blissful feeling that one is looking in the right direction.

This passage fades into conventionality and vagueness – 'somehow the blissful feeling' – and its metaphors don't do much to persuade us of the view. Nabokov's writing begins to suggest just the oppo-site of what its brave announcements claim. His 'one' who is wide awake seems pretty remote from the experience he invokes – a good deal more remote, in fact, than the 'I' who saw the silent and bothered dead in his dreams:

> I am aware of them, without any astonishment, in surroundings they never visited during their earthly existence, in the house of some friend of mine they never knew. They sit apart, frowning at the floor, as if death were a dark taint, a shameful family secret.

It is a family secret, and *Speak, Memory* is made up of its denial and return. 'Robust joy and achievement'; 'bravest movements'; 'nobody will die'; 'I confess I do not believe in time'. These are extravagant and embattled and touching claims, and to take them entirely literally would be to miss almost everything that matters about them. But if they are not simply to be accepted, they are not simply to be suspected either – as if suspicion was ever simple. The joy and the bravery are real; time and death don't have to be grovelled to. The poignancy in what Nabokov is doing, and in the way the structure of the haunting works, is that he must measure the loss of the time he wants to redeem, cannot do otherwise; that loss is the tune behind every survival and recapture.

One of the most interesting stylistic clues to this double motion is the book's regular recourse to reminders of the time and place of its writing; of this America (mainly) as well as that Russia. 'Time: a dim point in the first decade of this unpopular century. Place: latitude 59 degrees north from your equator, longitude 100 degrees east from my writing hand.' Our equator *and* his, we might think; but there's a faint hint here that he shares our longitudes but has other latitudes. Elsewhere he lets us know that it takes him two hours to describe 'a two-minute run' of his father's fluent handwriting. 'His drafts were the fair copies of immediate thought', unlike his son's, whose 'massacrous revisions and rewritings' not only slow him down but make the very idea of immediate thought seem a distant fantasy. In what ought to be a piece of maudlin whimsy but mysteriously isn't, Nabokov wonders what would happen if he telephoned 'right now' – that is, from Ithaca, New York, in 1949, or if we shift the writing time to the time of revision, from Montreux in 1965 – to his own old number in St Petersburg. '24-43, *dvadtsat' chetïre sorok tri*'. 'No answer? No such number? No such country?'. Or would the old family retainer – 'our wonderful, eminently bribable Ustin' – still be there to offer the old, respectful reply? This thought is saved from whimsy by the discretion (and the speed) with which it displaces its nostalgia, translates time into space. What looked like a call to a vanished past becomes a call to an unknown and certainly mangled present. The past is not a foreign country but an abolished one; the present of that past is a foreign country.

The most brilliant and intricate of these slides in time occurs at the end of a marvellous evocation of a Russian snowscape. The moon 'glazes the runner tracks left on the road, where every sparkling lump of snow is emphasized by a swollen shadow'. Nabokov continues:

Very lovely, very lonesome. But what am I doing in this stereoscopic dreamland? How did I get here? Somehow, the two sleighs have slipped away, leaving behind a passportless spy standing on the blue-white road in his New England snowboots and stormcoat. The vibration in my ears is no longer their receding bells, but only my old blood singing. All is still, spellbound, enthralled by the moon, fancy's rear-vision mirror. The snow is real, though, and as I bend to it and scoop up a handful, sixty years crumble to glittering frost-dust between my fingers.

The passage was rewritten for the 1966 edition of the book – the passportless spy and the rear-vision mirror make their appearance – but the beautiful slide effect was there from the start, involving forty-five years rather than sixty. Then *is* now, it is like the butterfly hunt through the marsh in reverse; the child *is* the adult spy in another country, the snow is real Russian *and* American snow, and it is time itself crumbling to frost-dust. But there is also the mirror, the moon is an instrument of fancy, there are still two scenes, two times and places, even as they seem to (and momentarily actually do) merge. Hence Nabokov's questions ('But what am I doing . . .? How did I get here?'). Time and difference disappear and fail to disappear; or more precisely, time's apparent abeyance, the fold in the magic carpet – the folding far more discreetly done here than on its announced occasion – is only, brilliantly, unforgettably apparent, the stereoscopic fulfilment of a wish in dreamland.

(ii)

It is perhaps time – more than time – to say something about the writing of the book as well as about its written effects, the writing of its writing, so to speak. *Speak, Memory* is at least four books, excluding versions in languages other than English and Russian and counting the English and American editions as a single work with two titles. There are:

(a) the chapters which appeared, in their entirety but in a different order from that of the book publication, in magazines published between 1936 and 1951: *Mesures*, Paris, 1936; the *New Yorker*, 1948-50; *Partisan Review*, 1949, 1951; *Harper's*, 1951. These chapters were written as follows: one (chapter five) in Paris in 1936; one (chapter three) in Colorado in 1947; four (chapters four, six, seven, nine) in Cambridge, Mass in 1947 and 1948; nine (chapters one, two, eight, ten, eleven, twelve, thirteen, fourteen, fifteen) in Ithaca, New York in 1948, 1949 and 1950. Nabokov says he had established the final (1951) order of the chapters from the very beginning, in 1936. There is no reason to disbelieve him, even if he does go on mischievously to suggest that his much later residence in Switzerland is already hinted at in his visit to an old Swiss governess in chapter five. But we may think that Nabokov had his reasons (which are none of our business, he would say) for writing his chapters in the order he did, and it is true that the book we compose by reading the work in the sequence of its composition is subtly different from the finished volume as we have it. The magazine versions were textually different, as Jane Grayson notes; but I'm thinking mainly of the difference the sequence creates.

(b) the English and American editions of 1951.

(c) Nabokov's (and his wife's) translation of this book into Russian, under the title *Drugie Berega, Other Shores*, 1954. Nabokov's description of work on this book is full of things not said; of implied travels between imaginary countries of just the kind the book itself specializes in:

> In the summer of 1953, at a ranch near Portal, Arizona, at a rented house in Ashland, Oregon, and at various motels in the West and Midwest, I managed, between butterfly-hunting and writing *Lolita* and *Pnin*, to translate *Speak, Memory*, with the help of my wife, into Russian . . .

(d) *Speak, Memory*, 1966, in English, subtitled 'An Autobiography Revisited', and incorporating further research and new memories, both Nabokov's own and those of members of his family who had read one of the earlier versions. Nabokov describes the final text as a 're-Englishing of a Russian re-version of what had been an English re-telling of Russian memories in the first place.' The mind spins; the snow crumbles to dust. Or it seems as if there is only snow here.

I don't want to make a large to-do out of the difference betwen the first of these works and the other three, although I do think experiments with the interpretation of sequence are always interesting, and much of the art of film, for instance, lies in just such experiments. In fact, I wouldn't pursue the difference at all here if it did not magnify and illustrate an interesting gap in the book itself, whatever the order of the chapters. It is a gap which returns us, with a difference, to the structure of haunting: the gap between design and mood, or between orchestration and feeling, which corresponds curiously to the way Nabokov writes about his father and the way he writes about his mother. The chief hint, or hinge, is the juxtaposition of chapters two and eleven in the first sequence: a chapter about the mother followed by a chapter about Nabokov's first poem – separated by nine chapters in the final versions.

Speak, Memory is strongly organized around the father's death. He floats in the air in the opening chapter, in a passage brilliantly discussed by Brian Boyd: the master of the house thrown aloft by local peasants in a traditional expression of gratitude, a man lying on the air like a figure in a painted paradise, while the coffin which is then evoked is veiled, abandoned perhaps by the immortal man. We have already seen how a duel affords both a premonition and a postponement of his death. The telephone announcing this death rings in chapter two; the death itself is formally reported, twice, in chapter nine; Nabokov's father's father dies, to the day, eighteen years before the writer's father. What is evoked here is not only the end of a man's life – Nabokov would frown at that 'only' – but an emblematic event, a crucial figure in the writer's magic carpet. This is death as interruption, absurdity and horror, as it always is in Nabokov; death as a grisly, freakish mistake, 'idiotic death', as Nabokov calls it later in the book. It is the senseless moment at the heart of Nabokov's sense-making, here as in *Pale Fire*. But it is also, perhaps because of its schematic importance and because Nabokov has not yet found a way to realize these horrors directly in fiction, a dry and oblique event, not an event *in the writing*, and Nabokov's whole relation with his father comes across like this. Of course, this stylistic fact doesn't necessarily or even probably reflect Nabokov's actual relation to his father, or what he thought about it, but it is what we have, what the writing (as distinct from the writer) says. Father and son, in the text, have an affectionate and admiring relation, full of friendliness and shared interests; but it is also slightly ceremonious. Nabokov's father isn't stuffy or pompous, but his very relaxation seems immaculately organized, as if he were a monarch on his day off, or a legend taking a break. He is dignity and honour and style marked out as history's target; proof that human folly and murderous chance are even more our enemies than time is.

Nabokov's mother, on the other hand, is loss itself, or rather she is loss and its survival, mistress of what her son calls 'unreal estate', and of the art of knowing what cannot be taken from one. 'As if feeling that in a few years the tangible part of her world would perish, she cultivated an extraordinary consciousness of the various time marks distributed throughout our country place.' And later, in Berlin:

> A soapbox covered with green cloth supported the dim little photographs in crumbling frames she liked to have near her couch. She did not really need them, for nothing had been lost. As a company of traveling players carry with them everywhere, while they still remember their lines, a windy heath, a misty castle, an enchanted island, so she had with her all that her soul had stored.

Nabokov inherits these intangible treasures from her, and better still, the habit of keeping such treasures. The mother is intimately associated with the writer's talent; the passages evoking her are full of rich and complex feelings, all very close to the surface of the prose.

Immediately after the simile of travelling players, Nabokov moves to the remarks I have already quoted about dreams and the dead; and from there, in the order of magazine publication, to a chapter in which he reads his mother his first poem. The time is 1914, the boy and his mother are in the country, the father detained in St Petersburg 'by the tension of approaching war'. The adult Nabokov is offhand about the content of the poem – 'It seems hardly worthwhile to add that, as themes go, my elegy dealt with the loss of a beloved mistress – Delia, Tamara or Lenore – whom I had never lost, never loved, never met but was all set to meet, love, lose' – but the boy is full of the achievement of the thing. He hasn't written it down, but it is 'so complete' in his head 'that even its punctuation marks were impressed on my brain like a pillow crease on a sleeper's flesh', and he doesn't doubt that his mother will greet his production with 'glad tears of pride'. He is right not to doubt this; wrong, the remembering Nabokov suggests, not to recognize that his mother might well have other things to think about. 'The possibility of her being much too engrossed, that particular night, in other events to listen to verse did not enter my mind at all.' She is engrossed, preoccupied by her husband's absence, but not too engrossed. The boy recites his poem, the mother weeps. 'Presently I finished reciting and looked up at her. She was smiling ecstatically through the tears that streamed down her face. "How wonderful, how beautiful," she said . . .'

The mother's tears, and her smile, are a form of grace, what one

has no right to expect. She is an image of the luck the boy doesn't
know he has. But she is also the perhaps unwitting agent of a revelation. She passes him a hand mirror so he can see the smear of blood
left by a mosquito he has crushed without noticing it.

> But I saw more than that. Looking into my own eyes, I had the
> shocking sensation of finding there the mere dregs of my usual self,
> odds and ends of an evaporated identity which it took my reason
> quite an effort to gather again in the glass.

Writing, the disappearance of ordinary identity into writing, is a
dissolution of the self, and this too, or the awareness of this, may be
part of Nabokov's legacy from his mother. She not only leaves him,
as we have seen, 'the beauty of intangible property, unreal estate . . .
a splendid training for the endurance of later losses', she allows him
to see that writing too is loss, a form of dishevelment. This is not
the way Nabokov usually talks about writing, or about himself, but
in this passage he is saying clearly that writing is a wreckage of self,
an act which leaves only 'dregs' and 'odds and ends' behind. Reason
recomposes the self in the mirror, and since this passage is so clear,
it is perhaps not oversubtle to suggest that Nabokov elsewhere insisted so much on the composed self because the 'shocking' truth of
writing continued to shock him. He didn't want to hide it, and he is
confessing it here. But he didn't want to parade it, and the bravery
of reconstruction appealed to him much more than the memory of
disarray.

I don't want to propose a simple, gendered allegory, where the
father is order and the mother dishevelled feeling. The mother is as
reasonable as anyone, and the father writes. But as guardian spirits,
the dear remembered dead – Elena Nabokov died just before the
Second World War – as figures in their son's text, they do draw different stories from him, and suggest different aspects of the project
of self-discovery or self-definition.

Both figures point us to the gap I mentioned earlier, betwen design and mood, or orchestration and feeling. We could think of the
scattered face in the mirror as lying in wait for the reciter of the
poem; of all poems. The very idea of autobiography falls into this
model – the entranced or artful assertion dogged by everything that
assertion forgets – and Nabokov seems to be playing the sort of
double game we shall see in *Pnin*. If we accept his assertions, he retains his privacy; if we go behind them, he will have been
understood. I think he didn't much expect the second response, and

perhaps didn't much want it. But he didn't wish to make understanding impossible.

This pattern is very clear, and the effect very moving, in the passage in the first chapter of *Speak, Memory* where Nabokov tells us what he thinks autobiography should be. He is describing the recurrence of what he calls 'the match theme' – the appearance of matches at different times and places, as if they were Proust's cakes or unequal paving stones – and he notes a number of such themes or reprises throughout the book: his grandfather is associated with the motif of throwing things or people out (a man out of a window, a cargo overboard); his father's lending Kerenski a car echoes an ancestor's lending his coach to Louis XVI and Marie-Antoinette; a piece of pottery the young Dmitri finds on the beach at Mentone fits and continues ('I do not doubt') the pattern of a piece Nabokov himself found there some thirty-five years earlier, and both pieces fit with a piece Nabokov's mother found there in 1882, and with a piece *her* mother found there in the 1830s: 'and so on, until this assortment of parts, if all had been preserved, might have been put together to make the complete, the absolutely complete, bowl, broken by some Italian child, God knows where and when, and now mended by *these* rivets of bronze.' These are the rivets of memory and will and imagination, and the complete bowl, of course, is a dream. It's the fit of even a few pieces that makes an autobiography for Nabokov.

What is striking about these 'thematic designs', as Nabokov calls them, is their flimsy and incidental nature. Or at least this is what strikes us if we resist Nabokov's stylish insistence on their importance, and our own attraction to the elegance of the coincidences. These coaches and matches and gestures are not large moments or bearers of grand meanings, and in the case of the pot there is not even a coincidence, only an act of the writer's mind. Yet the tracing of such designs, Nabokov says, 'should be . . . the true purpose of autobiography.' Is he saying that pattern – any pattern – is meaning? Or that pattern may compensate us for the absence of meaning? He is saying, I think, and may himself half-believe it, that pattern is a redemption of loss, and perhaps the only redemption of loss there is, however fragile and unlikely and insignificant the pattern may be. But he is also saying, or his text is saying, that loss is irredeemable, that loss goes on and on, an endlessly discomposed face in the mirror.

There is also an implication that loss may actually be sought, although not perversely, not for its own sake. As a five-year-old, travelling in Europe for a long spell, Nabokov sees the family estate in the country as an 'inexplicably nostalgic image of "home"' – 'inexplicably' because he is so young, and because he has no reason to think this home won't always be his. The grown man pictures the child's return to the estate in the summer of 1905 not as the homecoming that it was, and not even as a figure for the 'grand homecoming' which after 1917 couldn't take place, but as a 'rehearsal' for the 'constant dream' of this homecoming. It was his 'first *conscious* return' (Nabokov's italics), the forerunner of all the imagined returns.

Plainly hindsight and loss are part of the writing here; but there are also other signals. The child defines home as what has been taken from him, if only for a season; reality is a rehearsal for a dream, rather than the other way round. Regret is a kind of fulfilment rather than an accident. We shall meet these motions and tones again in *Ada*, and I don't want to suggest simply that Nabokov was in love with loss, as well as attached to its denial. What lurks in the prose of *Speak, Memory* is something more elusive, best tracked perhaps through the images of Nabokov's first love, whom he calls Tamara ('to give her a name concolourous with her real one').

The girl of the secret summer meetings is agreeable but conventional (her eye is 'merry' and her cheeks are 'blooming' and 'dusky'); the girl of their partings each night is livelier and more vividly imagined ('warm, wet eyelids and rain-chilled face'); and the girl of the 'last glimpse' is genuinely haunting ('as she turned on the steps to look back at me before descending into the jasmin-scented, cricket-mad dusk of a small station'). But the girl of the lost letters, the person whose letters, Nabokov believes, continue to reach the Crimea after he and his family have left for good, is the most moving creature of all, an emblem of homelessness understood not as a banishment from an old domain but as a forlorn quest for what cannot possibly be found:

> letters from Tamara would still be coming, miraculously and needlessly, to southern Crimea, and would search there for a fugitive addressee, and weakly flap about like bewildered butterflies set loose in an alien zone, at the wrong altitude, among an unfamiliar flora.

When Nabokov says that 'for several years ... the loss of my country was equated for me with the loss of my love', he is pointing us towards the role of Tamara in *Speak, Memory*, and perhaps in his life. He didn't love her in order to lose her, any more than he loved his country because he had lost it. But he loved them both most deeply in their loss, and his love is most alive in the imagining of those miraculous and bewildered letters, and of the Russia he will never see again. He loved the chance of loss, he loved what he *could* lose, which is perhaps what we really love in anyone or anything. Chance, with a terrible willingness to oblige, promptly turned itself into history.

All this is admirably delineated in the evocation of the match theme itself. A friend of the family, General Kuropatkin, visits the Nabokov house in St Petersburg – the year is 1904 – and shows the young Vladimir a rather feeble trick with some matches. Fifteen years later, after the Revolution, in flight through southern Russia, Vladimir's father is approached by an old man in a sheepskin coat who asks for a light. It is Kuropatkin. Nabokov adds

> I hope old Kuropatkin, in his rustic disguise, managed to evade Soviet imprisonment, but that is not the point. What pleases me is the evolution of the match theme: those magic ones he had shown me had been trifled with and mislaid, and his armies had also vanished, and everything had fallen through, like my toy trains that, in the winter of 1904-5, in Wiesbaden, I tried to run over the frozen puddles in the ground of the Horel Oranien.

Nabokov says the human story is not the point, and tells us what 'pleases' him. But the 'evolution of the match theme', ostensibly a mask and an answer for loss, leads directly to loss itself, to matches mislaid and trifled with. And more than matches are gone. 'Everything had fallen through': armies and toy trains – which in turn echo the actual Russian trains mentioned a paragraph or so above. The ice wouldn't bear their weight, and a world was swallowed. The purpose behind the purpose of autobiography, perhaps, is to tell us what the tracing of designs *can't* do for us.

There are losses which memory can't even record; memories which are lacerations, evocations of absence. Nabokov has remarkably few of these, but he would be a monster of happiness if he had none. An uncle left him a lot of money, but he continued as a child to adopt toward his benefactor 'the general attitude of smiling condescension that even those who liked him usually took'. Nabokov is so anxious to assure us that he doesn't care about money, about the later loss of his fabulous financial fortune, that he seems not to have appreciated the gift at all, and he now worries that he may have been ungrateful. As a kind of textual amend, he evokes Uncle Ruka affectionately in his book, although still with a touch of mockery, glancing at his 'high tenor voice', and 'asthma, palpitations, shiverings, a Proustian excoriation of the senses'. The uncle is then suddenly, and rather startlingly, linked to Nabokov's brother Sergey, 'who also stammered, and who is also now dead.' Many people stammer, and even more are dead. The unspoken association is that both men were homosexual, and the hovering implication is that Nabokov cannot alter or defend his distaste for that fact. This is what the Proustian hints are doing there, and this is what accounts for the sense of failed affection in the passage, of affection that wasn't enough.

This mood is even clearer in Nabokov's later, separate description of his brother. Nabokov himself speaks of Sebastian Knight here, comparing V's quest for his half-brother's 'real life' with his own awkward attempt to say something about Sergey. 'For various reasons I find it inordinately hard to speak about my other brother' – he has just spoken, easily, about his younger brother Kirill. Sergey was less than a year younger than Vladimir, and 'quiet and listless' while Vladimir was 'rowdy, adventurous and something of a bully'. They both studied at Cambridge, and, like V and Sebastian, saw something of each other in Paris. Then Vladimir and Véra and Dmitri escaped to America, and Sergey went to work in Berlin. 'A frank and fearless man', Vladimir Nabokov says, Sergey was arrested for criticising the regime, 'and sent to a Hamburg concentration camp where he died of inanition, on 10 January 1945'.

This death is distressing enough, but it is not the chief source of distress in these pages, and no source at all for Nabokov's writing difficulties. When the boys were 16 and 15, Vladimir discovered and read a section of Sergey's diary which 'abruptly provided a retroactive clarification of certain oddities of behaviour on his part', and which Vladimir, 'in stupid wonder', showed to his tutor, who in turn showed it to the boys' father. (Nabokov says 'my father', as if some sort of exclusion were still at work.) We are not told what happened next, and homosexuality is not explicitly mentioned. We are to intuit the mixture of shock, tolerance, displeasure, gentility and condescension with which the family did or did not tell Sergey they understood. Vladimir Nabokov meanwhile has confessed his stupidity and betrayal – and by implication his distaste – but it is all, inadvertently, about to happen again. Sergey's life and death announce a series of figures of separation and loneliness appearing again and again in Nabokov's fiction after *Pnin*. When Vladimir and his family get away from France in 1940, they are unable to inform Sergey, who is still in Paris, and their sense of freedom is complicated by an echoing regret and an intensely particular image: 'My bleakest recollections are associated with Paris, and the relief of leaving it was overwhelming, but I am sorry he had to stutter his astonishment to an indifferent concierge'. Who also stammered, and who is also now dead. Sergey's death was not caused by Vladimir's neglect or the distaste lurking in his genuine affection; but this death does underwrite and freeze the incompleteness and irresolution of Vladimir's feelings.

> It is one of those lives that hopelessly claim a belated something – compassion, understanding, no matter what – which the mere recognition of such a want can neither replace nor redeem.

What's missing from the memory is the real life of Sergey Nabokov.

Nabokov has another, more straightforward view of the 'purpose of autobiography', but it is pretty much confined to chapter five of *Speak, Memory*, written in 1936. Autobiography here is the opposite of the tracing of design. It is the rescue of the real from the uses the imagination might find for it. Nabokov says that pieces of his past lost their 'personal warmth', their 'retrospective appeal', once he gave them to characters in his fiction, becoming 'more closely identified with my novel than with my former self':

> Houses have crumbled in my memory as soundlessly as they did in the mute films of yore, and the portrait of my old French governess, whom I once lent to a boy in one of my books, is fading fast, now that it is engulfed in the description of a childhood entirely unrelated to my own. The man in me revolts against the fictionist, and here is my desperate attempt to save what is left of poor Mademoiselle.

He asks at the end of the chapter if he has 'really salvaged her from fiction'. He doesn't answer his question, but the implication is that he has perhaps saved *a* Mademoiselle, an awkward, unlikely and often disagreeable character evoked in brilliant detail; but that he may also have missed virtually everything in her except her misery. It is at this point that Nabokov arrives at the insight about loss and understanding which I quote in my preface:

> I catch myself wondering whether, during the year I knew her, I had

not kept utterly missing something in her that was far more she than her chins or even her French ... something, in short, that I could appreciate only after the things and beings that I had most loved in the security of my childhood had been turned to ashes or shot through the heart.

The 'something' is not named but is evoked in images: 'the radiant deceit' of the old girl's gratitude for a hearing-aid that doesn't really help her; a clumsy swan trying and failing to hoist itself into a moored boat, a creature, Nabokov says, 'whose agony was so much closer to artistic truth than a drooping dancer's pale arms'. This is like the child's understanding only much later that his mother might have been too worried to listen to his poem. Except that here the agency of learning is made clear. It took a world in ashes and his father's death for this gifted and confident person to grasp the ragged generosity of those of meagre means; the poignancy of awkwardness and failure; the fact that even your mother might not think of you *all* the time.

(iii)

If we ask about the purpose of an autobiography, we can also ask about its audience. We are Nabokov's audience, because we have bought or borrowed the book, and because, as we have seen, he speaks to us directly ('your equator'). But a little less than halfway through the book, we are displaced, invited to move over; or shown to have been eavesdropping all along, spying on a message meant for someone else. Nabokov starts to say 'You and I': 'you and I had been delighting in swarms' of butterflies, 'I lodged in two shabby rooms with you and our child', 'you and I have frequently remarked', 'we shall never forget, you and I'. He is addressing his wife Véra, the dedicatee of all his books, but here more closely inscribed in the text than usual. 'The years are passing, my dear, and presently nobody will know what you and I know'.

This address is real, of course, and so, I take it, is the sentiment. Yet both are also rhetorical, pieces of a performance. They conjure up a relation we cannot be part of, but they conjure it up *for us*. It is a flaunting of privacy which would be a betrayal of privacy if Nabokov and his wife did not disappear so thoroughly behind their graceful masks. There is an intimacy here, but it is the intimacy of a text, of reading; we can share the couple's feelings only if we don't invade them.

Masks are Nabokov's business, even as an autobiographer. Towards the end of *Speak, Memory*, he evokes the exiled Russian writers of his generation, including himself, rather oddly, impersonally identified only by his pseudonym, Sirin. In fact, if we don't know that Sirin is the name with which he signed his Russian novels, or to put that more forcefully, that Sirin was Nabokov's name when he was a Russian novelist, we shan't know he is talking about himself. There is arch mischief here, then, we are being teased. 'But the author that interested me most was naturally Sirin. He belonged to my generation'. Naturally. But the 'he' and the 'my' suggest that something else may be going on behind the self-regarding joke. Sirin is seen as others see him, or would have seen him – 'Just as Marxist publicists of the eighties in old Russia would have denounced his lack of concern with the economic structure of society, so the mystagogues of émigré letters deplored his lack of religious insight and moral preoccupation. Everything about him was bound to offend Russian conventions . . .' But then Sirin's admirers 'made much, perhaps too much, of his unusual style, brilliant precision, functional imagery'. And old fashioned readers were 'impressed by the mirror-like angles of his clear but weirdly misleading sentences, and by the fact that the real life of his books flowed in his figures of speech . . .' Were they too impressed; did the admirers really make too much of Sirin's unusual style? Nabokov's hints don't invite us to find any real modesty here; only the sense, perhaps, that others, friends and enemies, are always wrong. It's an elegant posture, and must be appealing if you like posturing. It looks like a help to worried critics too: the author returns from the dead to do a bit of oblique but official self-definition. But the grammar suggests that this writer is not the self; or only an old self. And the most important thing about Sirin, what lifts this passage out of self-regard into the kind of pathos we keep meeting in this nervous and arrogant book, is that he is gone, that 'he vanished as strangely as he had come'. He disappeared, that is, Nabokov-as-Russian-novelist disappeared, for the obvious, obscure and painful reasons we have already looked at, 'leaving nothing much else behind him than a vague sense of uneasiness'. In 1951, only two of Nabokov's Russian novels, *Laughter in the Dark*, 1936, and *Despair*, 1937, had been published in English, both in translations he later revised; but we may feel that the novels themselves, even when rescued, leave us chiefly with 'a vague sense of uneasiness', and we may feel this is a considerable achievement. What happens in the later work, in the work in English, is that the vagueness disappears and the uneasiness grows. Sirin *was* another writer, as Nabokov knew; an old self but also a different artist: a writer whose name in civilian life was Vladimir Nabokov but not yet the writer he was to be: *Vladimir Nabokov écrivain.*

Speak, Memory, as I have been suggesting, is full of cracks in apparently smooth surfaces, gaps that open wider and wider as you inspect them, and there is no better instance of this than the image that Nabokov offers in his opening pages. He invites us to equate the life before birth with the life after death, 'identical twins', he says, 'two eternities of darkness' on either side of 'a brief crack of light'. He goes on to say that we usually 'view the prenatal abyss' more calmly than the other one; and goes on to show, although his overarching, rather conventional rhetoric denies this, that the abysses are entirely different, that there is really no comparison between dying and not being born. It is not fear of death that haunts this book, and converts Nabokov into what he calls a 'chronophobiac'. It is the mastered but anxiously remembered fantasy of not having arrived in the world; one's journey cancelled, so to speak, before it starts.

> I know ... of a young chronophobiac who experienced something like panic when looking for the first time at homemade movies that had been taken a few weeks before his birth. He saw a world that was practically unchanged – the same house, the same people – and then realized that he did not exist there at all and that nobody mourned his absence. He caught a glimpse of his mother waving from an upstairs window, and that unfamiliar gesture disturbed him, as if it were some mysterious farewell. But what particularly frightened him was the sight of a brand-new baby carriage standing there on the porch, with the smug, encroaching air of a coffin; even that was empty, as if, in the reverse course of events, his very bones had disintegrated.

This empty pram is filled in the last pages of the book with a sequence of baby carriages for Nabokov's son Dmitri, mutating into push-chairs as time goes by. Children and books are marks to be left on the world without us, the world of our death; death can't be defeated but it can be accused, compromised. But if the first pram were never filled, there would be no children or books or anything else; and books at least can be seen as desperate attempts to cover up this most alarming of all possibilities. When Nabokov said the American title of the first edition was meant to suggest 'conclusive evidence of my having existed', he meant, as we have seen, evidence of having survived a history that took many others away, including his assassinated father, and his stammering brother. But he also meant, we now glimpse, evidence of having been in the world at all, of having entered the seemingly sealed realm of the home movie. His very life, without books or children, would be conclusive evidence of this, we might think; but no evidence is conclusive against fantasy, particularly when the fantasy involves your own permanent absence.

5

The Language of *Lolita*

I only write like this, you know,
since I stopped sinning years ago

Pushkin, *Eugene Onegin*

(i)

Lolita, like countless detective and horror stories, presents itself as a textual game, insists not only on its verbal but on its written quality. It is a novel pretending to be a memoir with a foreword; as *Pale Fire* is a novel pretending to be a critical edition of a poem; as many novels pretend to be biographies. The text of *Lolita* is itself full of reproduced or simulated texts: letters, poems, a class list, pages from magazines and reference books, shop signs, road signs, motel signs, excerpts from motel registers, fragments of a diary. A disturbance of Humbert's mind is pictured as an unsettling of print, where thoughts turn physically into words and are mirrored in something like water, or silk, or parchment: 'A breeze from wonderland had begun to affect my thoughts, and now they seemed couched in italics, as if the surface reflecting them were wrinkled by the phantasm of that breeze.'

Games are caught up in other games. Humbert Humbert offers us (or his imagined jury) a pocket diary for 1947 as 'Exhibit Number Two' (Number One was Humbert's experience of what the angels envied in Poe's poem 'Annabel Lee'). He then tells us the diary was destroyed five years ago, so that what we are reading is a reconstruction, albeit an accurate one, 'by courtesy of a photographic memory'. We sniff sceptically, but maybe our scepticism is premature:

> I remember the thing so exactly because I wrote it really twice. First I jotted down each entry in pencil (with many erasures and corrections) . . . then, I copied it out with obvious abbreviations in my smallest, most satanic hand . . .

Humbert gives us every reason to distrust this text, but we end up, I think, weirdly trusting it – the more so because he tells us when he feels the afterthoughts have crowded too thickly upon him: 'Beginning perhaps amended'; 'all this amended, perhaps'.

The same odd oscillation between trust and distrust occurs with Charlotte Haze's lamentable letter to her uninterested lodger:

> You see, there is no alternative. I have loved you from the minute I saw you. I am a passionate and lonely woman and you are the love of my life . . . Let me rave and ramble on for a teeny while more, my dearest, since I know this letter has been by now torn by you, and its pieces (illegible) in the vortex of the toilet. My dearest, *mon très, très cher*, what a world of love I have built up for you during this miraculous June!

There is, sadly, a genuine passion trying to speak through this drivel, but as the American critic F. W. Dupee notes, poor Charlotte is 'whatever it is that spoils the party and dampens the honeymoon all across America'. The letter these phrases come from occupies more than a page of print, and seems to be complete. It isn't: we have read only what Humbert remembers of it, although, in a wonderfully acrobatic twist on an already dizzying logic, what he remembers he remembers *verbatim*. 'It was at least twice longer. I have left out a lyrical passage which I more or less skipped at the time, concerning Lolita's brother who died at two when she was four, and how much I would have liked him'. The text is correct, then, but abridged. But is it correct? 'There is just a chance that "the vortex of the toilet" (where the letter did go) is my own matter-of-fact contribution. She probably begged me to make a special fire to consume it'. The text of the letter now seems uncertain, but the toilet acquires a positively Tolstoyan solidity, and on inspection we begin to see shifts and interferences in the style, Humbert's sardonic eloquence invading Charlotte's raving and rambling. How could we have thought 'vortex' was Charlotte's word? And doesn't 'been by now torn by you' have a faintly Humbertian cadence?

The point of textual pretences in their simpler forms must be plausibility, something verging on the actual deception of the reader, and Nabokov, as we have seen, gets something of that effect, albeit through a seemingly perverse double bluff. The larger effect of the games in *Lolita* is to make the text, or anything resembling a text, into a metaphor, an image for what is readable and misreadable in the world. Nabokov himself, in an essay on *Lolita* which is now included in most editions of the novel, fears that he must appear textually 'as an impersonation of Vladimir Nabokov talking about his own book'. Nabokov was presumably pretty sure as he wrote that he *was* Nabokov and not an impersonator. But the joke tells the literal truth of the textual game. Nabokov on the page, joined to the text of his novel, writing 'I', signing and dating his work, is no less ghostly than his characters or than any other author. The difference is that authors have flesh-and-blood histories, documentable lives which precede the traces they leave in words, and fictional characters don't. But the difference between a trace with a past and a trace without one is rather more interesting, less wide and less obvious, than the supposedly simple difference between fiction and fact.

We don't need to confuse the imagined Humbert with the un-imagined Nabokov, or rush into the notion that everything is fiction. We do need to see that the important differences between these figures are going to be textual (unless we happen to be friends of Nabokov or victims of Humbert), matters of reading. Humbert points for example to what seems to be the rigidity of textual characters, their hopeless inability to change their tune:

> No matter how many times we reopen 'King Lear', never shall we find the good king banging his tankard in high revelry, all woes for-gotten, at a jolly reunion, with all three daughters and their lapdogs. Never will Emma rally, revived by the sympathetic salts in Flau-bert's father's timely tear.

Humbert is echoing a very ancient complaint, and it is interesting that he should write of reopening *King Lear*, rather than of seeing the play again. 'Writing, you know,' Socrates says to Phaedrus,

> has this strange quality about it, which makes it really like painting: the painter's products stand before us quite as though they were alive; but if you question them, they maintain a solemn silence. So, too, with written words: you might think they spoke as though they made sense, but if you ask them anything about what they are say-ing, if you wish an explanation, they go on telling you the same thing, over and over forever. Once a thing is put in writing, it rolls about all over the place, falling into the hands of those who have no concern with it just as easily as under the notice of those who com-prehend; it has no notion of whom to address or whom to avoid. And when it is ill-treated or abused as illegitimate, it always needs its father to help it, being quite unable to protect or help itself.

Socrates seems to be saying that texts are both too fixed and too easily unfixed. Less luridly, we might say a text cannot do without interpretation, which may be secure or shaky, decent or disreputable, but will always be work (or play), cannot simply be *given*. Nabokov confirms Socrates' case with comic excess (and partly, like Plato giving us such an emphatic written Socrates, refutes the case in the way he makes it). He also anticipates and varies Derrida's famous claim that there is nothing outside the text, *il n'y a pas de hors-texte*. There is plenty outside the text, Nabokov would say, but the text is usually what we've got, and pretty much all we've got. Outside the text is silence. Or noise, but in any case not language. If King Lear could escape from his tragedy, he would only, in Humbert's scenario, find himself turned into Old King Cole. Not everything is a text, but a text is a good image for much of what we know – for everything we know that is beyond the reach of our own immediate experience, and for most of what we imagine is our immediate experience too. Literature is practice for, the practice of, such knowledge.

(ii)

Lolita's Foreword, the part of the game which allows us to believe we haven't started the novel when we have, is ascribed to one John Ray, Jr., Ph.D., the echoing initials and flaunted doctorate making clear that he is a figure of fun. He is an obtuse and self-admiring psychologist, author of the prize-winning *Do the Senses Make Sense?*, and a cousin of Humbert's lawyer, which is how he comes to be editing the manuscript. JR, Jr's closing words are a triumph of self-parody, almost enough to turn us away from virtue for good, and we would no doubt be laughing even louder if we hadn't, outside of novels, heard (and even offered) just this sort of lilting moral uplift in so many speeches and social sermons. Ray insists on the future 'ethical impact' of Humbert's memoir:

> for in this poignant personal study there lurks a general lesson; the wayward child, the egoistic mother, the panting maniac – these are not only vivid characters in a unique story; they warn us of dangerous trends; they point out potent evils. 'Lolita' should make all of us – parents, social workers, educators – apply ourselves with still greater vigilance and vision to the task of bringing up a better generation in a safer world.

106

Ethical impact, of course, is what Nabokov endlessly denied that he was seeking, and John Ray, Jr. stands for all the idiot readers and critics who are benighted enough to think that such stuff matters in literature. But Nabokov's irony in his fiction is lighter and more complex than the teasing postures of his prefaces and interviews. 'Despite John Ray's assertion,' Nabokov says, '*Lolita* has no moral in tow'. It has no moral John Ray would recognize, or that any of us could comfortably package. Humbert moralizes, we might say, Nabokov doesn't. But this is a book about a guilt which both glorifies itself and grovels in self-accusation, and can therefore scarcely avoid raising moral questions in the reader's mind – even if the whole once and still scandalous premise of the story didn't raise such questions. No simple lesson, then, and certainly no general lesson; but plenty of practice for the moral imagination, more than we can cope with, perhaps. Nabokov was closer to this sense of the work when he reacted rather sharply to Herbert Gold's suggestion that his 'sense of the immorality of the relationship between Humbert Humbert and Lolita is very strong':

> No, it is not *my* sense of the immorality of the Humbert Humbert-Lolita relationship that is strong; it is Humbert's sense. *He* cares, I do not.

Gold thought Humbert might be 'touching', but Nabokov disagreed:

> I would put it differently: Humbert Humbert is a vain and cruel wretch who manages to appear 'touching'. That epithet, in its true, tear-iridized sense, can only apply to my poor little girl.

Nabokov doesn't care, but is able to make eloquent moral judgements all the same. He is suggesting, I take it, not that moral questions are absent from his work, but that they are far from all there is, and that they are grotesquely easy to inflate and misrepresent – isn't there a moment, reading John Ray, when we are almost nodding in approval or ready to write 'How true' in the margin? Some of our laughter has to do with the narrowness of our escape.

The prose of Ray's Foreword is not uniform, and so provides us with some practice for our encounter with Humbert's mannered, Protean performance. Ray writes dully of Humbert's abnormality, says Humbert is 'not a gentleman', but 'a shining example of moral leprosy', a particularly charming mixed bunch of clichés. But he also uses, to describe Humbert's situation awaiting trial, the wonderful phrase 'legal captivity', suggesting a zoo rather than a prison, and pointing us discreetly to Nabokov's own remarks on the origins of *Lolita*:

> As far as I can recall, the initial shiver of inspiration was somehow prompted by a newspaper story about an ape in the Jardin des Plantes who, after months of coaxing by a scientist, produced the first drawing ever charcoaled by an animal: this sketch showed the bars of the poor creature's cage.

Nabokov also writes, in *Speak, Memory*, of 'captivity in the zoo of words'. Humbert, we are to think, has drawn not the world but what separates him from the world, and John Ray is now one of the posthumous bars of his cage. Not that Humbert couldn't have written Ray's lines, if he had been alive and allowed to. Indeed at moments he does seem to have written Ray's lines, to have infiltrated this stodgy style with a taste for alliteration and French phrases, and a lyricism quite alien to Ray's flat-footed thought. In this sentence, for example, Humbert seems to have made away with the first half, before Ray returns with the complacently balanced clauses of the end:

> But how magically his singing violin can conjure up a tendresse, a compassion for Lolita that makes us entranced with the book while abhorring its author!

The Foreword also gives us a few useful 'facts' which Humbert's memoir cannot know: news of Humbert's own death, for example, from a coronary thrombosis, on 16 November 1952; of Lolita's death in childbirth (the child, a girl, stillborn) on Christmas Day of the same year. It tells us names have been changed on grounds of 'taste' or 'compassion', and that Haze (Lolita's maiden name) 'only rhymes with the heroine's real surname.' For details of Humbert's crime, the murder of Clare Quilty, it refers us, in Stendhalian manner, to the newspapers for September 1952.

We can remind ourselves that these 'facts' are fictional – that there is no Lolita who could have a 'real surname' other than Haze – but we need to proceed rather carefully with our scepticism, since the novel needs some 'facts' of this kind for its very foundation. Modern fiction remorselessly teaches us doubt, but we have to doubt our doubt at times. The unreliable narrator so dear to so much criticism can't exist without some notion on our part of what can be relied on, and I have already hinted that this cannot be a sturdy realm of common sense beyond the text, a historical kingdom of certainty where fiction is unknown. Humbert Humbert – or John Ray, Jr, for that matter – is a narrator in the style of Fielding's or Sterne's, capricious in his storytelling, but committed to the existence of his characters beyond his narrative of them, to a Tom or a Tristram or a Lolita whom the narrator knows but has not created. It is true that Nabokov, like Beckett, endlessly reminds us that our faith in these characters *is* only faith, a precarious business and entirely up to us ('Imagine me; I shall not exist if you do not imagine me'). But both Nabokov and Beckett do ask this faith of us, in a way that more visibly fabricating, more algebraic novelists, like Thackeray or Gide, do not. In those cases the author reveals himself at the job of making a world, and can do without our faith: an undeceived willingness to see connections, to compare his world with ours, is enough. Thackeray and Gide are Brechtians, we might say; Nabokov and Beckett, for all their self-consciousness, closer to Chekhov. John Ray's speaking of Humbert's memoir as a novel and (twice) as a work of art wobbles this perspective a little, but doesn't banish it, since Humbert's 'reality' (life and crime and death) as the author of whatever it is remains unquestioned. Vladimir Nabokov himself is not going to show up anywhere here: there are only impersonations.

(iii)

'You can always count on a murderer for a fancy prose style', Humbert says on his first page. The fanciness in question at this moment is an elaborate indirection, a taste for riddles. Where in time are we to locate Humbert's first, Mediterranean love? 'About as many years before Lolita was born as my age was that summer.' The answer is 1923, when he was 12 going on 13. The riddle has its ornate relevance, since Lolita, who in Humbert's theory is a second version of this first love, is 12 when he meets her. 1947 repeats 1923; 1935, the date of Lolita's birth, is poised midway between them. Of course, not everyone likes this kind of game, and it certainly can't be all the rage among murderers. Humbert's 'You can always count' is like some stealthy irony out of Jane Austen ('It is a truth universally acknowledged . . .') which has gone wild and taken to the trees.

Less than a page later Humbert is wondering, none too apologet-ically, whether we can still stand his style – the offence this time being a bit of antiquated fine writing, a run of hoary and over-stretched metaphors ('the hollows and dells of memory, over which ... the sun of my infancy had set'). He adds that he is writing under observation, which presumably tells us to look out for codes and clues and beware of the literal; but mainly Humbert is giving him-self (and Nabokov) a sensational stylistic licence. He will, he is saying, overwrite when he feels like it, parody himself whenever he wants, and we shall applaud, or at least put up with him. The fancy prose style is a reversal of Count Mosca's dictum in *La Chartreuse de Parme* that assassins don't make puns. This one puns indefatig-ably. But then he is a special kind of assassin, as he is a special kind of stylist. His distinction is only slightly lessened by the fact that he is not as special as he thinks he is.

'Colloquial baroque' is Alfred Appel's phrase for the language of *Lolita*, and that is a good place to start. Humbert's English is fluently idiomatic, casually littered with linguistic small change from both sides of the Atlantic ('a stiff drink', 'a shake-up', 'knows the ropes', 'I dare say', 'Hell no', 'taken aback', 'gave me the creeps', 'I fell for it', 'in the family way', and so on). There is a faint flavour of irony in some of these instances, as if the European Humbert (Swiss father, English mother, childhood on the Riviera) were imitating us rather than joining us, but the flavour is very faint, and I'm sure would be undetectable if Humbert's prose didn't have other features to give us a lead. He is keen on the archaic, for example. He says 'Okay', but also 'anent', 'forsooth', 'in thrall', 'noon was nigh' and 'I would fain'. The effect is that of a parade of vaguely poetic fossils, as if Humbert were trying out on us the old-world charms we thought he had reserved for Charlotte Haze. It is only 'as if', I think, since Humbert presumably expects us to laugh with him at this dusty literary manner. At other times his language is not archaic but extraordinarily refined and recondite, inclined to words like 'favonian', 'pavonine', 'palpate', 'oculate', 'leporine'. There are mild misuses of English ('such ... that' instead of 'such ... as', 'on my part' instead of 'for my part', wobbly verb-phrase constructions like 'I really did not mind where to dwell ...'), and there is one curious, repeated error I would think was intentional if I could see any point in it, and if it wasn't made on one occasion by the all-American Lolita herself: why would she call a drug store a candy bar? Plausibility (if we care about it on this level) is preserved of course by the fact that the narrative is all Humbert's: he must have misheard or misremembered what Lolita said, the tiny touches of foreignness are perfectly in character. Nabokov himself offered an argument of this kind to Edmund Wilson, on the subject of *The Real Life of Sebastian Knight*, but also felt the defence was 'not quite fair' – meaning the errors were not a problem, but not part of the design either. My aim here in any case is to characterize Humbert's prose, not to correct it, and the odd genuine mistake seems to me to enhance the acrobatic fluency of the rest, and certainly sets us up for Humbert's inspired manglings of usage, as in 'scrambling across the Mexican border while the scrambling was good', or 'my west-door neighbour', or 'at first wince', or 'set all paradise loose'. 'Crippling' is his word for the way a wounded spider creeps; 'mauvemail' is a mild form of blackmail. We know what a 'sleep-talker' is. 'Let me tell you, however, something' anticipates the scrupulously awkward rhythms of *Transparent Things* ('Easy, you know, does it, son'), and spoofs through mangling a certain kind of American directness. As does this brilliantly excessive improvisation on a fragile phrase:

> This, to use an American term, in which discovery, retribution, torture, death, eternity appear in the shape of a singularly repulsive nutshell, was *it*.

Humbert likes joky off-rhymes (trips/traps, drumlins/gremlins/kremlins), alphabetical mirages (the visual echo in palaeopedology/Aeolian, the sense that 'ennui' and 'pneumonia' must be versions of each other, like 'ecru' and 'ochre'), and the meeting musics of disease and island in typhus and Corfu. This is not simply to say that illness finds its phonetic home only in fiction, or that *Lolita* is only words. It *is* only words ('Oh, my Lolita, I have only words to play with!' Humbert cries a touch too pathetically), but all literature lies in an *only* of this kind. Words are among our best routes to what is beyond words, and nature has been known to imitate art. What Nabokov/Humbert is doing with this Wildean thought is to tilt it away from paradox and towards something like miracle: if you have to die of typhus, Corfu would be the place to do it, and your untidy existence, even in death, would have responded to the chances of art, to what the poet John Shade, in *Pale Fire*, calls 'A feeling of fantastically planned,/Richly rhymed life.' Humbert suggests three times, once explicitly, that the difference between the rapist and therapist is a matter of conventions of spacing. Deep

111

truths in the alphabet, the much-therapied Humbert would claim; but then he is, as he also says, 'naïve as only a pervert can be'.

Humbert's dandyish taste for alliteration is so thoroughly indulged that he becomes almost unreadable at times. He is a prodigious stylist, capable of wonders. But he is also a fussy aesthete, capable of driving us crazy, and both aspects of his performance are important. Some of the alliteration is briskly comic, sardonically overwrought: 'garrulous, garlicky', 'tuberculosis in the tundra', 'hideous hieroglyphics', 'maroon morons', 'maudlin murals', 'bridge and bourbon', 'desire and dyspepsia', and the spectacular 'connubial catch-as-catch-can'. Other instances are parodies of a style which listens too fondly to itself: 'I spend my doleful days in dumps and dolours'; 'January was humid and warm, and February fooled the forsythia.' But then this style in turn fades easily into something which is no longer quite pastiche: 'a plethora of pain that would have hospitalized a Hercules (I should know by now)'; 'what crazy purchases were prompted by the poignant predilection Humbert had in those days'. Such lines (and there are a great many of them) are certainly fancy, but we are not, I think, invited to distance ourselves from them much. The effect is arty, but art can include artiness – only Philistines and Puritans, Nabokov would suggest, stolidly think otherwise. Lolita herself picks up the alliterating habit, although the example may indicate a heartlessness in her and in her mentor: 'Oh, a squashed squirrel,' she said. 'What a shame'. Unless of course she said nothing of the kind, and the unfortunate squirrel comes from the same suspect source as the vortex of Lolita's mother's toilet.

Humbert's other fussy habit is his constant dropping into fragments of French, and when Nabokov in an interview briefly borrows the habit from his creature, he reminds us how fussy it is: 'I am extremely *distrait* (as Humbert Humbert would put it in his affected manner) . . .' 'Do you mind very much cutting out the French?' Lolita says towards the end of their affair. 'It annoys everybody.' *Lolita*'s first publisher thought the same, and Nabokov agreed to degallicize the text a bit. It can have been only a bit, since there is still scarcely a page without a slither into French: '*Eh bien, pas du tout!*', '*pas tout à fait*', '*enfin seuls*', '*que sais-je!*' '*donc*', '*entre nous soit dit*', '*grand Dieu!*' '*le grand moment*', '*comme on dit*', '*c'est tout*', '*les yeux perdus*', '*mais je divague*', '*à titre documentaire*', '*dans la force de l'âge*', etcétera . . . The French works in fact very much like the 'forsooths' and 'anents'. It is not a real retreat into a foreign language – none of these phrases expresses anything

Humbert couldn't say in English, and indeed what is there that Humbert couldn't say in English? – but a signalling of strangeness, the equivalent of a carefully cultivated alien accent. Humbert is not to be confused with the natives. There is little danger of that, of course, and that is why the affectation is so splendidly comic.

It is in part because he is nothing like a native that Humbert can mimic the natives so well. Ramsdale, in New England, is 'the gem of an eastern state', and New England itself ('elms, white church') is just what our clichés thought it was, although they are not usually quite so laconic. 'What d'ye know, folks', jocular Humbert says, and indeed regularly addresses his readers in a whole array of voices: respectful, diffident, confidential, insulting. He pictures us as his judge and jury; as long-suffering *aficionados* of old-fashioned novels; as learned, male, female, bald, frigid, patient, human, angelic listeners to his sad story. Sometimes we are his lawyer Clarence Choate Clark ('I notice the slip of my pen . . . , but please do not correct it, Clarence'), once an inattentive printer, clumsily setting Humbert's pleading message but not acting on it:

> Don't think I can go on. Heart, head – everything. Lolita, Lolita, Lolita, Lolita, Lolita, Lolita, Lolita, Lolita. Repeat till the page is full, printer.

The stylistic mayhem really starts, though, when the mimicry is complicated, as in Joyce's parodies, by the presence of other, genuinely unruly voices. A house in that eastern gem of a town is described as 'a kind of ramshackle wooden château' – the ambitions of the last word ruined by the sorry state of the verbal path leading up to it. In the following example, Humbert's impatience gets the better of his literary laughter, which manages nevertheless ('my reader') to make a graceful comeback:

> When the bride is a widow and the groom is a widower; when the former has lived in Our Great Little Town for hardly two years, and the latter for hardly a month; when Monsieur wants to get the whole damned thing over with as quickly as possible, and Madame gives in with a tolerant smile; then, my reader, the wedding is generally a 'quiet' affair. The bride may dispense with a tiara of orange blossoms securing her finger-tip veil, nor does she carry a white orchid in a prayer book.

We shall see Humbert's language at work again, but I would like here to point to just one more feature of it, an aspect it seems to share with Nabokov's own – a place where style and signature come together. This feature is what we might call the evocation of a depraved and glorified fairy tale, a world of legend and hyperbole, playfully celebrated, then undermined and at last – ironies still clashing like swordsmen in a moat-and-dungeon romance – coolly endorsed. The mode allows for both comic and lyrical applications. Humbert, for example, says he has 'a cesspoolful of rotting monsters behind his slow boyish smile.' The American wilds are full of poisonous plants and riotous insects, of rustling snakes, '*que dis-je*, of semi-extinct dragons!' American toilets, especially in sleepless nights, are 'manly, energetic, deep-throated', and flush like falling Niagaras. Lolita playing tennis 'paws' the ground with her foot before she serves, smiles at the high-thrown ball before 'falling upon it with a clean resounding crack of her golden whip'. And here is Humbert meeting Lolita for the first time, the very reincarnation, he thinks, of his doomed (typhus-stricken) seaside love:

> It was the same child – the same frail, honey-hued shoulders, the same silky supple bare back, the same chestnut head of hair . . . And, as if I were the fairy-tale nurse of some little princess (lost, kidnapped, discovered in gypsy rags through which her nakedness smiled at the king and his hounds), I recognized the tiny dark-brown mole on her side. With awe and delight (the king crying for joy, the trumpets blaring, the nurse drunk) I saw again her lovely indrawn abdomen where my southbound mouth had briefly paused . . .

'Awe and delight' would be tame, and the fairy-tale merely winsome, if it were not for the discreet clarity of 'southbound', and that second, sudden bracket with its excited contents – above all the abrupt, blissful drunkenness of the dishevelled Nurse Humbert.

(iv)

The novel we are reading is called *Lolita*, and so is the imaginary memoir which makes up most of it. It opens with a famously elaborate invocation to a girl of that name:

> Lolita, light of my life, fire of my loins. My sin, my soul. Lo-lee-ta: the tip of the tongue taking a trip of three steps down the palate to tap, at three, on the teeth. Lo. Lee. Ta.

Lolita certainly seems to be the topic, yet some three-quarters of the way through his text, Humbert feels constrained to tell us, 'This book is about Lolita.' What he mainly means is that his 'three empty years' without her, after her departure with Quilty, are not part of this story, which is about her and not about him. But the emphasis is odd, invites us to quarrel a little. And even if we don't, Humbert is soon to tell us that he 'simply did not know a thing' about the girl's mind, and to conjecture, with dim and belated condescension, that 'quite possibly, behind the awful juvenile clichés, there was in her a garden and a twilight, and a palace gate . . .' 'It was always my habit and method to ignore Lolita's states of mind while comforting my own base self'. Touché, as Humbert might say. This book is not about Lolita, or only about Lolita in a peculiarly displaced or refracted way. It is about 'Lolita', about the obsessive dream of Lolita which captured the actual child and took her away. 'My own creation, another, fanciful Lolita,' as Humbert claims, ' – perhaps more real than Lolita . . .' Perhaps. The ape has drawn the bars of his cage.

Yet there is a rebound, or double-take. Once we have seen that the ape has drawn his bars we can also see that he has, miraculously, sketched a little of the world too, a fraction of the zoo community as it might look to less caged eyes. I want to go further and suggest that if Humbert has not evoked, however faintly or briefly, a Lolita as well as a 'Lolita', allowed us a glimpse of the substantial American child as well as the solipsized (Humbert's word) nymphet, there is no novel here that matters, only the brilliant, vain spinning of a mind hooked on nothing but its own figments. Humbert sees very little of Lolita through the haze of his obsession, but the little he sees is fresh and engaging. His memory, we might say, is better than his understanding.

Even so, the finicky Humbert is less of a snob than many of his scholarly readers, who have seen in Lolita a condemnation of America's shallow, mass-managed culture. Humbert likes the rising twang in her voice when she says 'I must go now, kiddo'. And he likes her slang too, recording it with a linguist's loyalty: 'beaut', 'swank', 'swell', 'peachy', 'sap', 'stinker', 'jerk', 'revolting', 'super', 'luscious', 'goon', 'drip'. 'You dull bulb', she says to Humbert; and, 'You must be confusing me with some other fast little article.' 'Do you sleep in your old room or in a heap with Mother?' '*Pardonnez*, Mother,' she sings out in mockery of poor Charlotte's French pretensions – and maybe in mockery of Humbert's little tic too. What Humbert doesn't like is what we might call the slang of her life, the slang he has to live with rather than merely admire as picturesque. In charge of Lolita, he finds himself weirdly siding with the late Charlotte against the disorderly girl, who he decides 'despite a certain brash alertness of manner and spurts of wit was not as intelligent as her IQ might suggest'. This is Humbert's impatience speaking, and his tyranny too. Would he recognize her intelligence if it took forms he liked better? 'Mentally, I found her to be a disgustingly conventional little girl.' She is 'the ideal consumer', Humbert says. 'She it was to whom ads were dedicated...' The horror, the horror: she likes pop music, fudge sundaes, movie magazines; she sulks at times, she moans, she clowns. She is, in short, an entirely ordinary child, unbearable, lovable, funny, moody and soon trapped in the circle of Humbert's obsession. His crime is not to ruin or abduct a genius, or a paragon of manners and culture. It is to lock this girl out of her history, to shut this lively but not exceptional person away from her time and her place and her peers. We see the liveliness in the following passage, and can judge for ourselves whether this is brash alertness or mobile intelligence. She is describing to Humbert her doings at summer camp.

'Well – I joined in all the activities that were offered.'
'*Ensuite?*'
'Ansooit, I was taught to live happily and richly with others and to develop a wholesome personality. Be a cake, in fact.'
'Yes, I saw something of the sort in the booklet.'
'We loved the sings around the fire in the big stone fireplace or under the darned stars, where every girl merged her own spirit of happiness with the voice of the group.'
'Your memory is excellent, Lo, but I must trouble you to leave out the swear words. Anything else?'
'The Girl Scout's motto,' said Lo rhapsodically, 'is also mine. I fill my life with worth-while deeds such as – well, never mind what. My duty is -, to be useful. I am a friend to male animals. I obey orders. I am cheerful ... I am thrifty and I am absolutely filthy in thought, word and deed.'
'Now I do hope that's all, you witty child.'
'Yep. That's all. No – wait a sec. We baked in a reflector oven. Isn't that terrific?'
'Well, that's better.'
'We washed zillions of dishes. "Zillions" you know is schoolmarm's slang for many-many-many-many. Oh yes, last but not least, as Mother says – Now let me see – what was it? I know: We made shadowgraphs. Gee, what fun.'

But can we sensibly speak, as I just have, of a substantial American child? Aren't all the characters made of words, here as everywhere else in literature? Yes, and of course we shouldn't go looking for a material Dolores Haze (second name changed from Hays perhaps – what other name will provide the rhyme?) whom the fictional Humbert has had his hands on. And I don't mean to suggest that Lolita is simply true to American life and therefore exists in a way that the unlikely Humbert cannot – although as Nabokov says 'a modicum of average "reality"' is needed in this as in most novels. No, Lolita is Humbert's obsession and what escapes it, she is its name and its boundary. The 'actual' Lolita is the person we see Humbert can't see, or can see only spasmodically. In this sense she is a product of reading, not because the reader makes her up or because she is just 'there' in the words, but because she is what a reading finds, and I would say needs to find, in order to see the range of what the book can do. She needs to be 'there', that is, and she needs to be found. This surely is what reading is: a modest mode of creation, a collaboration with other minds and pictured worlds.

We should take the same line, I think, about the rest of what Humbert sees: plenty of bars but also some remarkable perspectives on the zoo. He is a whimsical and mischievous narrator, planting traps and gags all over the place, and defying us to trust him. But this means we have to be careful with our trust, not blandly and conveniently distrust everything he says. He seems pretty reliable about his childhood and first marriage, for example, where the joke is so thoroughly on him it's hard to see why he would tell it if it weren't pretty close to the (fictional) facts; and about America at large, with its landscapes ('and all around alternating strips of quicksilverish water and harsh green corn, the whole arrangement opening like a fan, somewhere in Kansas') and humbugging headmistresses ('we insist you unveto her non-participation in the dramatic group'). We take such things as 'true' partly because we do recognize what is being evoked or parodied, but mainly because we have no reason at all not to. We can doubt them – we can doubt anything – but it isn't in our readerly interest to do so. Or to put that another way, we can't question Humbert's interpretations, as we often must, if we don't grant some sort of stability to the material he is interpreting, and some sort of meaning to what he denies, to what leaks through his obsessively waterproofed prose.

Thus we accept, as the ground floor, as Mary McCarthy said in another context, of the novel's reality, that Humbert's beautiful mother died in an improbable accident ('picnic, lightning'); that his father owned a hotel on the Riviera; that the child Humbert had a desperate, passionate romance with a girl his own age ('All at once we were madly, clumsily, shamelessly, agonizingly in love with each other'); that the adult Humbert can't keep his mind off little girls; that he marries an American woman and on her death becomes her daughter's dodgy guardian; that he kills someone, and is now in gaol, having been in the prison hospital's psychiatric ward. What we question is Humbert's arrangement of all this, which is hindsighted and deeply suspect, full of what he himself calls static – meaning the electrical interference of what is felt in what is reported. At a crucial moment he gives us a moving speech *verbatim*, and then says 'words to that effect'; and a moment later, 'to that effect'. He is only translating, or recreating. We are reading Humbert's novelisation of Humbert's life. His very name is what he arrives at after rejecting Otto Otto, Mesmer Mesmer and Lambert Lambert as pseudonyms: 'for some reason I think my choice expresses the nastiness best'.

The method is roughly that of Gogol's *Diary of a Madman*, where a Russian character comes to think he is the missing King of Spain. Across his crazed narrative we pick up all the details of his being locked up and ill-treated (strange they should do this to the King of Spain, the madman thinks), as well as the fact that the King of Spain really is missing: the madman understands the newspapers, as Humbert understands America. Humbert's madness is very different and may not be madness at all, but the interpretative principle is the same. We read the reading as well as what is read, and probably need as much practice as we can get in this line. As René Girard has pointed out, if we take accounts of witch trials, for example, as traditional criticism takes a text – authorial intention, meanings which are manifestly 'there' – we shall always find the supposed witches guilty, because only the accusers and judges write of them. We need, Girard suggests, to hear the hysteria in the apparently authoritative pronouncements, the unreason hiding in the stern formalities. We shan't always find it; but often we shall and thereby strike a blow (better too late than absolutely never) for the historical innocence of these women. The author is not dead in Barthes' sense: just crazy, or conspiratorial, like the narrators we are looking at. This is an attractive model for reading, since it spares us both the tyranny of intention and the lure of endless undecidability.

Some of Humbert's fictional touches are distinctly minor, but interesting all the same. Was his childhood love really called Annabel Leigh, or is this a verbal mask borrowed from Poe's poem, with a crafty alteration in the spelling? Certainly the adult Humbert is very keen on connecting Poe's story with his own; alludes to the said poem on his first page, mentions Poe when he can ('Virginia was not quite fourteen when Harry Edgar possessed her. He gave her lessons in algebra. *Je m'imagine cela*'), preferably in the company of Dante ('Oh, Lolita, you are my girl, as Vee was Poe's and Bea Dante's'). He tells the Ramsdale *Journal* that his name is Edgar H Humbert ('I threw in the Edgar just for the heck of it') – although I'm not sure J Edgar Hoover isn't more prominent in this gag than Poe is. 'Annabel Leigh' on this reading would have drifted in from Humbert's later life, a graceful disguise for the dead girl. But perhaps she just *was* called Annabel Leigh, daughter of the bald, brown and English Mr Leigh – there are far wilder coincidences both in the book, and outside it – in which case Humbert's early life would have prepared one of those symmetries or prophecies he and Nabokov are so fond of. Other invitations to precisely the same double reading are: Lolita's spending a summer at Camp Q (near Lakes Onyx, Eryx and Climax) before either she or Humbert meets Quilty; Humbert cooking up an Aunt Clare as part of the ordinary family life he plans not to have; the hotel room of Humbert's and Lolita's first night together having the same number (342) as the Haze house in Ramsdale. Humbert's authorial hand or life's little ironies? (Let's leave Nabokov out of it for a moment.) I'm not inclined to decide, because nothing depends on the decision, and there is plenty of fun in both directions – and both clearly belong to Nabokov's moral geography, his sense of a world which is infinitely reworked and rejigged and also very quirky in the first place.

More serious is Humbert's theory of what he calls his perversion. He is asking us to believe that Annabel prefigures Lolita; that the interruption of his affair with Annabel at just the wrong moment caused his fixation on little girls, opened the obsession into which Lolita will fall. We can accept the first proposition without being much persuaded by the second. 'There might have been no Lolita at all had I not loved, one summer, a certain initial girl-child'; 'I am convinced . . . that in a certain magic and fateful way Lolita began with Annabel'. 'Might have been' is cautious enough, but 'magic and fateful' look like a mystification, as does Humbert's later talk of 'a fatal consequence'. 'No Lolita at all' is an interesting overstatement, meaning not no Dolores Haze but no Lolita-haunted story.

Humbert describes Lolita at first meeting as 'the little Herr Doktor who was to cure me of all my aches', and the territory begins to look a little more familiar. This is Gogol's story with a twist: the madman is sane enough to identify his affliction, and is widely read in the literature of the clinic.

> I discovered there was an endless source of robust enjoyment in tri-fling with psychiatrists: cunningly leading them on; never letting them see that you know all the tricks of the trade; inventing for them elaborate dreams, pure classics in style (which make *them*, the dream-extortionists, dream and wake up shrieking); teasing them with fake 'primal scenes'; and never allowing them the slightest glimpse of one's real sexual predicament.

There is, I think, something slightly crazy, as well as very funny, about this determined enjoyment, a slight echo perhaps of the be-haviour of the hero of Italo Svevo's *Confessions of Zeno*, who gets a certificate of sanity to impress his father. Tears of distress appear in the father's eyes as he says, 'Ah, then you really are mad!'

Of course we become the teased psychiatrists the moment we seek to diagnose Humbert – or indeed the moment we accept his diagnosis. There is much malarkey along these lines. We shall want to know, Humbert suggests – 'the able psychiatrist who studied my case' will want to know – when he took Lolita to the seaside in order to 'find there, at last, the "gratification" of a lifetime urge, and release from the "subconscious" obsession of incomplete child-hood romance with the initial Miss Lee'. Freudians and Poe scholars will note the spelling. Humbert's answer is surprising, though, even for wary readers. 'Well, comrade,' he says, 'let me tell you that I *did* look for a beach', but by that time the chase was too conscious, 'the rational pursuit of a purely theoretical thrill', and the beaches were disappointing, too muddy on the Atlantic, too foggy on the Pacific, and too windy on the Gulf. More important, the exorcism had already taken place at the first glimpse of little Doktor Haze, as she sunbathed in Ramsdale, 'golden and brown, kneeling, looking up, on that shoddy veranda, in a kind of ficti-tious, dishonest, but eminently satisfactory seaside arrangement . . .'

This is complicated mischief. The patient is boasting of what the patient in supposed to hide; worse, actually enjoys what he is sup-posed to have repressed. What use is a trauma when it's the patient's own pet theory, and what is a humble analyst to do? We might unravel the game (Humbert's and Nabokov's) in this way: psychiatric explanations of behaviour are often idiotic, and are easily faked, but certain psychological realities are undeniable – the past does haunt the present, for example. Perhaps we can't explain these realities at all, and in Nabokov's world definitely can't explain them without being laughed at, and maybe laughing ourselves at the sheer plodding plausibility of what we have proposed. All this means, though, is that we need to listen to the laughter as well as the explanations – the irony could come, as it does for a character in Henry James, not from impatience but from 'having so much imagination'. We are left with the feeling, not that the Annabel affair simply set the pattern for Humbert's later life, but that he pretty much believes that it did, in spite of his doctor-baiting antics – and to that extent it actually does set the pattern. Humbert's showy self-consciousness, I think, adds up to something less than scepticism: he really is saying what he pretends he is only pretending to say.

This reading of Humbert's manoeuvres allows us a new look at Nabokov's repeated attacks on Freud and psychoanalysis. There is scarcely a preface written in the 1960s and 1970s, when his Russian works were being translated and/or reprinted, in which the 'Viennese delegation' or the 'Viennese witch-doctor' are not taunted, for all the world as if this were Humbert having a bit of robust fun in the hospital. I shall not suggest that Nabokov secretly admires and agrees with the Freud he is attacking – that would be to become a Nabokovian parody of a Freudian – or even, more delicately, with Richard Rorty, that Freud is Nabokov's denied and resented forerunner, 'the precursor who may already have written all one's best lines'. But it is clear that Nabokov's making Humbert a sort of Freudian *malgré lui* deepens the apparently silly contest. Nabokov, let's say, would be the sceptic Humbert can't manage to be; a sceptic who knows there is something to be disbelieved: a false or ludicrous view of serious things. Freud is more of a rival than he looks, and needs to be caricatured as the fool who rushes in where Nabokov plans delicately to tread. The ground is not empty, but sacred; that is why the angels and the slightly less fearful novelist are going softly.

Humbert's theory of his art merges with his theory of his perversion, and asks for the same sort of reading. 'I am not concerned with so-called "sex" at all,' he says. 'A great endeavour lures me on: to fix once for all the perilous magic of nymphets'. He struggles to analyse Lolita's walk and why it charms him:

A faint suggestion of turned-in toes. A kind of wiggly looseness below the knee prolonged to the end of each footfall. The ghost of a drag. Very infantile, infinitely meretricious.

That's one endeavour. The other is to secure for Lolita and himself the shared immortality of literature: 'I am thinking of aurochs and angels, the secret of durable pigments, prophetic sonnets, the refuge of art.' Aurochs are extinct, and angels little seen, but paintings and sonnets have been known to last. Humbert is hoping, guessing, explicitly sees himself as an artist. He is trying out Shakespeare's gesture but understandably lacks Shakespeare's confidence. And the two endeavours come together in the myth he has invented for his obsession. He will become immortal as a certain kind of artist and madman – the sad and splendid irony being that it is only as a failure in this respect, only as a man whose glamour is finally a kind of buffoonery, whose fate is a farce, that he has any chance of a literary afterlife. Like Don Quixote, he will survive a long time because he comically misses his high vocation.

> Between the ages of nine and fourteen there occur maidens who, to certain bewitched travellers, twice or many times older than they, reveal their true nature which is not human, but nymphic (that is, demoniac) . . . Between those age limits, are all girl-children nymphets? Of course not. Otherwise, we who are in the know, we lone voyagers, we nympholepts, would have long gone insane. Neither are good looks any criterion . . . You have to be an artist and a madman, a creature of infinite melancholy . . . in order to discern at once, by ineffable signs . . . the little deadly demon among the wholesome children . . .

This is fancy prose indeed for a liking for little girls, and the complacent stance – elegantly draped between Yorick and Jacques – makes us laugh at its ambitions. But there is something appealing here too, an oblique definition of what seem to be less crazily specialized affections. Romantic love itself, the suggestion runs, *is* crazily specialised, the banishment of all smiles, gestures, hair and habits in the world save those of a single person. Every loved being has a second, secret, demonic nature which arbitrarily and categorically separates him or her from people who seem and perhaps really are very similar. Humbert is speaking of a class of persons, and that is an error, a compulsion, he will later say he regrets, but the rest goes for most of us. He is claiming, overgrandly, that his perversion is a proof of art – this indeed is one of his favourite and most maudlin defences – but Nabokov, I take it, is intimating that love, like art, is a feat and a travail of the peculiarly concentrated imagination. We may want to remember that Nabokov (following Proust, as Lucy Maddox has pointed out) defines art as 'curiosity, tenderness, kindness, ecstasy', and doesn't restrict it to what is officially called art – life itself will have it in moments of grace. There is much sense to be sifted from Humbert's madness; but of course we shan't see it unless we see the madness too.

Humbert's madness, or the possibility of his madness, is important *as* madness, as well as for the sense it contains, for it is through his constantly implied questions about Humbert's sanity that Nabokov most firmly signs and invents the world of *Lolita*. We can, if we wish, tame some of the unlikelier twists in the book in the manner I have suggested. Camp Q, Annabel Leigh, Room 342 and Aunt Clare would be the posterior work of Humbert the writer, laying tracks and making shapes. Certainly his memo of the '342 hotels, motels and tourist homes' he registered at while pursuing Lolita and Quilty looks to be faked by an excess of memory or of art. Humbert's thought that the fire which burns down a house in Ramsdale just before he arrives is caused by his own feverish excitement during the night ('the synchronous conflagration that had been raging . . . in my veins') is a simple flight of fancy, an overeagerness of metaphor. The long hike Lolita turns out to be away on with her fellow campers (Humbert having invented the story that she was away on a long hike with her fellow campers) is a little less manageable in reasonable terms. So are the builders who roll up to ruin Humbert's view in Beardsley, unobliging agents, it seems, either of the fretting superego or of Humbert's comically coordinated bad luck. There is a gap between the houses across the street, and he plans to perch in his bedroom and watch the girls in the school playground – Lolita, but also any other nymphets worth the connoisseur's while.

> Unfortunately, on the very first day of school, workmen arrived and put up a fence some way down the gap, and in no time a construction of tawny wood maliciously arose . . . utterly blocking my magic vista; and as soon as they had erected a sufficient amount of material to spoil everything those absurd builders suspended their work and never appeared again.

Coincidence is the word we reach for when reason can't cope and won't let go, but many of Nabokov's arrangements are only half-coincidences, or no coincidences at all. The name of the hotel where Humbert and Lolita spend their first night together is *The Enchanted Hunters*, and Lolita's school play has the same name. Humbert sometimes gets the name wrong (*The Hunted Enchanters*), but does remark on the 'coincidence', which he finds 'pleasant in a sad little way'. Lolita, who has met the author of the play after long admiring him from afar, knows the apparent coincidence is a joke. Quilty himself has a weakness for little girls, has been 'almost jailed once' on that score, and happened (a touch of coincidence after all) to be at the hotel when Humbert and Lolita were. He is the man in the dining room who Lolita thinks looks like Quilty, as well he may. He seems even then to have fancied Lolita, and to have had a hunch about brooding Humbert's tastes and intentions. On the other hand we may note that the enchanted hunters sound rather like the bewitched travellers in Humbert's myth of the nature of nymphets. The possibilities then are (please tick one or more of your preferences) that this name game reflects: life's joke on Humbert; Humbert's plagiarism of a hotel sign; Humbert's joke on us, and a posthumous trick on the dead Quilty; a sign of Nabokov's combinational art; Nabokov's joke on art and Humbert and us. Some of the jokes in *Lolita* are buried very deep. When Lolita says, *à propos des bottes*, that she is not a lady and does not like lightning, Humbert cannot possibly understand her allusion, since he has (at this stage) no knowledge of Quilty's works, which include *The Lady who Loved Lightning*, written (*tiens!*) in collaboration with the anagrammatic Vivian Darkbloom. Lolita is amusing herself – another instance of her wit that Humbert records but does not see – and Nabokov is wondering whether we are awake. Even Humbert seems to have forgotten his mother, killed by lightning.

Humbert and Quilty have an extraordinary conversation on the occasion of their first meeting. Humbert doesn't know and can't see Quilty, and only his erratic and learned style ('That child of yours needs a lot of sleep. Sleep is a rose, as the Persians say. Smoke?') reveals him to us. The two men are sitting on the hotel porch, and Quilty is drinking, and drunk. He says:

> 'Where the devil did you get her?'
> 'I beg your pardon?'
> 'I said: the weather is getting better.'
> 'Seems so.'
> 'Who's the lassie?'

'My daughter.'
'You lie – she's not.'
'I beg your pardon?'
'I said July was hot. Where's her mother?'
'Dead.'
'I see. Sorry . . .'

This is either Quilty's verbal fun or Humbert's anxiety getting into the sound of Quilty's words. Everything we subsequently learn about Quilty tilts us towards the first reading, but the important thing is that it is the stranger one: more plausible in context but indicative for that reason of how odd the context is. Humbert's guilt makes psychological and moral sense of this scene, and would be enough in another novel. The presence in this particular hotel, on this night of all nights, of a disreputable, joking Humbertian twin ('a fellow of my age in tweeds', as Humbert notes, and we know that Lolita thinks Humbert looks like Quilty) suggests that life (alias Humbert's mocking fate, alias Nabokov) is distinctly up to something.

All of Quilty's appearances have this flavour. We first find him for example in one of the few books in Humbert's prison's library, *Who's Who in the Limelight* (1946): 'Quilty, Clare. American dramatist. Born Ocean City, N.J., 1911 . . . His many plays for children are notable. *Little Nymph* (1940) travelled 14,000 miles and played 280 performances on the road . . .' The entry is full of tinny echoes, slightly off-pitch. Humbert was born in Paris, in 1910, but Ocean City seems to glance at his Riviera childhood. Quilty's *Little Nymph II* (1949), played live and not on stage, travelled quite a bit, and starred Humbert and Lolita, along with Quilty himself in a succession of rented cars.

Does this man really trail Humbert and Lolita more than halfway across America just for the hell of it? It would be madness to think so; but he does. 'It would have been too foolish even for a lunatic', Humbert says, 'to suppose another Humbert was avidly following Humbert and Humbert's nymphet . . . over the great and ugly plains'. This figure must be a hallucination, Humbert thinks; or a detective, some delegate of the Mann Act; or no one at all ('for a day or two I enjoyed the mental emphasis with which I told myself that we were not, and never had been followed'); or some unbelievably frolicsome and patient prankster. Early in his story, as we have seen, Humbert inclines to the defensive on the subject of his mental condition – 'I had another bout with insanity (if to melancholia and a sense of insufferable oppression that cruel term must be applied)' – but now he would rather be crazy than be tortured by a dream of being hunted. No enchantment in this prospect. *O lente currite noctis equi!* Humbert cries in an inspired misapprehension of Ovid via Faustus. 'O softly run, nightmares!'

> After all, gentlemen, it was becoming abundantly clear that all those identical detectives in prismatically changing cars were figments of my persecution mania, recurrent images based on coincidence and chance resemblance. *Soyons logiques*, crowed the cocky Gallic part of my brain . . .

Nabokov's world is very close to Hitchcock's here, and indeed Hitchcock did, in 1964, invite Nabokov to work on a movie with him. Nabokov expressed cautious interest, but nothing came of the venture. In Nabokov as in Hitchcock, apparently innocent landscapes are infested with suspicion. Any car on the roads of America might contain a pursuing Quilty; every name in a motel register could be a Quiltyan gag. On the other hand many of those 'verbal phantoms' might also just be 'living vacationists', entirely innocent after all. Quilty's hand is clear in the signatures 'Donald Quix, Sierra, Nev.', 'Lucas Picador, Merrymay, Pa.', but what about 'Johnny Randall, Ramble, Ohio'? Not everyone is Quilty; it's just that anyone could be. A crazy, frightened mistrust of the world is presented to us as manifestly crazy (in most circumstances) and merely the truth (in these circumstances). Logic is wrong and foolishness is right. Even paranoids have enemies, as the old joke goes, and Nabokov and Hitchcock make art out of that joke. The terrible, the ludicrous Quilty is 'tuned' to Humbert's 'mind and manner', as the victim says; as those vanishing builders were tuned to Humbert's spectatorly designs on the school playground. 'The tone of his brain', Humbert says, 'had affinities with my own . . . His allusions were definitely highbrow. He was well-read. He knew French. He was versed in logodaedaly and logomancy . . .' Even when he has killed Quilty, Humbert still feels he may be caught in Quilty's script: 'This, I said to myself, was the end of the ingenious play staged for me by Quilty.' Quilty, Clare. American dramatist.

What is happening here? Is Quilty Humbert's sleazy *alter ego*, his monstrous dream-double, the home-movie made by his guilt and shame? Yes. But he is not, alas, a mere projection of Humbert's oppressed mind, a figment like Banquo's ghost or Macbeth's dagger. He is that mind's nasty analogue, a material *semblable* and *frère*. He is an aspect of Humbert's self-image which has got loose, seceded, and taken over a part of the plot. Or he is Nabokov's answer to Humbert, the case Humbert can't make against himself. Either way he has plenty of independent life, and we need a full sense of how resilient this life is if we are to understand the manner of Quilty's dying, and to respond at all to what is perhaps the strangest moment in the whole book, when Humbert recounts his weird contentment at learning the name of his tormentor. Lolita tells him, he says, 'the name that the astute reader has guessed long ago'.

> I, too, had known it, without knowing it, all along. There was no shock, no surprise. Quietly [we almost hear Quilty's name] the fusion took place, and everything fell into order, into the pattern of branches that I have woven throughout this memoir with the express purpose of having the ripe fruit fall at the right moment; yes, with the express and perverse purpose of rendering – she was talking but I sat melting in my golden peace – of rendering that golden and monstrous peace through the satisfaction of local recognition, which my most inimical reader should experience now.

We have had a comic trial run for this experience in Humbert's account of his first marriage. 'There is another man in my life,' his wife says, Humbert translating for us 'from her French which was, I imagine, a translation in its turn of some Slavic platitude'. He bundles her into a taxi, and angrily insists on knowing who the fellow is. She rattles on about her misery and about wanting a divorce, and finally, mutely, points to the taxi driver. 'He pulled up at a small cafe and introduced himself.' Here the seemingly accidental is reclaimed for the main plot; the apparent extra turns out to be a principal character. With the revelation of Quilty's name almost every scattered sign in Humbert's life assumes significance, the random is banished, meaning blossoms everywhere. Fusion; order; golden peace. But the order is perverse, the order of a gigantic mockery, and we need to linger a little on this lyrical and scaring paradox, this travesty of the triumph of art.

I can think of only two other expressions of this sentiment. They are very disparate, but oddly relevant. One appears in Kafka's 'Letter to his Father': 'I was very despairing and in such moments all my bad experiences in all areas came gloriously together.' Glorious is *grossartig*, and could be a bitter sarcasm, of course. But it really seems to register a genuine, if paranoid, pleasure: the pure perfection of everything going entirely wrong; the perfection overcoming the wrongness. My other instance has the voice of Harry Gold, the Russian spy supposedly connected with the Rosenbergs, and pretty much Humbert's contemporary. Confessing the 'authenticity and enormity' of his crime, Gold said:

> The manner in which all of the pieces of the giant jigsaw puzzle, of which I was a part, are falling ever so gloriously into place – to reveal the whole picture – has added a tremendous zest and sense of achievement to my life.

Enormity and zest: we can scarcely hold the thought together. Zest is not what Humbert is conjuring up for us, but his peace is just as hard to take. Not that we don't understand him. On the contrary: we understand and would rather not. This is the happiness of abdication, a demonic parody of religious submission. In anyone's will is our peace, if that will encompasses and disposes of our diffusion. Fortunately Humbert sees that his mood is monstrous as well as golden; and we see that Quilty is neither God nor Humbert's hallucination but a sort of tempter. He is the way we feel when we feel things are against us; the paranoid's enemy; objective proof (in the world of the novel) of the conspiracy we thought we had only dreamed.

I seem to have slithered over the element of literary parody in all this, but that is easier to see. *Lolita* is not only a book with a manically material double in it, it is a joke about books which allow such creatures any sort of run. Nabokov would expect us to remember Dostoyevsky, who wrote a novel called *The Double* and whose reputation in the West, Nabokov thought, was hugely inflated. That inflation itself might have seemed to secure the allusion, even if we didn't know that Stavrogin's almost unnameable sin, in *The Possessed*, is the molestation of a little girl; and Humbert himself, in case we need a hint, says he feels a 'Dostoyevskian grin dawning . . . like a distant and terrible sun'. The clue to Conrad, another specialist in doubling, is stealthier. Humbert imagines Quilty as 'that secret agent, or secret lover, or prankster, or hallucination, or whatever he was'. 'Secret sharer' is the phrase Humbert has left out, but he wouldn't want us to prompt him. When Humbert speaks of Quilty as 'my brother', the fun piles up in several tiers. If we are still not sure about casting Quilty as Humbert's double, we pounce on the words, wondering mildly why Humbert/Nabokov is suddenly being so helpful. We should wonder more, since Humbert is only referring to the fact that Quilty, taking Lolita away, pretended to be her uncle, hence his brother, and the symbolists among us are stuck in mid air. Or are we? It's not as if Humbert is any less literary than we are.

These are good games, but it would be a mistake to close the perspective with the smiling novelist and his cultivated readers, as if there were nowhere to go beyond the knowledge that art is art. I want to say a word about the grotesque comedy associated with the figure of Quilty, and about the peculiar, agnostic sense of fate which makes the joking artist (Humbert, Quilty, life as an arranger of material events, Nabokov as the arranger of that life and the inventor of those who live it) somehow the servant of his own jokes, emblems of a truth which is not only stranger than fiction but neater, addicted to the coincidences fiction can't afford.

(v)

Philip Roth once told me, in relation to the tilt towards what feels like vulgarity in his writing, that he could do the delicate stuff but had to go where the energy was. Words to that effect. I can think of no better introduction to the comedy of Quilty – except possibly Peter Sellers' performance in Kubrick's film *Lolita*. There are lunatic energies abroad here, and although they help to confirm the suggestion of Quilty as a too perfectly placed double, an ideal of inventive awfulness, they can't entirely be reclaimed by this or any other scheme of interpretation. Nabokov spoke of 'the secret points', 'the nerves of the novel', meaning the images he himself remembered with most pleasure – he mentioned the taxi-driving lover, the class list of Lolita's school in Ramsdale, Lolita playing tennis, Lolita stalking dreamily up to the suitcase full of presents Humbert has bought her, one or two other scenes – and many readers linger on just the same moments when they rerun the book in their minds. But I would want to add a few pieces of the Quilty material: the trail of riddling clues and pseudonyms he leaves in the motel registers of America, for example (we have seen Donald Quix and Lucas Picador, but there are plenty more: 'N. Petit, Larousse, Ill.', 'D. Orgon, Elmira, NY', 'Arthur Rainbow', 'Morris Schmetterling'; licence numbers like 'WS 1564' and 'SH 1616'); and the florid and protracted and hilarious scene of his murder.

What is the pleasure here? What are we remembering, or looking forward to in our rereading? An escape from Humbert, I think; and even perhaps an escape from Nabokov, at least in his more lordly or fastidious registers. 'Goodness, what a tease the poor fellow was', Humbert says of Quilty. 'His main trait was his passion for tantalization'. You would have to be little crazy to delight so in such games: who but a madman would get such fun from mocking another madman? Quilty is the artist not only as manic plotter of infinite details but as the superfluous, gratuitous subject, master of finely tuned and quite pointless skills. This is art for no sake at all, not even art's; and this is why he eludes our schemes; why we enjoy him; and why he is almost impossible to kill.

Talking once about the Marx Brothers, Nabokov went into such detail about a scene from *Night at the Opera* – the amazing pile-up in Groucho's exiguous cabin – that the interviewer didn't even try to summarize it. A scene of 'pure genius', Nabokov called it – not a phrase he threw around lightly – and Quilty has something of this anarchic genius, a chaotic disregard for the proper and the probable. He wisecracks the way Groucho Marx does, and the point in both cases is less that the gags are funny (some are, some aren't, and some don't even get near) than that they are made, and made constantly, as if the determination to crack jokes was a habit and a vow and a disease and a victory all at once. 'This is the only way to travel', Groucho says in *Duck Soup* when Harpo has stranded him on an unmoving vehicle for the third time. It's not much of a line, but anyone else would have been speechless.

'Grey-faced, baggy-eyed, fluffily dishevelled in a scanty balding way', Quilty is doped and maybe drunk when Humbert catches up with him in his sprawling house. He takes Humbert at first for a man from the telephone company, but soon changes his mind:

> 'You have a funny accent, Captain . . . You are some foreign literary agent. A Frenchman once translated my *Proud Flesh* as *La Fierté de la Chair*. Absurd.'

Humbert is still trying to play his melodrama straight. 'She was my child, Quilty', he says. Quilty looks a little wary, and says,

> 'I'm very fond of children myself, and fathers are among my best friends . . . What do you want? Are you French, mister? Woolly-woo-boo-are? . . . Say! that's a swell little gun you've got there. What d'you want for her? . . . You recall Kipling: *une femme est une femme, mais un Caporal est une cigarette*?'

Quilty reaches for Humbert's gun, then makes a dive for it, and the two men find themselves grotesquely wrestling, Humbert's whole impersonation of the cool avenger gone up in Kipling's smoke, toppled into burlesque.

> We rolled all over the floor, in each other's arms, like two huge help-less children. He was naked and goatish under his robe, and I felt suffocated as he rolled over me. I rolled over him. We rolled over me. They rolled over him. We rolled over us . . . He and I were two large dummies, stuffed with dirty cotton and rags. It was a silent, soft, formless tussle on the part of two literati, one of whom was utterly disorganized by a drug while the other was handicapped by a heart condition and too much gin.

Not, as Humbert notes, the great slug-out, 'the obligatory scene', we find at the end of Westerns. He retrieves his gun, and forces Quilty to read out his own death sentence, 'a neat typescript' containing Humbert's parody of the opening section of Eliot's 'Ash Wednesday':

> Because you took advantage of a sinner
> Because you took advantage
> Because you took
> Because you took advantage of my disadvantage . . .

Quilty adds jovial comments to his reading – 'That's damned good', 'Oh, grand stuff!', 'Didn't get that', 'A little repetitious, what?' and hands the typescript back: 'Well, sir, this is certainly a fine poem. Your best as far as I am concerned.' He eyes the gun, and makes a speech, alternately clear-headed and confused, and in its way courageous – or is it just that he cannot really believe what is happening to him?

> 'Now look here, Mac . . . You are drunk and I am a sick man. Let us postpone the matter. I need quiet. I have to nurse my impotence . . . This pistol-packing farce is becoming a frightful nuisance. We are men of the world, in everything – sex, free verse, marksmanship . . . My memory and my eloquence are not at their best today but really, my dear Mr Humbert, you were not an ideal stepfather and I did not force your little protégée to join me . . . This house . . . is yours, gratis . . . Now, *soyons raisonnables*. You will only wound me hideously and then rot in jail while I recuperate in a tropical setting. I promise you . . . you will be happy here, with a magnificent cellar, and all the

royalties from my next play – I have not much at the bank right now
but I propose to borrow – you know, as the Bard said, with that cold
in his head, to borrow and to borrow and to borrow. There are other
advantages . . . Now drop that pistol like a good fellow . . . I knew
your dear wife slightly. You may use my wardrobe . . . I can arrange
for you to attend executions, not everybody knows that the chair is
painted yellow – '

Humbert fires and misses. Quilty scrambles into the next room and
begins to play the piano. Humbert fires again and manages to hit
him.

he rose from his chair higher and higher, like old, grey, mad Nijin-
ski, like Old Faithful, like some old nightmare of mine, to a
phenomenal altitude, or so it seemed – as he rent the air – still shak-
ing with the rich black music – head thrown back in a howl, hand
pressed to his brow, and with his other hand clutching his armpit as
if stung by a hornet . . .

Quilty can still scurry away, though, and now Humbert wounds
him three or four times. The pain is real enough, but Quilty is still
joking, playing Sidney Greenstreet out of *The Maltese Falcon*: 'he
shivered every time a bullet hit him as if I were tickling him, and . . .
he would say under his breath, with a phoney British accent . . .
"Ah, that hurts, sir, enough! Ah, that hurts atrociously, my dear
fellow. I pray you, desist. Ah – very painful, very painful, indeed . . ."' Quilty climbs into his bed and wraps himself up.
Humbert shoots him some more and finally seems to kill him. Even
then Quilty manages to crawl out on to the landing before he gives
up the histrionic ghost.

A whole generation of black comedy comes from this scene, and
of course Nabokov is brilliantly showing us how hard it is to put
old nightmares down. 'Do not pity C. Q.', Humbert says, addressing Lolita in his imagination. 'One had to choose between him and
H.H. . .' But we do pity Quilty – or we would if we weren't caught
up in another, more complicated emotion – and the choice is not
easy. It is not easy even for Humbert, since we may take the almost
unfinishable murder as a narrative metaphor for other difficulties.
There is nothing attractive about Quilty. He is goatish like
Groucho, and a good deal kinkier, as his interest in executions suggests. But it is not a matter of our liking him. He is Nabokov's least
simplified portrait of the forces which wreck the order and happiness of the world, and the question is not so much whether we can

get rid of him as whether we can actually do without him, whether we should not miss our contact with the prodigious misrule he represents. 'Banish plump Jack,' Falstaff says, 'and banish all the world.' Prince Hal replies, 'I do. I will.' Banish plump Jack, he means, but the grammar makes him ready to banish all the world too. Falstaff is not all the world, and he is not a lot more attractive than Quilty – not the charming, always forgivable scoundrel of popular mythology. He is dangerous disorder, but even so, or just for this reason, the world without him may not be much of a world.

(vi)

Destiny is quite often another name for narrative, the order we retrospectively find in scattered events. Sometimes that is all it is. Much of the work of Gabriel García Márquez, for example, is a comic and haunting demonstration of this human habit. We orchestrate a whole history and then imprison ourselves in the score, as if someone else had written it. Even Hardy, in *Tess of the D'Urbevilles* and many of his poems, can be seen as a master builder of metaphors of persecution rather than a serious believer in fatality.

Nabokov goes further than García Márquez and is craftier than Hardy. He takes the traditional notion of God as the author of the world's text and wonders what sort of author God is. This is not a theological curiosity – Nabokov is too sceptical for that – but it is a philosophical one, and none the less philosophical for being playful and oblique. God becomes a figure for whatever order there is in the world – really is, beyond our constructions, the narrative prior to our narrative, destiny's destiny. We can impose orders readily enough. 'It is a brave affair,' as the poet Wallace Stevens says. 'But to impose is not /To discover':

> From this the poem springs: that we live in a place
> That is not our own . . .

There may be no such order, or none that we can find or recognize, but curiosity requires only the possibility, the door that is not fast closed.

In *Lolita* the curiosity takes distinctly mischievous forms. What if God the author were not an epic poet, like Homer say, or Milton, and not a formidable novelist like Tolstoy, but a lighter, more whimsical writer, like Sterne or Lewis Carroll? If he were particularly fond of the unlikely, keener on miracles than on the laws of physics? The real and the fantastic, in literature and in the world, would not then merge as the Surrealists hoped they would: they would just change places. So-called realism would be the most wishful of all modes of art, because it would depict normality where there are only freaks, and normality itself would be a distant dream masquerading as the state of things. In *The Enchanter*, his first (1939) run at the subject of *Lolita*, Nabokov is still dedicated to an old plausibility, in spite of his difficult and dangerous theme. The mother of his nymphet gets ill and dies; the tortured protagonist flings himself into a suicidal accident to end his story. In *Lolita* the full resources of an acrobatic art are deployed to signal wild improbability and then to justify it as true. True, that is, to a particular sense of the world, or to the world as it may appear to us at particular moments. Paranoids do have enemies: why should the precious instants when the enemies show up be less real than the endless hours when they are only imagined?

The plot of *Lolita*, Humbert's plan for the girl, Nabokov's narrative need, require the death of the girl's mother, as in *The Enchanter*. Nabokov first plays with our guess that Humbert will murder Charlotte Haze. He does think of it; finds the necessary occasion and the means and what he thinks is the freedom from observation. He will tug her under the water of Hourglass Lake (Our Glass Lake, as he at first thinks it is), and hold her down until she is dead. 'The setting was really perfect for a brisk bubbling murder . . .' But he can't do it, doesn't do it. 'Poets never kill', he insists, which as we have just seen is not strictly true, unless Humbert's terrible poetry takes him out of the class of poets altogether. What he means is clear enough, though: he can kill an enemy and a tormentor and destroy his own life in the process; he can't kill poor harmless Charlotte just to get her out of the way. It's as well for him that he can't, since Charlotte's friend Jean Farlow has been watching them swimming and could even see that Humbert was wearing his wrist watch. A present from Charlotte: 'Waterproof,' she says proudly.

No murder then. Charlotte will either have to stay alive and alter the story or meet with the proverbial bad accident. Only a very confident novelist would proceed to arrange the accident in all its obviousness, and have his narrator call it 'a bad accident'. The very notion of an arranged accident raises dizzying questions about fiction. Distressed by learning of Humbert's distaste for her and his designs on her daughter, blinded by tears, Charlotte rushes out to post her farewell letter and is killed by a car which has mounted the sidewalk to avoid a wandering dog. Even then Charlotte might not have been hit if the sidewalk had not been wet and slippery. We have glimpsed the dog before: Humbert's limousine almost ran over it on the day of his arrival at 342 Lawn Street.

'I had actually seen the agent of fate,' Humbert thinks after a ludicrous conversation with the driver of the car, but goes on immediately to break fate down into its detailed ingredients: 'hurrying housewife, slippery pavement, a pest of a dog, steep grade, big car, baboon at its wheel'. He doesn't forget his own 'vile contribution', the diary Charlotte has found and been so upset by. Even so the ingredients mean nothing, make nothing happen, except in a particular mixture, and Humbert is thus able after all to speak of 'precise fate, that synchronizing phantom', the scenarist who places dog and car and Charlotte and wet street and her tears together at just this right/wrong juncture of space and time.

Fate is still a phantom, a metaphor; but a metaphor Nabokov has made virtually irresistible. An accident as elaborate as this – but perhaps all accidents are elaborate when we look at them closely – can't look like an accident. We are in the world of apparent coincidences set up by Quilty, and Humbert, and . . . Nabokov. Only Nabokov can be suspected here. This accident is even more convenient for him than it is for Humbert, and there is something spectacular about his so royally treating himself to it. But there is more. The strings of the puppet-characters dangle thickly in the air, but the puppets *as* puppets hint at a further truth. 'Life's nonsense pierces us with strange relation', Stevens says, and the nonsense of Charlotte's death *is* its claim on our mind and our emotions. The tricky novelist mimes the trick of circumstances when they have abandoned plausibility, as they so often do. Destiny is not narrative here; just a picture of life behaving like a novel. Of course you have to be a particular kind of writer – God or Nabokov – to catch the relation and the nonsense.

(vii)

'I shall be remembered,' Nabokov said, 'by *Lolita* and my work on *Eugene Onegin*.' The first part of this remark is almost certainly true; the second probably needs reversing. His wilful and appealing work on *Onegin* will no doubt be remembered because it is his. One of the things we shall most remember in *Lolita* is Humbert's desolate and draining last encounter with the rediscovered girl. Nabokov either triumphs here or makes a brilliant near-miss; either does or does not transcend the fastidious cleverness which is his besetting limit. I think he triumphs, but the case is worth arguing, since it is an extremely close thing.

Lolita has abandoned Humbert for Clare Quilty, has refused the latter's more freakish sexual demands and been thrown out by him. She has drifted for almost two years, making a living by washing dishes, and has married Dick Schiller, a youthful war veteran. She is pregnant, looks worn and helpless and hollow-cheeked. She seems calm and kindly, weirdly resigned to her peculiar past and shabby present. She and Dick live in an urban American waste land some eight hundred miles from New York, their clapboard shack surrounded by 'withered weeds', lost in a region of 'dump and ditch, and wormy vegetable garden . . . and grey drizzle, and red mud, and several smoking stacks in the distance.' The drizzle is presumably laid on by the pathetic fallacy, but the rest must be there in all weathers. She still thinks of the obscene Quilty as 'a great guy', and grants that Humbert was 'a good father', as if that was all he had been. This dazed tolerance is more terrible than resentment or rage because it belongs to a person who is past surprise, who has lived with more human strangeness – Humbert's obsession, Quilty's pranks and kinks – than anyone should have to. 'Yes,' Humbert reports her as wearily saying, 'this world was just one gag after another.' She is still only seventeen, and the reader knows, as no one in the story does, that she will be dead in just over three months.

Much of the power of this chapter of the novel rests not on the depth or complexity of Lolita's character, or on her having acquired such a character, as David Rampton attractively argues, but on her sheer ruined ordinariness, her old lost ordinariness found again only as a ruin. Life with Humbert was a cage, a travelling prison, a dreary round of sexual duty. Quilty looked like glamour and romance and freedom, but turned out to be only quirky Sadeian games. Even so Lolita regards Quilty as 'full of fun', and Humbert as a remote, hardly remembered nuisance:

> She considered me as if grasping all at once the incredible – and somehow tedious, confusing and unnecessary – fact that the distant, elegant, slender, forty-year-old valetudinarian in velvet coat sitting beside her had known and adored every pore and follicle of her pubescent body. In her washed-out grey eyes, strangely spectacled, our poor romance was for a moment reflected, pondered upon, and dismissed like a dull party, like a rainy picnic to which only the dullest bores had come, like a humdrum exercise, like a bit of dry mud caking her childhood.

Our poor romance is his poor romance, no romance at all for her. The sadness of Lolita's story, as Humbert later realizes, is that she hasn't had the childhood he casually evokes here in metaphor: only the mud and the spoiled picnic, followed by her escapade with Quilty and sudden adulthood. Just one gag after another.

Lolita may well be happier than Humbert (or we) can imagine, but she seems stunned and flattened, almost erased by the life she has led, and for Humbert, of course, this scene is dominated by the thought that the whole sad story is his work, that he has brought Lolita to this. He compares his hands to those of Dick Schiller and thinks: 'I have hurt too much too many bodies with my twisted poor hands to be proud of them.' We remember his hitting Lolita, twisting her wrist; his tormenting of his first wife, Valeria. Trying to make small talk, he almost asks Lolita about one of her old class-mates in Ramsdale, 'I wonder sometimes what has become of the little McCoo girl . . .?', but doesn't, for fear of Lolita's responding, 'I wonder sometimes what has become of the little Haze girl . . .' Lolita won't say this, of course, only the ventriloquism of Humbert's guilt speaks. Similarly, when Lolita starts (but does not finish) a comparison between Quilty and Humbert – 'I would sooner go back to Cue. I mean – ' – it is Humbert who mentally supplies the lurid novelistic words: '*He* broke my heart. *You* merely broke my life'.

Is this sensitivity new in Humbert? It is not new in the book, which is littered with expressions of compunction – entirely un-availing, not in the least acted on, to be sure. After Charlotte Haze's death and Humbert's first night with Lolita:

> More and more uncomfortable did Humbert feel. It was something quite special, that feeling: an oppressive, hideous constraint as if I were sitting with the small ghost of somebody I had just killed.

At the end of their first set of all-American travels:

> We had been everywhere. We had really seen nothing. And I catch myself thinking today that our long journey had only defiled with a sinuous trail of slime the lovely, trustful, dreamy, enormous country that by then, in retrospect, was no more to us than a collection of dog-eared maps, ruined tour books, old tyres, and her sobs in the night – every night, every night – the moment I feigned sleep.

There is a certain amount of narrative complication here. Humbert is 'thinking today' throughout his text, but the constraint, the sobs and the feigned sleep belong to the lived past. What he is suggesting, I think, is that his guilt was always with him, but his perpetual desire and fear wouldn't allow him to concentrate on it, and in any case it was a different guilt, associated with a publicly identifiable crime, that of cohabitation with a minor. What he wants to evoke and renounce in his last meeting with Lolita is the guilt not of having slept with her but of having treated her as a sample or a treasure, a hoarded specimen of nymphetry, rather than as a person. It is this person, Lolita then *and* now, he insists he loves:

> there she was with her ruined looks and her adult, rope-veined narrow hands and her goose-flesh white arms, and her shallow ears, and her unkempt armpits, there she was (my Lolita!), hopelessly worn at seventeen, with that baby, dreaming already in her of becoming a big shot and retiring around A.D. 2020 – and I looked and looked at her, and knew as clearly as I know I am to die, that I loved her more than anything I had ever seen or imagined on earth, or hoped for anywhere else . . . You may jeer at me, and threaten to clear the court, but until I am gagged and half-throttled, I will shout my poor truth. I insist the world know how much I loved my Lolita, *this* Lolita, pale and polluted, and big with another's child, but still grey-eyed, still sooty-lashed, still auburn and almond, still Carmencita, still mine . . .

This is the end of a maniac, the projected birth of a hero. Humbert rejects his past specialization, his obsessive interest in a *class* of little girls, the charms Lolita could only grow out of: 'sterile and selfish vice, all *that* I cancelled and cursed.' His conversion comes far too late, of course, but it would always have been too late, a one-sided love story, Tristan without Isolde. What Humbert is busily, desperately doing is to convert a ragged and tantalising tale of physical possession and loss into a great romance. This is the function of the clustering references to *Carmen*, once a tender allusion for Humbert, then an unwanted joke between him and Quilty, now a touch of literary orchestration, a hoisting of his 'poor romance' into famous sentimental company. This is not Nabokov's parody of Mérimée, it is Humbert's bid for Mérimée's help – although we may glimpse, somewhere off in the margin, Nabokov's smile at Humbert's conventional taste. Humbert *is* Don Jose, Lolita *is* Carmen: a replay. '*Changeons de vie, ma Carmen, allons vivre quelque part où nous ne serons jamais séparés . . . Carmen, voulez-vous venir avec moi?*' There is a difference, though, which Humbert carefully exploits.

> I could not kill *her*, of course, as some have thought . . . Then I
> pulled out my automatic – I mean, this is the kind of fool thing a
> reader might suppose I did . . .

Don Jose killed Carmen; Humbert kills the bullfighter. And Humbert's prose, of course, is more various than Mérimée's: histrionic, self-regarding ('pale and polluted', 'I looked and looked', 'my poor truth'), but also casual ('big shot') and heartrendingly exact ('rope-veined', 'sooty-lashed').

What are we to make of all this? Readers and critics have rightly focused much attention on this troubling scene. Michael Long thinks Nabokov is trying to change key and hasn't got the voice for it, as Flaubert and Joyce have: 'It is hardly possible for the hero of such an exuberant work of fictional artifice to turn, at the last, into the weeping figure from whom these fragments are torn.' Appel and Rampton wonder whether we believe in Nabokov's new order of love; conclude that we do, albeit with difficulty. I think Long gets closer to the centre of the problem. I can't believe in Humbert's new love partly because there is nothing in his self-portrait to suggest he can rise to it, and partly because he is protesting too much, hooked on his version of *Carmen*, too anxious for us to *see* the change in him ('You may jeer at me, and threaten to clear the court . . .'). I can't believe in his repentance because the language of his renunciation is the language of gloating – as indeed his language throughout, however guilty he feels or says he felt, is full of relished remembrance, like that of Dante's lovers Paolo and Francesca enjoying the rerun of what took them down to hell.

> She was only the faint violet whiff and dead echo of the nymphet I
> had rolled myself upon with such cries in the past; an echo on the
> brink of a russet ravine, with a far wood under a white sky, and
> brown leaves choking the brook, and one last cricket in the crisp
> weeds . . .

This is (overwritten) nostalgia, not regret. Humbert calls his old vice sterile and selfish, but a *grand péché radieux*, as he also names it, can't be so easy to moralize, let alone give up. The same goes for his later intimations of remorse: his talk of his 'foul lust', 'total evil', 'bestial cohabitation'; his sense that his life with Lolita had been only a 'parody of incest'; his self-sentencing ('Had I come before myself, I would have given Humbert at least thirty-five years for rape, and dismissed the rest of the charges'); his listening to 'the melody of children at play':

> I stood listening to that musical vibration from my lofty slope, to those flashes of separate cries with a kind of demure murmur for background, and then I knew that the hopelessly poignant thing was not Lolita's absence from my side, but the absence of her voice from that concord.

This perception is surely morally correct. Humbert's crime is the Jamesian one *par excellence*, the theft of another's freedom – in this case, the freedom to be the ordinary, lively, vulgar American kid we have intermittently seen. But coming from Humbert the claim seems mawkish and self-regarding, altogether too good to be true, 'dictated by some principle of compensation', as Dupee says. Humbert's fussy prose, elsewhere so resourceful and acrobatic, here manages to seem both artful and hackneyed.

One of Humbert's afterthoughts is slightly more convincing, because it offers an argument and anticipates the queer moral indifference of the second generation of *Lolita*'s readers (after the outrage, the lazy tolerance – and after that, the vigilantes again):

> Unless it can be proven to me – to me as I am now, today, with my heart and my beard, and my putrefaction – that in the infinite run it does not matter a jot that a North American girl-child named Dolores Haze had been deprived of her childhood by a maniac, unless this can be proven (and if it can, then life is a joke), I see nothing for the treatment of my misery but the melancholy and very local palliative of articulate art.

We can agree that this deprivation does matter, and more than a jot; that life is not this kind of joke. But even here Humbert ends on *his* misery, and is still glamorizing his misdemeanours: the one thing worse than being a serious malefactor would be to be nobody, a negligible miscreant.

We might go further and say that while Humbert writes wonderfully about his own deviance, he can't write himself straight; and that the thinness of his repentance is a measure of the weird, lingering humanity of his crime. He has been involved in 'intricately sordid situations', as Dupee says, but somehow 'his horrid scrapes become our scrapes'. Not literally or legally, we hope, but closely enough for all but saints and hypocrites. Love itself, of the least deviant kind, is scarcely less possessive or crazed than Humbert's mania.

> No matter, even if those eyes of hers would fade to myopic fish, and her nipples swell and crack, and her lovely young velvety delicate delta be tainted and torn – even then I would go mad with tenderness at the mere sight of your dear wan face, at the mere sound of your raucous young voice, my Lolita.

The wan face, the raucous voice, the eyes like myopic fish, the velvety delicate delta are the notations of desperate love, and Humbert writes here the purest, most precise Nabokovian prose. What we question is not his passion but its supposed new respectability. The whole of this book has been asking us to trust Humbert's obsession, even as we are repelled by it. We can't leave off trusting it now, especially when it speaks in these accents, so lyrically mourning what it claims it won't miss.

Still, it may not be necessary for us to believe what Humbert believes at the end. Indeed we may understand his crime more fully if we are sceptical about his repentance and altered love. What is unmistakable is his desire to see himself, and to project himself, as supremely conscious of his grisly errors, as the sort of grovelling Dostoyevskian sinner Nabokov so detested. It is easy to confess, as Appel says, and it may actually be to Humbert's credit that he is not entirely convincing in this line, in spite of his ambitions. And of course what finally fuels this whole great scene, what makes it moving, with all its disconcerting, criss-crossing antics, is not the moral issue, important as it is. We need to work through our scepticism, I think, but then we can let it go, because we can all, without question, believe in Humbert's loss, his sense of dereliction. 'I believe in my abandonment,' a figure cries in a Geoffrey Hill poem, 'since it is what I have.' Humbert's loss is what he has; we can't, so to speak, take that away from him. His shabby selfishness, his alternately brilliant and inflated prose, his unavailing bid to lift himself into high romance, all add to the sadness rather than lessen it. We don't have to admire Humbert in order to feel his pain, and he does become, briefly and ambiguously, in his overacted way, the kind of character we find in Joyce and Flaubert, one whose lamentable lack of grandeur stirs us perhaps more than the grand tragedy of some others. The shift is pictured in this chapter in a beautifully placed, entirely banal American word. Humbert repeats his request that Lolita/Carmen come away with him ('*Carmen, voulez-vous . . .?*'), and she says 'No, honey, no.' Humbert reflects, 'She had never called me honey before.' She couldn't call him honey before because she didn't think of him fondly enough or casually enough: banality was outlawed from their life, which was only romance and torture (for him), drudgery and quarantine (for her). For a moment Humbert seems to glimpse the attraction of the acceptable and the familiar, of the way other people daily talk and live – the realm of shared feeling which inhabits cliché, and which cliché serves. Of course he can only recognise the feeling because he is excluded from it, but the recognition is something, since it matters that even this tiny and perfunctory brand of tenderness was missing from his relation with Lolita. Missing on both sides, we might add, in spite of Humbert's liking for tenderness as a word; as kindness is often missing from romantic love.

It is a very short-lived recognition, though, and Humbert is soon driving off through 'the drizzle of the dying day', wrapped again in an imagery of pathos, and on his way to kill Quilty among the bedrooms and bathrooms of grotesque comedy, where Humbert and his style meet their extravagant match.

6

The Poem of the Past:
Eugene Onegin

> *Then practice losing farther, losing faster:*
> *places, and names, and where it was you*
> *meant to travel.*

> Elizabeth Bishop, 'One Art'

(i)

The Russian title of *Invitation to a Beheading*, Nabokov tells us, was literally *Invitation to an Execution*. He didn't like the rhyme in English, but would have put up with it if he had to. 'On the other hand', he adds, *Invitation to a Decapitation (Priglashenie na otsechenie golovi)*, is what he would have said in the first place if he had 'not been stopped by a similar stutter' (*shenie/chenie*). He finds in English what he lost in Russian; translation is serendipity and rewriting, a discovery in the attic of old intentions. The implication, I think, is not only that some writers are lucky and the author isn't dead at all, but that languages can help each other out in curious ways. If translation is in one sense impossible, it is also what languages cry out for, the voice of their own incompletion or self-encumbrance. This looks like the argument of Walter Benjamin's well-known but very difficult essay 'The Task of the Translator', 1923: 'Languages are not strangers to one another, but are, a priori and apart from all historical relationships, interrelated in what they want to express.'

There are differences, though. Benjamin's a priori is strange, as is the idea of languages wanting to express things (*was sie sagen wollen*). What Nabokov's practice suggests – I'm thinking both of his work as a translator and of the interplay of languages, chiefly Russian, French and English, in his fiction – is that languages can meet up and do need each other, but the encounters are contingent

and magical, rather than necessary and metaphysical. The preco-
cious heroine of *Ada*, as a girl of twelve, devises a double
translation, sound and sense, of King Lear's fivefold 'Never'. The
sense isn't too hard. It's true that 'never' and 'jamais' don't have
quite the same resonances – you can't say *à tout jamais* in English,
or never-never in French – but the meanings are as close as interlingual meanings are going to get. Translation does involve travel
and difference; wouldn't be translation otherwise. But an equiv-
alence of sound is another matter:

> *Ce beau jardin fleurit en mai,*
> *Mais en hiver*
> *Jamais, jamais, jamais, jamais, jamais*
> *N'est vert, n'est vert, n'est vert, n'est vert, n'est vert.*

This is not exactly nonsense verse – it says, grammatically, that this
garden blooms in May, but in winter never is green – but it does
work by a virtual cancellation of the French meaning of the last
line, so that *jamais* and *n'est vert*, in juxtaposition, produce a kind
of cross-Channel echo, as if the French were speaking English
without knowing it – with a French accent. The game is the one
played several times by Raymond Queneau (in *Exercices de Style*
and *Zazie dans le Métro*, for example), and by the successful series
of books called *Mots d'Heures Gousse Rames*, alias *Mother Goose
Rhymes*. What is comically articulated here is not a 'central reciprocal relationship between languages', as Benjamin puts it, but a
sense that the shared world of noise can be raided for different
national meanings; that any language could always be shadowed or
possessed by another.

Language is a haunting for Nabokov, even when it's his own;
always pursued or accompanied by other languages. Humbert
overdoes the French, but French is also the language spoken by
Russians in the opening pages of *War and Peace*, 'that elaborately
choice French, in which our forefathers not only spoke but
thought'. More precisely, they are said, in Russian, to be speaking
French; just as Pushkin, in *Eugene Onegin* 'translates' the French
prose of his heroine's letter into Russian verse. The text and the
story speak different languages, although both are Russian, and
both speak only Russian on the page: an emblem of cultural complication. Translation becomes a metaphor for missing things, even
when there's nothing to miss, and all the more so when there is.
'Here's/an incomplete, feeble translation', Pushkin says of his rendering of Tatiana's letter, 'a pallid copy of a vivid picture,/or

Freischütz executed /by timid female learners' fingers' (Nabokov's version). There's much mischief here: Pushkin the poet becomes the girlish amateur pianist, and the romantic girl becomes a musical master; Russian becomes a stumbling sort of French. Pushkin presumably believed something like the opposite, but it's not clear where the swirl of jokes ends. It is clear that translation is a figure of absence, and Pushkin later uses a similar figure when he says he can't translate the English word 'vulgar'.

In *The Real Life of Sebastian Knight*, when V reproduces for us Sebastian's last letter, he both translates and transliterates: 'stuck' [*zasstrianoo*], 'fed up' [*osskomina*], 'shed snake-skins' [*vypolziny*], 'destined' [*prednaznachalos*], 'bore' [*dokoochayou*]. The effect must be different for different readers, but it would be different again if the Russian words were missing, or were given in Cyrillic. This way we can all read them if we want to, in at least one sense of 'read'. Russian speakers will recognize the words (won't they?), many anglophone readers will perhaps skip the words altogether, or take them in as some sort of typographical buzz. I sometimes do that, but when I can slow myself down I do pronounce the words, as best I can. Then I travel briefly, not into the Russian language, of course, but into an imaginary Russia, into a Russian haunting of my English. I experience, however crudely, another language which is an *otherness* of language; words behind words.

It's salutary to remember that there *is* no Russian text here, no act of translation taking place beyond the fiction; just as there is no French dialogue in the text at the start of *War and Peace*, no actual letter in French prose that Tatiana sent to Onegin, beyond the Russian verse letter we read. These are textual figments, like much of the stuff in *Lolita*. Nabokov wrote *The Real Life of Sebastian Knight* in English; the translation from Russian is a translation into Russian. The supposed original language is an illusion, an emblem of loss, what Sebastian returned to, and what Nabokov, in this very text, is giving up. This is a way of saying that the fiction, as fiction, mirrors a disappearance, that the language fades even as it makes its ostensible comeback. But it also comments on the other, new language; not because it is untranslatable, but because it also exists, reminds us that there are other, different ways of naming these same moods and effects.

The Russian language often works this way in Nabokov's fiction in English, particularly in *Ada*. It is always translated and transliterated, remote from itself, so to speak, a language without a home, neither here nor there. It sits by the side of its translation like an image of otherness, functioning as a stark and delicate form of distancing, a making strange of the page and the linguistic scene. Nabokov presumably hears the language as his; sees it as alien, because transcribed in a foreign alphabet; pictures it through our eyes as weird, perhaps spectacular, perhaps barbaric; hears in advance our mangling of its pronunciation; gives us an English translation – or perhaps only pretends to do this, having found, for stylistic reasons, that he needed the Russian ghosts of the English words he already had. The most astonishing effect of this kind occurs when Van Veen, in *Ada*, devastated by the news of his young mistress' infidelities, expresses his pain through the apparently bare bones of a language lesson, a literal translation. There is also an echo of *Lolita* here, so the movement, minimally, is from English to Russian to English, but I suspect it's even more complicated than that; certain rhythms, of thought and music, seem to float between languages. Humbert imagines Lolita leaving him, and ending up as a waitress in some dismal mid-Western diner, 'and everything soiled, torn, dead'. Van Veen, after seeking to distract himself by remembering Tolstoy's use of inner monologue in *Anna Karenina*, cannot keep his mind from circling back to his torment. He translates a coachman's speech from Russian into English, carefully, slowly, as if this simple task could stave off all thought. '*Etu*: this (that). *Frantsúzskuyu*: French (adj., accus). *Dévku*: wench.' Then, impelled perhaps by the word 'wench' or perhaps just by the sheer weight of his misery, he continues translating, beyond anything the coachman has said: '*Úzshas, otcháyenie*: horror, despair. *Zhálost*: pity. *Kóncheno, zagázheno, rastérzano*: finished, fouled, torn to shreds'. Three nouns, three past participles; two languages; boundless distress. An invitation to a beheading.

(ii)

'I shall be remembered by *Lolita* and my work on *Eugene Onegin*.' 'Work' here presumably means not only Nabokov's idiosyncratic translation, but the whole package of his English-language edition: foreword, scholarly introduction, note on the Russian calendar, note on transliteration and pronunciation, translation, copious index, long, long commentary, and in the first edition, Russian text. Nabokov dreamed up the fictional editorial excesses of *Pale Fire* while he was labouring on this pious and perverse task, but we also need to see how *Pale Fire* comments on the translation. 'Flaubert speaks in one of his letters', Nabokov said in an interview, 'about the difficulty of painting *couleur sur couleur*. This in a way is what I tried to do in retwisting my own experience when inventing Kinbote'. Kinbote is the narrator/editor of *Pale Fire*, and his work is the crazy imaginative twin of what Nabokov thought of as an act of stubborn historical sanity. The mad commentator in the novel takes over a defenceless poem, the novelist as commentator seeks only to serve Pushkin, but Nabokov would want us to recognize how close sanity is to madness here, and to see that the *book* in both cases is not just the poem. The poem can't do without the commentary in *Pale Fire* because it takes both (and a foreword and an index) to make the novel; and the translation of *Eugene Onegin* can't do without the commentary because only the commentary can begin to tell us how much is lost.

Alexander Gerschenkron suggested that 'Nabokov's translation can and indeed should be studied, but despite all the cleverness and brilliance it cannot be read.' This is an exaggeration. The translation is far more readable than it used to seem, and at times is actually more readable than Charles Johnston's excellent 1977 version, which in any case owes and acknowledges a great debt to Nabokov. But it's important to realize that Nabokov would have taken the remark as a compliment, however unintended. The readable, for Nabokov as for Benjamin, is precisely what a translation should avoid. '"Readable", indeed', Nabokov snorts, roughing up the phrase 'It reads smoothly': 'In other words, the hack who has never read the original, and does not know its language, praises an imitation as readable because easy platitudes have replaced in it the intricacies of which he is unaware'. Benjamin's line is that since works of art are never intended for their receivers, but only, the implication is, for the attention and memory of God, we can't aim translations at their audience either. Benjamin is quibbling about 'intention' here, means we can't get at the deep imperatives of art or life through a survey of consumer habits. And Nabokov invents an ignorant hack because he doesn't want to deal with an opponent who might know something. But both point to a significant fact about the language of the work of art, and indeed about much ordinary language, when it takes on any degree of complexity, as it does in jokes or ironies. Poems and novels and figures of speech are scarcely ever simply readable; when they feel as if they are, it's because we've got used to them, or because their prejudices are indistinguishable from our own. A translation, in this light, would need to be doubly unreadable: first to show that it *is* a translation, that it's not part of its job to make the original redundant; second to record and evoke the original's own interesting unreadability, whatever it was that made it stand out from the linguistic company it kept, and seem worth translating.

This is an austere theory, and will appeal only to those who like to think different languages have lives of their own, and to feel that even in translation something of an alien life might flicker through. The wish to learn about other cultures is different from the willingness to naturalize all other cultures as our own, and these appetites feed on different styles. We might even, if we were not Nabokov or Benjamin, enjoy both styles, feel drawn to the austere theory but recognize others. Douglas Robinson calls Benjamin and Nabokov 'aversionists' in their notion of translation – they turn away from the reader of the second language, and ultimately from themselves as readers of the first language:

> You always came too late; the author whose masterpiece you read will always have gone before you, lived a life that you were born too late to partake in, had experiences you will never know, meant more than you will ever understand.

This is certainly how Nabokov thinks of anglophone readers of Pushkin, and of the language of his own translation; the translation itself seems designed to tell just this story. His strange word orders ('And dreams a wondrous dream Tatiana', 'Disturbs her the ache of jealousy', 'On sensing the corpse, snort/and jib the horses') and recondite vocabulary ('dolent', 'joyance', 'larmoyant', 'ancientry') take us to a place that was late before it even started – and Nabokov's idea of English slang ('chap', 'pal', 'tosh') makes him sound like Humbert Humbert trying to go stylistically straight.

Fortunately it isn't all like this, the translation has wonderful moments, like the evocation of Onegin's 'sharp, chilled mind', and Tatiana's youthful yearning, shadowed like a 'scarce-born day', and the thirty-year-old Pushkin's sense of the death of the world of feeling:

> But at a late and barren age,
> at the turn of the years,
> sad is the trace of a dead passion . . .
> Thus storms of the cold autumn
> into a marsh transform the meadow
> and strip the woods around.

And there is the rest of the 'work', the heroic, perhaps absurd attempt to make Pushkin accessible to readers who know almost nothing of his world and absolutely nothing of his language. Well, not just accessible: Nabokov seeks to make us inhabitants of Pushkin's world, in so far as people who need an interpreter and come 125 years too late can enter such a territory. And of course, Nabokov has no aversion at all for himself as a reader of Pushkin. He has every confidence in his ability to share Pushkin's experiences, not a trace of a feeling of lateness. 'I, too', he says, walked as a child in the Jardin d'Eté in St Petersburg; his family owned an estate where Pushkin may once have fought a duel. He dresses Pushkin's characters in his mind – 'I imagine he wore to that particular ball (winter, 1819) not simply a black *frac* but (following London rather than Paris), a brass-buttoned, velvet-collared, sky-blue coat' – and licks his lips over the food Pushkin sets before us: a vol-au-vent is 'an ethereal crust filled with braised white of chicken and cut-up mushrooms . . . or with oysters poached in white wine . . . and there are several other varieties, all delicious'. Of course there is plenty of research (and eating) behind these guesses and instructions, and we could read Nabokov's *Eugene Onegin* as a kind of companion to *Speak, Memory*, with its paradoxical structure reversed as if in a mirror. You can't deny loss without naming it; you can't enumerate the detail of what's lost without bringing something back. The autobiography tells a story of pattern and preservation which conceals a deeper story of dispersion; the translation and commentary register dispersion, even disappearance, but insist on the miracle of preservation, the vivid actuality of ancient history perceived in its resurrected bits and pieces.

I have used the word 'original', which is anathema in current translation theory, and I had better pause over it, since this is where common sense and sophisticated thinking seem furthest apart, and where genuinely interesting philosophical questions lurk. Of course there's an original, common sense says, what else would we be translating; Nabokov writes of 'rendering . . . the exact contextual meaning of the original'. He agrees we might be able only to approach this meaning ('as closely as the associative and syntactical capacities of another language allow'), but he doesn't doubt its existence. But what if we are not sure what 'exact' and 'original' mean in relation to a historically soaked, semantically overdetermined literary language? Deconstruction, it seems, might actually mean more pay: if there is no such thing as an 'original' work, if everything is intertextuality, echo and deferment, there is no reason for translators to think of themselves as secondary and put up with such lousy rates. Unless of course the deconstruction of the original means *no one* gets paid.

There is a confusion here, or rather two good points conspire to occlude a third; and common sense is not wrong, but only a little baggy, or in Nabokov's case a little too confident. It's true that translation is a difficult art, and that the pay should be better; also true that 'originality' is a highly questionable term, intimately related to the hallowed concepts ('creativity and genius, eternal value and mystery') which Benjamin, in 1936, thought could only be helpful to Fascism. (Benjamin's attractive error, it now seems, was to think there are concepts which *couldn't* be helpful to Fascism.) But there is a first and a second instance in translation, there is translation *from* and translation *to*, and we don't have to think of the first instance as absolute or pristine in order to get to work on it; or to see that it is there before the second. What we have, in all cases of translation, is a complex, historically placed linguistic act, for which another, no less historical home is sought, possessing as many parallels as possible to the first. You can't change homes without loss, but this is not a reason for settling for anything or never moving. What's interesting in translation is the nature and extent of the loss; and when we're lucky, the range of the finds too, since loss isn't all there is, you can find the old beheading you thought had gone for ever. Johnston has a character in *Eugene Onegin* feeding on 'hope's deceptive dinner' where Nabokov, presumably closer to Pushkin, simply says 'Hope nursed him'; while Nabokov's 'monotonous family,/all sons of avid boredom', already pretty good, becomes in Johnston 'a monotonous breed/begot by boredom out of greed'. We can argue about whether translators' 'finds' are to be welcomed, whether loyalty to a (dead) poet doesn't require us to stick with our losses, to make sure there *are* no finds; but that is an argument about accuracy, not about originality or quality.

Here are Nabokov's and Johnston's versions of a death in Pushkin. Nabokov:

> now, as in a deserted house,
> all in it is both still and dark,
> it has become forever silent.
> The window boards are shut. The panes with chalk
> are whitened over. The chatelaine is gone.
> But where, God wot. All trace is lost.

Johnston:

> but now the mansion is forsaken;
> shutters are up, and all is pale
> and still within, behind the veil
> of chalk the window-panes have taken.
> The lady of the house is fled.
> Where to, God knows. The trail is dead.

Johnston adds the idea of taking the veil and loses the notion of 'forever silent'; but then he doesn't have the arch chatelaine or the ludicrous 'God wot'. Neither of these passages can be as good as their predecessor in Pushkin, but not because the original is perfect and holy – perhaps it could have been even more wonderful – only because some poets are better than others, and Pushkin was a great poet. The chief point concerns not originality but the travel of meaning between languages, and in this respect even Nabokov's literal version must spill as much as it manages to keep. Well, I suppose it sometimes spills a lot and sometimes spills less; and certainly *adds* less than any rhyming version. My interest, though, is not in the quality of Nabokov's translation, but in what it and his commentary tell us about language – about the language of his novels, principally, but also about the language in which we discuss novels and many other things.

The literal translation, for Nabokov, is distinguished from the 'paraphrastic' ('offering a free version of the original, with omissions and additions prompted by the exigencies of form, the conventions attributed to the consumer, and the translator's ignorance') and the 'lexical' ('rendering the basic meaning of words'). The literal is 'true translation' because it aims, as we have seen, at the 'exact contextual meaning of the original'. The sin of rhyme is that it forces translators to add material, or to change metaphors, and Nabokov will have none of it. Even when a rhyme presents itself unproblematically, without risk of compromise, he forswears it. He knows a primrose path when he sees one: 'the incorruptible translator should resist such temptations', should insist on 'the ruthless and triumphant elimination of rhyme'. Does he protest too much? Yes; especially since he has failed to eliminate the awful rhyme dit and Kit. He is imitating a Russian folk-carol, but even so.

Rhythm on the other hand appears to be part of contextual meaning, and although Nabokov's lines in *Eugene Onegin* are not all of equal length, he has taken some pains to make them scan, to 'iambize' them, as he says; 'to achieve some semblance of English construction and retain some vestige of Russian rhythm'. He discusses the 'melody' of the lines in his notes. Even so, meaning is not mood, there is a sort of tyranny of sense here, to the exclusion of all kinds of other things that language and poetry possess. And meaning itself, however rich in its first context, can only be guessed at by the reader of a translation. Guessed at rather than read; like pronouncing the transliterated Russian words in *Ada* and *The Real Life of Sebastian Knight* and trying to guess at the meaning that lies behind the translations we are given. We could argue (but I won't now) that understanding even our native language works like this: we intuit whole fields of meaning, then restrict them, cut them up, impoverish them, in the light of particular needs and situations. Translation is a form of reading *and* writing, interpretation as visible action. The best translation is the one that allows the best guesses, or causes the least impoverishment.

This is pretty much what Nabokov's commentary keeps saying, almost in spite of itself. He worries at meaning as if he were Empson starting all over again with his seven types of ambiguity. He translates *gulyál* as 'promenaded', yet says the word not only means 'saunter', 'stroll', but also 'to go on a spree'. 'There is no exact equivalent in English', he says, for *razuveryat*: 'The verb means to unpersuade, to unconvince, to dispel or change another's belief . . .' 'No single word in English renders all the shades of *toska*', which ranges from 'great spiritual anguish' to 'a dull ache of the soul' to 'nostalgia, lovesickness', and 'ennui, boredom'. '*Shum* implies a more sustained and uniform auditory effect than the English "noise". It is also a shade more remote and confused'. 'The verb *rvat'sya* . . . implies the violent agitation of a person who is restrained by others while indulging in a passion of grief, seeking an issue in desperate writhings and other wild motions.' Some verb. There is much, much more of this kind of thing. At times Nabokov distinguishes among Russian words without any real reference to English – or with English only as the language he is making the distinctions in *Mgla*, for instance, a word for darkness, 'is murkier and foggier' than its competitors *sumrak* and *mrak*, which offer 'not unfrequently pleasurable and poetic glooms'. Sometimes he frankly says words are 'untranslatable'; although often he can find a French locution which comes close, and in many cases is the 'original' of the Russian idiom. It is an essential part of Nabokov's provocative but plausible argument that Pushkin's access to English and German literature was exclusively through French translations; and that if French was a Russian language, as I have suggested, Russia was in many respects a French culture. The world of Pushkin's poem is 'a stylized Russia, which would disintegrate at once if the French props were removed and if the French impersonators of English and German writers stopped prompting the Russian-speaking heroes and heroines', and 'it is curious that even a Russian winter comes to Pushkin through French poems, or from French versions of English poems'. The literalist is even willing to read silence, to suggest an 'exact contextual meaning' for that. He speculates that an apparent gap in Pushkin's manuscript may be an intentional one, a device 'with some musical value – the artifice of a wistful pause, the imitation of a missed heartbeat, the mirage of an emotional horizon, the false asterisks of false suspense'. This is a wonderful idea, and fine writing; but something has happened to the translator's austerity.

What has happened, I think, is that language, as so often in Nabokov, has found its energies in what almost eludes it, in meanings or a memory that must fade, that cannot outlive the writer's consciousness, or the consciousness of those who understand language as he does, remember what he remembers. Translation is an act of memory, the Russian language is seen again in the failure of English to live up to those murky or brilliant riches. If it is impossible to love two languages, as Nabokov suggests, it may also have been impossible for him to live with only one, and it is striking for a man so keen on control that he should speak of his 'greatest happiness' in writing as appearing 'when I feel I cannot understand, or rather catch myself not understanding (without the presupposition of an already existing creation) how or why that image or structural move or exact formulation of phrase has just come to me'. This is an experience we can have without being distinguished writers, although we don't always think of it as happiness. How do we know we have found the word we were looking for? After all, we hadn't lost it; didn't know it was the one we needed until it presented itself. It's as if we had translated from a language we don't know into one we do; but how could we translate in such a way? We catch ourselves not understanding at the very moment the word arrives. We may feel baffled, but the writer or talker in us is happy; and the other language, the one we don't know or the one we are not speaking now, is an image for all the words we are not hearing, a promise of sense in what seems to be noise and nonsense, even in what George Eliot in *Middlemarch* called the roar on the other side of silence.

(iii)

In his Foreword to his translation Nabokov glances at the 'piped-in background music' of our 'era of inept and ignorant imitations', and we seem already to be hearing the voice of Kinbote, in *Pale Fire*, driven crazy by the tinny music of his America. Nabokov's commentary is a work of scholarship, and of pedantry in the sense defended by the essayist Hazlitt: 'He who is not in some measure a pedant, though he may be a wise, cannot be a very happy man' (Nabokov's quotation). But it is also a stylistic performance, full of jokes ('this may be splitting dyed hairs', 'the comic naivetés in his running, or rather stumbling, commentary', 'I am satisfied . . . that I know as little about economics as Pushkin did') and alliterations ('a vivid vibration of v's', 'a cardboard Kiev', 'strident strings', 'campestral cure', 'a rake, and a rape, and rural roses'), and we see Nabokov's mood change as the work goes on. The haughty purist, for example, the person who thinks biographical speculation is idle, becomes the eager detective once he gets a feeling for the game. The commentator becomes a satirist:

> Tatiana faded out of Russian literature, and Russian life, just before the revolution of November, 1917, the leadership of which was taken over by matter-of-fact, heavily booted men. In Soviet literature, the image of Tatiana has been superseded by that of her sister Olga, now grown buxom, ruddy-cheeked, noisily cheerful. Olga is the good girl of Soviet fiction; she is the one who straightens things out at the factory, discovers sabotage, makes speeches, and radiates perfect health.
> This business of 'types' may be quite entertaining if approached in the right spirit.

The scholar tells us not only about pies and coats and old St Petersburg and hundreds of literary references, but about the options for dealing with ennui, and his meticulously stored memory of winter lights in a snowy Russian street, evoked by Pushkin as 'rainbows'.

> Judging by a number of early-nineteenth-century English and French novels that I have perused, the four main outlets or cures for ennui found by the characters suffering from it were: (1) making a nuisance of oneself; (2) committing suicide; (3) joining some well-organized religious group; and (4) quietly submitting to the situation.

154

This is like a David Levine cartoon of suffering romantic heroes such as René or Werther or Adolphe; I'm still trying to think of an example of (4). Here is the rainbow:

> My own sixty-year-old remembrance is not so much of prismatic colors cast upon snowdrifts by the two lateral lanterns of a brougham as of iridescent spicules around blurry street lights coming through its frost-foliated windows and breaking along the rim of the glass.

Spicules, frost-foliated. The literalist writes his own untranslatable poem. And Nabokov gets friskier and friskier. 'Pushkin played an average game', he says of the poet's chess, 'and would probably have been beaten by Tolstoy'. Above all he registers from the very beginning that 'the pursuit of reminiscences may become a form of insanity on the scholiast's part'. He means literary reminiscences, echoes and parallels in one's own reading that may have no match in anything the poet set his eyes on. But we almost see the birth of Kinbote here.

We also see glimmerings of Pnin, in the shape of the historical Professor Chizhevksi (Nabokov's transliteration), of Harvard and Marburg, author of a commentary on *Eugene Onegin*, 1953, a Russian in America, and a man with a knack for getting things wrong. Chizhevksi is 'again moved to misinform the reader', Nabokov says about a repeated mistake, and offers this merciless gloss on the mistake's first appearance:

> Grandison, the hero of *Clarissa Harlowe* [wrong novel] is familiar to the mother only as the nickname of a Moscow sergeant [mistranslation]! . . . The development of old Larina from a sensitive girl into a strict mistress [ambiguous] was a familiar experience for both men [very ambiguous] and women in Russia.

But these are only glimmerings, and unkind ones: Pnin as seen by his enemies. All the sympathy which Nabokov displays (and displaces) for the protagonist of his next work of fiction has still to be found, and is found, perhaps, in the intuition that not Chizhevski but Nabokov, not the man who got things wrong but the man who pedantically got them right, was out of the place in the fumbling world of the mid-century. Pnin is actually halfway between these exiles – he makes comic mistakes, but he is not a laughing stock, or he shouldn't be. He is 'least of all a clown', Nabokov said in a letter; and we are about to see how Nabokov himself, or a 'stylized' version of himself, to borrow the term he uses for Pushkin's repeated appearances in *Eugene Onegin*, shows up in the novel in a very harsh light.

7
Pnin's Revenge

I have discovered that China and Spain are
really one and the same country ... If you
don't believe me, then try and write
'Spain' and you'll end up writing 'China'

Gogol, *Diary of a Madman*

'"My name is so-and-so," I said.' We have already looked at some of the ways in which the narrator of *The Real Life of Sebastian Knight* avoids giving his name, but not at this particular formulation. It seems unproblematic at first glance; we know what he means, and we transpose the sentence into indirect speech. He said his name was so-and-so, he mentioned then a name he's not mentioning now. He gave a false name, perhaps, which he doesn't wish to remember or reveal. Except that this isn't quite what he says he says, and a slower inspection of the sentence can induce a mild vertigo, the sort of shaky feeling we get when George Burns or Groucho Marx simultaneously addresses us and someone in the story. A name like so-and-so is unusual enough to ruffle any conversation a little.

> 'My name is so-and-so,' I said.
> 'And mine,' he cried, 'is Pahl Pahlich Rechnoy ...'

Two times and two places are beautifully elided, a narrative now creeps into the narrated then, and a well established, virtually sovereign convention about the truthfulness, or at least the plausibility, of reported speech is quietly broken. The effect is like falling through a mirror into another mirror, a reminder not only that we are readers but that as readers we make complicated deals with mixed bunches of words. The effect is very stealthy, though. It is only when we see how easily it could have been dispensed with that we realize how eerie and mischievous it is. The same narrator's later strategy – 'My name is [I mentioned my name]' – is awkward but

157

not troubling; and 'I gave him my name', would have caused no dizziness at all.

The narrative world of *Pnin* seems miles away from such tricks, a realm of easy omniscience and old-fashioned readerly comfort. Professor Timofey Pnin is first glimpsed as 'the elderly passenger sitting on the north-window side of that inexorably moving railway coach', and is described as 'he might appear to a fellow passenger'. There aren't any fellow passengers, though, and the slightly surprising 'inexorably' hints at the fact that Pnin is on the wrong train. The narrator knows this, as Pnin doesn't; as the narrator knows that even now the conductor ('a grey-headed fatherly person with steel spectacles placed rather low on his simple, functional nose and a bit of soiled adhesive tape on his thumb') is proceeding along the train towards our hero, but still three coaches away. The 'imagined observer', so dear to Balzac and Thackeray and Stendhal and so many nineteenth-century writers, puts in several appearances in this novel, strategically placed for a God's eye view.

> Presently all were asleep again. It was a pity nobody saw the display in the empty street, where the auroral breeze wrinkled a large luminous puddle, making of the telephone wires reflected in it illegible lines of black zigzags.

There is perhaps a faint touch of pastiche in this angle of vision. We seem to become not gods but ghosts or nonentities in relation to the pictured world: our name is so-and-so. But let's stay for a moment with the suggestions of comfort.

The narrator amiably refers to the central character as 'our friend' and 'our poor friend'; offers benign and thoughtful judgements in the manner of George Eliot ('It was very pleasant to see the two men discuss a legend or a religion . . .' , 'Joan . . . used the word "pathetic" perhaps a little too much'). Sometimes he is rather more emphatic ('Genius is non-conformity'); sometimes jocular ('This is 1953 – how time flies!'). He reflects now and again on the business of storytelling: 'Technically speaking, the narrator's art of integrating telephone conversations still lags far behind that of rendering dialogues conducted from room to room . . .'; and in one very beautiful modulation allows the illusion he has created to melt into a question about illusion. A couple stand silhouetted against the evening sky, and 'one' can't quite tell who they are, or indeed if they are anyone at all we know from the world of the fiction, 'or merely an emblematic couple placed with easy art on the last page of Pnin's fading day'. The easy art seems graceful as well as facile, and the collapsing of Pnin's day into the narrator's page recalls some of the textual conjuring of *Lolita*. The move doesn't shake our confidence in the narrator, though; just makes us feel he may be more subtle than we thought, deeper in his old-fashioned way.

I am cheating slightly for the sake of clarity of exposition. Our confidence in the narrator is not shaken here because it has already been shaken by more dramatic disturbances, notably the revelation that he is not a remote Tolstoyan presence but an entangled character, a man who is about to take Pnin's job and who in the past had an affair with the woman who became Pnin's wife. We reread him warily, and sure enough, the prose begins to sprout quiet peculiarities. Here are the opening sentences of the novel, already quoted in part:

> The elderly passenger sitting on the north-window side of that inex-orably moving railway coach, next to an empty seat and facing two empty ones, was none other than Professor Timofey Pnin. Ideally bald, sun-tanned, and clean shaven, he began rather impressively with that great brown dome of his ... but ended, somewhat dis-appointingly, in a pair of spindly legs ... and frail-looking, almost feminine feet.

'That ... coach', 'none other than', 'that ... dome of his' suggest not the leisurely opening of a nineteenth-century novel but the con-tinuation of an anecdote – or the start of another anecdote about a person we already know. 'Ideally bald' is particularly delicate, I think. The notion appears later with the same connotations ('his in-clined head would demonstrate its ideal baldness') and suggests not that Pnin or anyone would ideally like to be bald but that if you are going to be bald you might as well aim for a certain purity, and more to our narrative point, that Pnin is exactly as bald as we want him to be, that he is a perfect visual fit for the role we have cast him in.

The narrator likes to play with and cancel stereotypes:

> Pnin, it should be particularly stressed, was anything but the type of the good-natured German platitude of last century, *der zerstreute Professor*. On the contrary, he was perhaps too wary, too persis-tently on the look-out for diabolical pitfalls ... It was the world that was absent-minded and it was Pnin whose business it was to set it straight.

This is funny but the result, if not a new, reversed stereotype, is something less than a person: an obvious protagonist of comic legend, a delightful foreigner, certainly some kind of cousin of the absent-minded platitude. I am not suggesting that Pnin, as the novel develops, *is* less than a person – on the contrary, as I hope to show, he is far more of a person than the narrator bargains for – only that most of the writing conspires to keep him in his helpless and amusing place, hold him to the status of lovable comic object. It is in this way that we see his 'heavy tortoise-shell reading glasses', parked above his 'Russian potato nose'; are told that 'he was more of a poltergeist than a lodger', conducting 'a passionate intrigue' with a washing machine, which he loves to watch at its revolving work: 'Although forbidden to come near it, he would be caught trespassing again and again. Casting aside all decorum and caution, he would feed it anything that happened to be at hand . . .' His English is a triumph of meticulous mispronunciation, an occasion of broad interlingual jokes. 'I search, John,' he says, 'for the viscous and sawdust.' 'John' is how he pronounces (how the narrator spells the way Pnin pronounces) 'Joan', but Joan knows that, as she also recognizes the whisky and soda he is after. Pnin's joy at his new full set of false teeth ('It was a revelation, it was a sunrise, it was a firm mouthful of efficient, alabastrine, humane America. At night he kept his treasure in a special glass of special fluid where it smiled to itself, pink and pearly') is both foolish and touching; and Pnin playing croquet, it turns out, is an altered man:

> From his habitual, slow, ponderous, rather rigid self, he changed into a terrifically mobile, scampering, mute, sly-visaged hunchback. It seemed to be always his turn to play . . .

The portrait is not simple and is often tender, but it remains tuned to a myth and to our expectations. Pnin is the 'ideal' Russian in America, an unassimilated victim of history, who can be both laughed at and pitied, treated as a pet, even loved if the unfortunate really can be loved by the fortunate; but never regarded as casually, entirely one of us. By us, I mean not Americans (although Pnin's notion that in 'two-three years' he will be taken for an American causes tremendous hilarity among his friends) and not exactly just humans but whatever grouping it is that makes laughter reciprocal among us, and pity impossible. There is no charity (in its modern sense) among equals. Of course we can all become Pnin, even without revolution and exile – become pitiable, that is, and pitied, and laughable and laughed at. But I am interested in the way the exclusion works: the odd 'idealization' of the unlucky, which allows us (or them if we are the unlucky ones at the given moment) to construct an object and feel the certainty of its difference. As I say, the movement is not unkind, indeed is usually generous, and that is why it is awkward to complain about it. But I wouldn't have started on the subject at all if Nabokov had not simultaneously endowed his narrator with all his own literary gifts (and some of his own history: nationality, writing and teaching career, name and patronymic and interest in butterflies) and invited us to view him with the deepest moral suspicion.

The literary gifts are dazzling. The narrator has Humbert Humbert's breezy familiarity with his adopted language – Pnin has 'a great time' and the college bells are said to be 'still going strong' – and a similar taste for trumping old idioms. Pnin in conversation is described as 'missing one bus but boarding the next'; most of the Russians in America have 'seen sixty and trudged on'. The clothes in Pnin's beloved washing machine look like 'an endless tumble of dolphins with the staggers'. Even when it is not dabbling in the colloquial, the prose is very sharp, a model of observant wit. A refrigerator gives off a 'bright Arctic light'; a rooster's cry is 'jagged and gaudy – a vocal coxcomb'. A phrase which tells us that Pnin 'swam in state' round a river basin manages to recall both a state visit and lying in state: Pnin swims like a monarch and a mummy. And in what I have always found the funniest phrase of the whole book, a character flushing the toilet is discreetly said to have 'brought down the house'. The sound of applause in a theatre mimics the noise of the water system, but the image also evokes a rickety American house seemingly threatened by the noise or even perhaps just by the vigorous pulling of the chain. We may also think of the terrible toilets of Humbert's sleepless night at the Enchanted Hunters hotel, all 'gurgle and gush and . . . long afterflow'.

It is not all that easy to resist such a stylist, but we have had a little practice with Humbert, and the narrator of *Pnin* himself spills quite a few clues to the limits of his charm. In Paris in the twenties, Liza Bogolepov, soon to become Pnin's wife, tries suicide ('a pharmacopoeial attempt', the narrator says with a grisly dip towards the dictionary) 'because of a rather silly affair with a littérateur who is now – But no matter'. No matter what? we ask, and then forget our question. This littérateur, it turns out, is none other, as he would say, than our narrator, who nonchalantly describes Liza's near-death as a 'contretemps', and coolly tells us of the desperate and idiotic ultimatum she sent to him after the event. 'This is an offer of marriage I have received,' Liza's missive says. 'I shall wait till midnight. If I don't hear from you, I shall accept it'. Of course she doesn't hear from him, and (of course) the offer is from Pnin. The narrator describes it as a 'tremendous love letter' and indeed has kept it among his papers, letting us see it now. 'I am not handsome, I am not interesting, I am not talented', it partly runs. 'I am not even rich. But Lise [Pnin uses the French form of her name, the narrator speculates, because it allows him to avoid both the too familiar and the too formal alternatives of the Russian], I offer you everything I have, to the last blood corpuscle, to the last tear, everything'. Pnin's love is entirely misplaced – but then how much well placed love do we know of? – because Liza is stupid and vain and cruel, and very soon deserts him; only returning to visit him briefly in America because she wants him to help support her son in school. But his love is his own. Like his sorrow, according to his own theory: 'Is sorrow not . . . the only thing in the world people really possess?' Not quite the only thing, perhaps. Pnin possesses his love, with all its good and ill luck. Certainly Pnin's abject and unquestioning surrender is a good deal more attractive than the narrator's haughty philandering; and may come to seem less 'pathetic' than it did, if we continue to scrutinize the narrator's edgy poise.

The narrator arrives at Waindell College, where Pnin teaches Russian ('a somewhat provincial institution characterized by an artificial lake in the middle of a landscaped campus, by ivied galleries connecting the various halls, by murals displaying recognizable members of the faculty in the act of passing on the torch of knowledge from Aristotle, Shakespeare, and Pasteur to a lot of monstrously built farm boys and farm girls . . .'). He is the character referred to by others (and indeed by himself when he reports such talk) as 'a prominent Anglo-Russian writer' and one of Pnin's 'most brilliant compatriots, a really fascinating lecturer'. His appearance makes Pnin redundant, but in the spirit of *noblesse oblige* (as long as it is not too inconvenient, and especially if it will create a sense of obligation in the recipient of the kindness) he has stipulated that Pnin is to remain. 'With this confirmed, I wrote to Timofey Pnin offering him, in the most cordial terms I could muster, to assist me in any way and to any extent he desired'. We may wonder faintly why he should need to muster cordial terms, why they don't come of their own accord, but Pnin doesn't even wonder. He replies curtly, refusing, telling the narrator he is through with teaching and will have left Waindell before the new lecturer arrives. We have been warned by his reaction to the news of his compatriot's appointment. 'Yes, I know him thirty years or more. We are friends, but there is one thing perfectly certain. I will never work under him'.

Professional pride on Pnin's part? Rather poorly judged if it is, given the relative successes of himself and the narrator in adapting to America. Lingering resentment, belated jealousy over the Liza affair? But Pnin doesn't seem at all given to these sentiments. No, he is on firmer ground. Pnin thinks the narrator is a liar and a scoundrel; wishes to free himself from this man's interest and patronage; and does. This is what I want to call Pnin's revenge, an escape from pity and from comedy; a flight from the very design of the fiction, and a picture of what human liberty might be in the un-fictional world. Of course this flight from the design must also, at a second level, be among the fiction's designs, but we can handle a little vertigo, and liberty will always look complicated and unlikely when seen from a world of cages. Let's step slowly over this terrain.

One of our measures of Pnin, which we may set against the narrator's haughty self-regard, is his ready kindness, which appears to be both instinctive and reasoned. He frequents a restaurant in Waindell 'from sheer sympathy with failure'; remembers, even in the midst of deep distress over his lost job, a dog he sometimes feeds, because 'there was no reason a human's misfortune should interfere with a canine's pleasure'. Visited and abandoned again by Liza, Pnin finds himself weeping in a public park while 'politely' operating a drinking fountain for a thirsty squirrel. The squirrel, described as a rodent, has an 'unpleasant eye', looks at Pnin 'with contempt' and departs after a good long drink 'without the least sign of gratitude.' No Disney touch here, and Pnin is too absorbed in his grief to care about gratitude or ingratitude. But then his response to the creature's casual need is all the more impressive: a tiny definition of disinterestedness.

The narrator is a contemporary writer building an apparently old-fashioned novel around the mythological aspects of his friend Pnin. This relation surfaces quite abruptly in the first chapter, for example, with the mention of a letter about Yalta Pnin has written to the *New York Times* 'with my help'. Later we hear of a fact that 'Pnin and I had long since accepted'. The traditional 'our friend' of old narratology begins to shade into 'my friend', and 'my friend and compatriot'. 'My poor friend', and 'My poor Pnin', in the context we are beginning to recognize, sound genuinely sympathetic without ceasing to sound a little patronizing. But then disagreements arise. The narrator first met Pnin, he tells us, in St Petersburg 'on a spring Sunday in 1911', when he was 12 and Pnin 13. Pnin's father is an opthalmologist, and the narrator-as-child has a speck of coal dust in his eye. Pnin *fils* appears in the doctor's office, and the proud father boasts of his son's academic achievements ('This boy has just got a Five Plus . . . in the Algebra examination'). Five years later, Pnin and narrator meet again during a country summer near the Baltic, where Pnin takes part in a play put on in an old barn on the property of the narrator's aunt. Or so the narrator says.

Pnin doesn't dispute the meetings in Paris in the twenties ('I know him thirty years or more'), but denies having met our narrator at all before. He vaguely recalls the narrator's aunt, but says his father never showed him off to patients, and in any case he was always poor at algebra. He was in the summer play, but not in the part the narrator ascribed to him. There are other very slight oddities in the narrator's report. Five years after he is twelve, for instance, he is only sixteen, the age he gives himself at the time of the summer meeting. Has he taken those five years from the five plus he allotted Pnin for algebra? More suspiciously still, an officer in the waiting room of Pnin's father appears to be conducting a romantic scene from the play produced five years later. These points may be meaningless, but the narrator is insisting on the accuracy of his memory, and the shadowy author, the narrator's inventor, is not at all given to wasting details.

The narrator treats Pnin's denial of these early meetings as a mild contribution to a 'little discussion', rather grandly 'noticing how reluctant he was to recognize his own past'. On a later occasion, though, Pnin gets agitated and tells a friend not to believe a word our narrator says. 'He makes up everything. He once invented that we were schoolmates in Russia and cribbed at examinations. He is a dreadful inventor (*on uzhasniy vïdumshchik*)'. *Pnin* is a mild-mannered book in spite of the narrator's brilliance, but the textual quandary here is deeper than anything in *Lolita*. Whom are we to believe? The narrator, surely. This is his story, we are in the habit of believing narrators unless broad hints tell us not to, and people do quite often wish to hide their pasts, or pieces of their past. On the other hand, what possible interest could Pnin have in lying about his marks in algebra, and is there anything in the novel to suggest that he lies at all? Many of his problems proceed from his scrupulous, awkward directness, and in the end it makes most sense to believe Pnin in spite of the stacked narrative odds.

The narrator likes to patronize Pnin when he can. His telling us that as a child he had a toy plane similar to Pnin's 'but twice bigger,

bought in Biarritz,' is vulgar showing off, and his recollections of
their supposed first meetings are offered, he says, 'to amuse him
and other people around us with the unusual lucidity and strength
of my memory'. For amuse we no doubt have to read impress; and
for memory perhaps something more oblique: an unusual ability to
invent details, to make inventions look like memories. That is one
way (not a bad way) of saying what a novelist does; only this novelist seems to be trying out his hand away from the written page. We
are only guessing, of course, could be over-reading. But the situation is similar to that of the witches in René Girard's example. We
have to do what we can for Pnin. On the night of his arrival in
Waindell the narrator rings Pnin up, although the poor fellow is
supposed to have left. 'I was foolishly eager to say something
friendly to my good Timofey Pahlich . . .' After the curt refusal of
the offer of a job, a response which 'surprised and hurt me'? 'Foolishly' gestures towards the implausible idea of reckless good nature
in our narrator, and the rest of the sentence drips with condescension, rather in the vein of Henry James being nice to 'good little
Thomas Hardy'. Does the narrator himself believe what he is saying? Does he expect us to?

These are the sort of questions criticism has taught itself to equi-
vocate confidently about. We all know the answer is yes *and* no.
But that easy, only apparently sophisticated response is not good
enough. We might, as some critics do in similar situations, separate
the author from the narrator round about here, so that we would
see a spectral (and less cavalier) Nabokov standing behind the cad-
dish Nabokovian impersonation. On this model the narrator plays
it straight and the author gets all the ironies. The defect of the
model is that it drastically simplifies the narrator, and leaves us with
an author who is too vulnerable a construction, too much just what
we want him or her to be, everything we can't assign to anyone else.
There is a case for seeing the author (as I have just done in speaking
of the narrator's inventor) as the architect of a fictional world, but
that is another story, and an author could be that and still leave
quite a bit of complication to the narrator. What I want to suggest is
that this narrator, like many nervous, ostensibly secure characters
in and out of fiction, courts our belief and our disbelief, is waiting
for the verdict he claims to have anticipated. The answer then
would be that he doesn't entirely, at present, believe what he is saying. But he will if we will. The novel is not confessional from
Nabokov's point of view (we guess that it isn't), but it is from the
narrator's, in spite of its objective appearances; and confessions, as

Paul de Man has shown, easily become excuses. The point about excuses is that they *are made*, like Quilty's and Groucho's jokes. What happens to them is a story not about their truthfulness (if an excuse were merely truthful, it would cease to be an excuse and become history) but about their context, their reception.

The narrator's situation is more complicated than he openly admits: that is clear. What I think we can't settle in any organized way – and perhaps really don't need to settle – is the strict level of intention in the narrator's address to us, as distinct from the picture of operative strategy sketched out above. We can read his linguistic behaviour, that is, and be pretty sure that 'my good Timofey' *is* condescending, without being at all sure the utterer knows just how condescending it is. Everything will depend on the way we construe the narrator's mind, and his problem remains. Can he stop patronizing Pnin (assuming that he wants to) merely by implicitly accusing himself of the act; and without falling into an opposite, sentimental error?

One of his difficulties is that his written relation of Pnin has a sort of oral twin in the novel in the performances of one Jack Cockerell, head of the English department at Waindell, and a specialist in side-splitting imitations of our displaced hero. Cockerell does Pnin 'to perfection', the narrator finds himself admitting:

> Pnin teaching, Pnin eating, Pnin ogling a co-ed, Pnin narrating the epic of the electric fan he had imprudently set going on a glass shelf right above the bathtub into which its own vibration had almost caused it to fall ... It was all built, of course, around the Pninian gesture and the Pninian wild English ... We got Pnin in the Stacks, and Pnin on the Campus Lake. We heard Pnin criticize the various rooms he had successively rented. We listened to Pnin's account of his learning to drive a car ...

The narrator finally doesn't find this compulsive, if brilliant stuff all that funny: 'the whole thing grew to be such a bore that I fell wondering if by some poetical vengeance this Pnin business had not become with Cockerell the kind of fatal obsession which substitutes its own victim for that of the initial ridicule'. His own narrative is too close to this kind of show for his comfort, and he must wonder if he is not in danger of becoming his victim's victim. Not that he ever calls Pnin his victim, and I don't want to overdo my evocation of his air of superiority. It is there, he draws our attention to it himself, but a real kindness is there too, he is far more generous and less repetitive than the mocking Cockerell. And of course it is through him that we know all we know about Pnin, including the features which allow us to prefer the narratee to the narrator. Even so, a benign version of the poetical vengeance he wonders about is just what I mean by Pnin's revenge; and he does need Pnin to stay in place as a figure of fun. Until he shifts him carefully into a new place as an ex-figure of fun.

This is precisely the character the narrator sees at the end of the novel when he thinks he catches sight of Pnin leaving Waindell in his small car, held up in the traffic then springing away, heading south in emblematic acceleration:

> the little sedan boldly swung past the front truck and, free at last, spurted up the shining road, which one could make out narrowing to a thread of gold in the soft mist where hill after hill made beauty of distance, and where there was simply no saying what miracle might happen.

Who speaks? as Beckett might say. What is going on? Shining road, thread of gold, soft mist, simply no saying, miracle. We have seen this sort of language once before in *Pnin*, but it was quickly spotted and turned back towards irony:

> Above the distant ... hills there lingered, under a cloud bank, a depth of tortoise-shell sky. The heart-rending lights of Waindell-ville, throbbing in a fold of those dusky hills, were putting on their usual magic ...

All is well, if a little soupy, until we get to 'dusky', which is too much for our self-conscious stylist, who corrects for over-acting, and reaches for the knowing, unfooled phrase 'their usual magic'. At the end of the novel, though, there is nothing after the hills and the possible miracle except a return to Jack Cockerell, 'a British breakfast of depressing kidney and fish', and some more remorseless Pnin imitations. The narrator's choice is between a travesty of Pnin and a sentimental compensation for all such travesties, a belated idyll bestowed on the comic hero, the way Chaplin used to give himself lyrical walks into the sunrise, accompanied at last by Paulette Goddard. Meanwhile, *our* Pnin, the human creature who has been evoked in the spaces and against the designs of this narrative, who can't at this stage even be talked to, escapes the idyll and

167

the travesty, takes off not into a romance of the road but into his own absence.

Escapes? Who can this Pnin be if not a product of the narrative we have read, and therefore the narrator's creation? This is close to our question about the actual Lolita and the world beyond the bars of Humbert's cage. And just as there is a Lolita whom Humbert can record but hardly see, so there is a Pnin, whom the narrator, more or less against his will, despatches into the freedom of the reader's imagination. 'Against his will' is a metaphor, of course, a name for a Nabokovian effect. But the metaphor helps, I think, because the Pnin we are discussing seems to emerge only when the narrator's will is not on full patrol. The narrator is noisily full of self, aware of that fact and willing to signal it to us, but more important he is intermittently capable of forgetting self, and of becoming the novelist whose inventions are larger and more varied than he is. It is not a question of the character's escaping the author's control – Nabokov was rightly scornful of such tropes – but of that control itself stretching to include something quite beyond its ordinary reach. This is to say that there are moments in *Pnin* when we lose all sense of ridicule, even of the gentlest kind. There aren't many of them and they rapidly topple back into the ludicrous; but they are there, and one of them, I would say, is central not only to this novel but to Nabokov's whole work.

The moments usually concern death, or memory, or a lost Russia. Pnin suddenly sees his long-deceased parents and other past companions in an American auditorium as he is about to give a lecture: 'Murdered, forgotten, unrevenged, incorrupt, immortal, many old friends were scattered about the dim hall among more recent people . . .' Later he falls back into a distant summer in the country – the same summer in which the narrator claims to have met him, complete with amateur theatricals – and sees everything as if it were intensely present. He believes, we are told, 'dimly, in a democracy of ghosts', a mournful figure for a loyal and troublesome memory – for a memory that will not accept death as the end of loved ones. Remembering for Pnin is associated with a strange behaviour of the heart ('not pain or palpitation, but rather an awful feeling of sinking and melting into one's physical surroundings') and at times it is literally intolerable. Mira Belochkin, the love of Pnin's Russian youth, died in Buchenwald, and the image of her end is more than his reason can manage, even for a moment:

In order to exist rationally, Pnin had taught himself, during the last ten years, never to remember Mira Belochkin – not because, in itself, the evocation of a youthful love affair, banal and brief, threatened his peace of mind . . . but because, if one were quite sincere with oneself, no conscience, and hence no consciousness, could be expected to subsist in a world where such things as Mira's death were possible. One had to forget – because one could not live with the thought that this graceful, fragile, tender young woman with those eyes, that smile, those gardens and snows in the background, had been brought in a cattle car to an extermination camp and killed by an injection of phenol into the heart . . .

'Those eyes, that smile': we see the face quite clearly. The abrupt absence of adjectives, the sudden discretion of the elsewhere so busily specifying novelist, signal a startling new fidelity of the narrator to Pnin's feelings; and make the young woman our thought as well as Pnin's, arrived at without description or instruction, or with only the preliminary, generic clues of 'graceful, fragile, tender', qualities we picture more precisely from our own fund of instances. 'Never to remember', 'had to forget': these are the paradoxes, the terrors of memory. It is only for the truly unforgettable that we ever feel we need such desperate, lying stratagems. The pretence of forgetting governs and distorts everything we choose openly to remember, and Pnin's fussy life, with all its eccentricities, now seems an anxious scheme of avoidance. 'Peace of mind' must be a ready-made phrase for mere bearable sanity, and itself a mild act of verbal evasion. The same note is sounded less darkly (because it is securely kept within the realm of Pninian comedy) in the course on tyranny Pnin is planning to teach (but never will) at Waindell. 'The history of man is the history of pain,' Pnin says enthusiastically. His friend and boss pats him on the knee and says, intending no irony, 'You are a wonderful romantic, Timofey . . .' We might add, following Pnin's logic, with its interesting inversion of the usual relations of conscience and consciousness, that this history is more particularly one of grotesque and arbitrary pain, pain unredeemed by order or sense. Mira Belochkin is every innocent creature smashed for no reason, caught up and mangled by the precise opposite of fate: raw, murderous, ungraspable circumstance, the cruelty of chance. Here are none of the patterns Nabokov and his characters love, not even failed patterns, which at least are a bid for meaning: just the mindless procession of what is beyond the mind.

The implication of this scene for the rest of Nabokov's work is that all his symmetries and shapes and coincidences are perhaps not a primary taste – an aspect of his temperament, a straightforward liking – but a response to an insight like Pnin's about the brutal meaninglessness of history. Even cruel jokes are better than empty cruelty, and we have seen how Humbert was drawn to the strange peace of this preference. I'm not suggesting a simple reaction of fantasy/consolation on Nabokov's part; more like an imaginative exploration of the comforts we can't have. 'But don't you think', a character in *Pnin* says of an unnamed practitioner, 'that what he is trying to do . . . practically in all his novels . . . is . . . to express the fantastic recurrence of certain situations?' Recurrence is not meaning, but here as in *Speak, Memory*, it may help to stave off absolute insignificance. The shapes Nabokov presents would be sceptical wishes, images of what a thoroughly designed world might look like. They would be *only* shapes, mere appearances of sense rather than sense itself. The appearance would not be enough, of course, but it would be what there is, and better than the stark, unaccommodated mess the shapes are drawn across.

Alex de Jonge in a very interesting essay mentions 'a notion that Nabokov never more than hints at, that there is no pattern without a pattern-maker'. This is well put, but I'm not sure Nabokov even makes this particular hint very often. Isn't it rather that there certainly *are* patterns without a pattern-maker, and that those are the patterns we mostly have? It's just that the echo or mirage of a maker, the phantom thrown up by de Jonge's impeccable logic, is a welcome guest; not a hope but a candidate for the special nostalgia we feel for what there never was. 'All Nature is but Art, unknown to thee;/All Chance, Direction, which thou canst not see', Pope says in *An Essay on Man*. Nabokov is plainly much attracted by this theory. But it is an attraction to a metaphor rather than a tenet, an attraction experienced by a sceptical modern, an heir to Schopenhauer and Nietzsche (Nabokov would have hated the association, but ghosts don't always get to choose their company, and the connection is not arbitrary). 'Only as an aesthetic phenomenon,' Nietzsche notoriously wrote, 'are existence and the world seen to be justified.' 'Only . . . aesthetic', as Michael Silk and Peter Stern suggest, implies not art for art's sake but a pointed contrast to the moral (and specifically Christian) interpretation of existence and the world. 'If life is defensible at all,' they write in commentary on Nietzsche's argument, 'it can only be defended in the way that one creator might justify his handiwork to another: ethically unedifying, but marvellous to look at.' Nature is beautiful but not meaningful; ordered but not morally ordered; full of what feels like and effectively is chance for us. The snag for Nietzsche, and I think for Nabokov, is that the prodigious creator is dead, scarcely available even as a metaphor; the handiwork is unowned. Much of Nabokov's art is devoted to lending quirky artificial life to this defunct figure: not as an achieved resurrection or an article of confirmed faith, but as a provocative question. Can we really imagine or tolerate the undesigned world – the world which has no particular designs for us – which is probably the world we have? Pope's age seems remote not because it is preposterous or heartless, as John Shade thinks in *Pale Fire*, but because it is confident: quite as willing to entertain doubts as we are, but considerably more willing to resolve them.

Occasionally, Nabokov did go a little further than this. Asked about organized religion he usually expressed his disbelief or lack of interest. Asked once if he believed in God he said: 'To be quite candid . . . I know more than I can express in words, and the little I can express would not have been expressed, had I not known more.' The remark is gnomic enough to take all kinds of interpretations, and must have been drafted for that purpose. But minimally it must mean that Nabokov's words depend upon a sizeable fund of silence ('James Joyce's mistake,' Nabokov also said, 'consists in that he gives too much verbal body to thoughts'). We might then want to think of God as a name for this silence. God would be the inexistent, eagerly dreamed-of pattern-maker; or the actual pattern-maker, real enough but perpetually absent, always invisible to our cobwebbed eyes. By 'belief' Nabokov may mean a willingness to imagine this second possibility. This will seem slim to other believers, of all kinds; but it is a lot for a sceptic, and would certainly fill Nabokov's silence with things he could not say.

The patterns in *Pnin* are not so arcane, and this is one of Nabokov's least patterned novels, prompting some critics to wonder whether it is a novel at all. What I hope I have suggested is that it is a sequence of stories which is altered, which becomes a novel, once we pay serious attention to the storyteller. It also has its tricky little patterns, and they feed on a curious modern prejudice about narrative. The narrator slips into sentimentality at the end because he can't cope with a Pnin who gets away, and this not only because he feels comedy is comedy but also because his sense of story can't do without failure and mishap. Tolstoy's famous first sentence of *Anna Karenina* is this man's creed: all happy families are alike and there is no story in happiness.

> Some people – and I am one of them – hate happy ends. We feel
> cheated. Harm is the norm. Doom should not jam. The avalanche
> stopping in its tracks a few feet above the cowering village behaves
> not only unnaturally but unethically . . .

There is more than a touch of sardonic exaggeration here, and the
thump of harm/norm/doom/jam sounds like a deliberately clumsy
word game – an imitation of the stalled avalanche perhaps. But
there is quite a bit to think about. Many people love happy ends,
some people hate them, and the second set feels more sophisticated,
although it might admit to being more unscrupulous in its appetite
for disaster. The second set would also claim to be appealing to
probability, to a sounder sense of life's odds, but no doubt relies as
much as the first set on narrative desire, on a yearning for just those
plots which meet particular habits and needs. Happiness *and* harm,
at this level, are only stories, a matter of guesses and wishes; and
both are easily contradicted by actuality at any given moment.

Having set up this question the narrator later proceeds to demonstrate that we do share his taste in stories, even if we express it less
gloatingly. Pnin has been given a large punch bowl of 'brilliant
aquamarine glass', and it has been the star of a happy party he gives.
Afterwards, alone, doing the washing up, he drops a pair of nut-
crackers into the soapy water and hears the horrible sound of
breaking glass. We know this must be the cherished bowl, and are
ready to feel very sorry for Pnin, even as we sagely congratulate
ourselves on knowing that this is, alas, just the sort of thing that
does happen. Harm is the norm. In fact the bowl is safe, it was a
wine glass that broke: the avalanche has stopped above the village.
Are we pleased? We are delighted, but also obscurely disappointed,
because all uncracked punch bowls are alike, and part of us would
rather pity Pnin than share his relief. His whole role in the novel is
to have things go wrong for him. These murky impulses of ours say
a lot about our investment in fiction, our need for misadventure,
our rage for gloomily plausible order. Doom and harm are ways of
making things ethically sound, of making them match our supposedly sensible assessments. But if we need to tidy up even here,
cannnot stand uncertainty in modest, imagined scenes, what shall
we do when the random assumes its violent and ugly historical
forms, threatening all stories, happy and harm-ridden, because no
conscience or consciousness or narrative can be expected to subsist
in a world which remembers what Pnin has taught himself to forget?

8

The Demons of our Pity:
Pale Fire

*I have been too unhappy, I thought, it cannot
last, being so unhappy would kill you.*

Jean Rhys, *Wide Sargasso Sea*

(i)

Pnin is briefly mentioned several times in *Pale Fire*, but oddly
transformed into 'a regular martinet in regard to his underlings'.
The underlings are perhaps even more surprising than the stance of
the martinet. Pnin is now Head of the 'bloated Russian Department' at Wordsmith College, in New Wye, Appalachia. We may
recognize him as the 'grotesque "perfectionist"' he is called here,
although the phrase, with its jeering quotation marks, seems
strangely hostile; as does a later reference to him as 'a farcical
pedant of whom the less said the better'. Other features are more
familiar. Colleagues have trouble pronouncing his pname, and he
must be the irrelevant extra seen in the Wordsmith Library towards
the end of the novel, a 'baldheaded suntanned professor in a
Hawaiian shirt . . . reading with an ironic expression on his face a
Russian book'. The very word order seems to have been taken over
by Pnin.

Has Pnin really become a martinet? The joke is so light that it
seems dangerous to linger over it, but the general suggestion, I
think, is that we should be wary of imposing fixed personalities on
people in and out of fiction – think of King Lear and Emma Bovary, evoked as rigid textual effigies in *Lolita*. Pnin could change,
and so could we. More locally and quite in opposition to this reading, our old sense of Pnin (there couldn't be two Pnins in academic
America, could there?) invites us to suspect the judgement of
anyone who could call him a martinet, and indeed there are plenty

of other grounds for suspecting this person. These grounds, we might say, are the subject of *Pale Fire*.

There is a more intimate and far-reaching connection between *Pnin* and *Pale Fire*. Liza's son Victor, donor of the punch-bowl we have just looked at, is a lonely and talented boy of fourteen who visits Pnin at Waindell. The two solitaries don't have much to say to each other, and Pnin, dismayed to learn that Victor doesn't care for games at all, has discreetly thrown away a new football, his intended gift. Nevertheless, they get on well enough, and meet up on an unexpected wave-length. In his sleep Pnin finds himself on a beach which, although he doesn't know it, belongs to Victor's dream world. 'Pnin saw himself fantastically cloaked, fleeing through great pools of ink under a cloud-barred moon from a chimerical palace, and then pacing a desolate strand . . .' In Victor's waking fancy a King, refusing to abdicate, is forced to flee and waits for a friend at Tempest Point, on 'a beach on the Bohemian Sea.' The King is Victor's imaginary father. The idea, I take it, is not to urge telepathy on us, but to offer a delicate metaphor for an order of kindness and goodwill which cannot make its way into speech or clear action. More, the suggestion may be that the lexicon of loneliness really is quite limited, that a certain monotony of beaches characterizes the imagination of sadness. Tolstoy's sentence is turned round: *un*happy families are alike, caught in a predictable, dreary circle of misery and misunderstanding. This reversal literally occupies the first lines of *Ada*: 'All happy families are more or less dissimilar; all unhappy ones are more or less alike'. We need to catch the joke about mistranslation, along with the graceless vagueness of the double 'more or less'. This, Nabokov implies, is roughly the level of accuracy we get when we read the Russians. But he is also mischievously, and I think bravely, rewriting Tolstoy. The hopeless misreading is also an original argument. Happiness *is* varied and multiple; pain and its friends *are* repetitive, derivative, forever wearing the same stiff, stubborn faces.

We see far more of these faces in *Pale Fire* than in *Pnin*, and notably in the distress of the narrator and central character. He is one Charles Kinbote, editor of a longish poem by the American John Shade, a dishevelled, distinguished figure who trails in reputation, as he himself says, 'one oozy footstep' behind Robert Frost. Shade resembles Frost a little: in looks; slow, sly style of wit; fund of wily common sense. He is a milder character than Frost, though; kinder; and a lot more than a footstep behind him as a poet. The book we read is ostensibly a text and commentary: foreword,

Shade's poem *Pale Fire*, extensive notes, index. Kinbote is a pseudonym, its owner tells us, eagerly letting us in on the secret that he is none other than Charles Xavier the Beloved of Zembla, forced into exile by a farcical and unnecessary revolution in his country. Kinbote in Zemblan means regicide, 'a king's destroyer', he says, 'longing to explain that a king who sinks his identity in the mirror of exile is in a sense just that'. The eerie thing is that Kinbote has escaped from his homeland via a very close relative of Victor's and Pnin's beach, and Zembla itself seems to have been cobbled together from Victor's daydreams and Pnin's past. Or as Nabokov put it, saying the same thing in reverse and with inside knowledge, 'the boy ... and Pnin dream of a passage from my drafts of *Pale Fire* ...' Brian Boyd suggests the dates of writing don't quite confirm this claim, but then the fiction behind the fiction gets even wilder, and more interesting: the boy and Pnin dream of passages from a book yet to be written.

Victor's fantasy is very clearly marked as such. His Middle European King, with a capital situated 'at the heart of a cross whose arms terminated in Trieste, Graz, Budapest and Zagreb', is a 'more plausible father' than the 'cranky refugee doctor', Liza's second husband, who actually begot him; and the sources of Victor's imaginings are meticulously listed:

An Italian film made in Berlin for American consumption, with a wild-eyed youngster in rumpled shorts, pursued through slums and ruins and a brothel or two by a multiple agent; a version of *The Scarlet Pimpernel*, recently staged at ... the nearest girls' school; an anonymous Kafkaesque story in a *ci-devant avant-garde* magazine ...; and, not least the residue of various family allusions of long standing to the flight of Russian intellectuals from Lenin's regime thirty-five years ago ...

Pnin's history, of course, overlaps precisely with the last item.

Kinbote's geography is different, but we might think his sources are pretty much the same, maybe adding in *The Prisoner of Zenda* and a handful of other Ruritanian romances. Zembla is a Baltic Kingdom, capital Onhava, a peninsula divided by a high mountain range, and cut off by a canal from 'the mainland of madness' – alias Russia, but also maybe the whole historical world. From the highest of these mountains 'one can distinguish on clear days, far out to the east, beyond the Gulf of Surprise, a dim iridescence which some

175

say is Russia'. I wonder what the others say. Kruschchev is planning to visit Zembla during the time of the novel's action (July to October 1959), but Kinbote's gloss on the name of the country, 'a corruption not of the Russian *zemlya*, but of Semblerland, a land of reflections, of "resemblers", tends to push the place back towards the imaginary. There is a Novaya Zemlya in the atlas, an island not a peninsula; but it doesn't have even an ex-king, or, as far as I know, any of the glittering, slightly decadent civilization Kinbote so lovingly evokes. It does have a 'Nabokov's River', since the area was explored by the writer's great-grandfather Nikolay Aleksandrovich; and Zembla appears in Pope's *Essay on Man*.

Kinbote tells us he fed his fantastic story to John Shade over the few months of their acquaintance, and expected to find his Zemblan material, transformed but gleaming, in the work he knows the poet has been writing. But nothing of his grand romance appears in Shade's poem, and Kinbote has to fight off a 'bitter hot mist of disappointment' when he finds himself, at the poet's death, possessed of the manuscript.

> I started to read the poem. I read faster and faster. I sped through it, snarling, as a furious young heir through an old deceiver's testament. Where were the battlements of my sunset castle? Where was Zembla the Fair? Where her spine of mountains? . . . The complex contribution I had been pressing upon him with a hypnotist's patience and a lover's urge was simply not there.

Kinbote's story, ostensibly historical, bears all the signs of fantasy, including a splendid slip into excessive enthusiasm for the invented realm:

> That King's reign (1936-1958) will be remembered by at least a few discerning historians as a peaceful and elegant one . . . Harmony . . . was the reign's password. The polite arts and pure sciences flourished . . . The climate seemed to be improving. Taxation had become a thing of beauty.

Hard to see how the revolution could take hold. Later Kinbote makes a revealing slip, but covers himself brilliantly: 'had I been a northern king – or rather had I still been a king (exile becomes a bad habit) . . .' But is this a slip, is this all a fantasy? What are the signs of fantasy? If there is fantasy here, we have to say we don't know where it begins and ends, or what 'reality' it has replaced, as we do know with Victor's: 'Actually, Victor's father was . . .' There is no 'actually' in *Pale Fire*.

When it first appeared *Pale Fire* was widely read as a dazzling riddle, and of course in part it is that. 'A Jack-in-the-box, a Fabergé gem, a clockwork toy, a chess problem,' Mary McCarthy said at the beginning of her essay, 'an infernal machine, a trap to catch reviewers, a cat-and-mouse game, a do-it-yourself kit'. If we look up *Crown Jewels*, for example, in the eccentric index, we are directed consecutively to *Hiding Place*, *potaynik*, *taynik* and back to *Crown Jewels*: a false trail of concealment. What do we make of the strangely prominent 'Botkin, V., American scholar of Russian descent', who cuts a figure in the index quite out of proportion to the two casual references to him the commentary, and keeps throwing odd verbal shadows when least expected? The index sends us first to this conversation, where Botkin appears only obliquely:

> Professor Pardon now spoke to me: 'I was under the impression that you were born in Russia, and that your name was a kind of anagram of Botkin or Botkine?'
>
> Kinbote: 'You are confusing me with some refugeee from Nova Zembla' [sarcastically stressing the 'Nova'].

On the other hand, in a mention which is not in the index, we learn that 'happily, Prof Botkin . . . was not subordinated' to that martinet Pnin. Happily? Whose happiness is this? The name Botkin, we are told, comes from the profession of 'one who makes bottekins, fancy footwear' (this trade is in the index). Botkin is said to be the correct spelling of Hamlet's bare bodkin. The index also informs us of the Russian words *bot*, plop, and *boteliy*, big-bellied. John Shade's wife Sybil calls Kinbote 'a king-sized botfly', and the index diligently notes 'king-bot, a maggot of extinct fly that once bred in mammoths and is thought to have hastened their phylogenetic end'.

There is a smart answer to this riddle, and critics have pounced on it. I must say I did, when I first read this book. Botkin is the name which is not supposed to appear and yet keeps appearing, as we so often suddenly mention the very topic we have sworn to avoid. Hence all the seemingly irrelevant echoes: they are what has crept past the censor. Kinbote *is* Botkin; Russian not Zemblan. Zembla doesn't exist, at least not as the romantic region Kinbote describes, and he is not its king. He is a fussy, disliked, exiled, Russian academic in America, sadder than Pnin and much nastier than the narrator of Pnin's story. There are difficulties with this reading, as we might imagine. Nabokov was a chess-player, and unlikely not to have foreseen our interpretative moves, especially the ones we regard as pretty clever. Thus if Kinbote is Botkin, he must have rewritten every mention of himself throughout the text, where he is regularly addressed as 'Charles', 'Kinbote', 'Dr Kinbote'. Indeed the idea of Professor Pardon's asking someone called Botkin if his name is an anagram of Botkin makes the hair stand on end. This fellow would have pushed the principle of 'My name is so-and-so' to the verge of delirium. It is easy enough to think of a narrator who doctors the conversations he reports (easier than thinking of one who doesn't, as a matter of fact); or of a narrator who fabricates his whole story. But if Kinbote is Botkin we can't place the narrative at all. The material will have been radically redrafted, but still seems to rely on, to allude to, a substratum of 'fact'. As with *Lolita* and Nabokov's other works, we cannot retreat into a safe zone where all is fiction; but the 'reality' here is much harder to establish. Kinbote/Botkin makes Humbert look like a mine of easy information.

I'd like to believe that all this is a lure: Botkin is not Kinbote, he is a mere weird verbal cousin, an accidental 'resembler', just one of those alphabetical things. But there is too much activity around the name for that, too much ado about a character who is scarcely there. Botkin is the static in Kinbote's story, the buzz and the hum of repression, the self Kinbote has buried. What we must say though, I think, is that we don't know enough about Botkin to treat him as the 'real', founding person, the man behind the mask. Kinbote has buried Botkin pretty successfully; only a few shreds of his former self cling to his new invention, so his new invention is what we have. Botkin's role in the novel is not to tell the hidden truth, deliver the crown jewels, but to remind us, eerily, that Kinbote's self *is* invented, precarious; that it has a past or has a double.

Similar questions arise about Zembla, which is manifestly a fiction, but whose? On the one hand, we can talk about a 'real Zembla', as Lucy Maddox does, because the place is registered in the world of John Shade as well as the world of Kinbote: characters in the novel discuss it as real, look it up in an encyclopaedia, read about it in the newspapers. Kruschchev is due to visit. We have only Kinbote's word for any of this, of course, but we have only Kinbote's word for everything in the novel, including the text of the poem, and as with Humbert, we have to hang our beliefs somewhere, even in fiction. On the other hand, much of what we learn about Zembla seems so frankly, so self-indulgently fantastic, so stickily Kinbotian in tone that we feel sure we have abandoned even the fictional 'reality'. It's just that we can't quite say where we crossed over, left one (imaginary) world for another. We don't need to identify the border – Nabokov's interest, I think, is in making the identification pretty much impossible – but we do need to see that much of the material in the novel is fantastic by any standards, invites the sort of cross-reading, the 'going behind', that the understanding of fantasy so often requires; and also that we shall not get very far through merely reductive readings, by tagging what we think is real and using it as an explanation for the rest. The real is not an explanation, it is a (disputed) territory.

We may feel, for example, that Kinbote's story is a fantasy because it reads like a tale of dream and need, an extravagant, displaced autobiography, what Stendhalians would call an imaginary revenge, an endowing of the self with what it most conspicuously lacks. We guess at Kinbote's failure and misery *because* of the rather tinny glamour and success he keeps reporting. This is the note we find in much of the Zemblan material – in so much of it that the novel at times threatens to topple into the very genre it is spoofing. Thus the escaping king meets a fairy-tale farmer and his wife. The farmer is 'gnarled' (and later places his 'gnarled hand' on a 'gnarled balustrade'), the wife is plump and heard 'crooning an ancient song' among her pots and pans. There are 'gossamer gleams of sunlight' on the forest path, a hillside is 'gay with gentians'. We have been here before, but not outside of literature. Is Kinbote sentimentalizing some sort of 'reality' or is he making the whole thing up?

A key passage in the novel offers a literary view of madness as a way of contemplating such questions. Madness, John Shade says, is not the right word for the condition of the old man at the railway station who thought he was God and started redirecting the trains. 'One should not apply it to a person who deliberately peels off a drab and unhappy past and replaces it with a brilliant invention. That's merely turning a new leaf with the left hand'. Shade calls the old man at the station a poet, and Kinbote meaningfully says, 'We all are, in a sense, poets.' He is alluding to his secret, royal life, but also pathetically and perhaps unintentionally to his continuing construction of his initial mask. Botkin is the past Kinbote has peeled off.

Shade's interpretation of madness is kindly, and combats a stigma; it even understands drabness and unhappiness. But it doesn't make them go away. They haunt the very inventions they

179

provoke. And Kinbote continues bewildered, asserting that he has 'personally ... not known any lunatics', but also rather eagerly placing himself among the famous men, mentioned in Shade's poem, whose 'minds ... died' before they did. 'Dark, disturbing thoughts', he writes; as if madness were not only a remedy for misery but itself a form of glamour.

The form of *Pale Fire* hardly seems to invite pathos. Of course we know it is not a real critical edition because it has been advertised and sold as (and indeed is) a novel by Nabokov. The poem of course is real in its way, not quite grand or strong enough for the reputation the novel imputes to its author, but witty and skillfully put together, and genuinely moving in places:

> And all the time, and all the time, my love,
> You too are there, beneath the word, above
> The syllable ...

> For we die every day; oblivion thrives
> Not on dry thighbones but on blood-ripe lives,
> And our best yesterdays are now foul piles
> Of crumpled names, phone numbers and foxed files.

The poem takes its title, although this is one of the things its editor doesn't know, from *Timon of Athens*, and almost finds the name of one of Nabokov's future novels in the process:

> But *this* transparent thingum does require
> Some moondrop title. Help me, Will! *Pale Fire.*

'The moon's an arrant thief,' the relevant lines tell us, 'And her pale fire she snatches from the sun.' Kinbote the editor is going to snatch as much fire as he can from the poet's sun, although the poet's name perhaps hints at the faintness of his chances. Kinbote has literally, arrantly, stolen the poem, gone off with the index cards it is written on; and metaphorically stolen it too, since he wants to endow it with a meaning which is all his own. The second theft doesn't in the end come off, because Kinbote, in spite of understandable temptations towards forgery and fixing, is too loyal to his text. He would like it to tell his story, but he knows it doesn't. The one variant that seems to carry a serious hint of the Zemblan romance ('Ah, I must not forget to say something/That my friend told me of a certain king') turns out not to scan and to have been faked by a disappointed Kinbote, who tells us this himself. He is a fantasist and possibly crazy, but he is not, in the end, going to lie to us about literature.

The commentary at times does do a perfectly ordinary job: gives us biographical information about Shade and his family, points to the poem's parallels in Hardy and Goethe (the word 'stillicide' borrowed from the first, the rhythm of 'The Erlking' from the second), tells us what a shagbark tree is (a hickory), and offers genteel exclamations of applause ('The loveliest couplet in this canto'). It also, less helpfully, identifies Sherlock Holmes as if no one had ever heard of him, and misses several broad jokes Nabokov expects us to get – like the one about Hurricane Lolita striking America in 1958. Even so, we don't advance more than a few lines into the book before we realize something very strange is going on. We wonder at first, I think, what kind of text this is; but soon wonder more seriously whose text it is, and what is the matter with him. The foreword, and the novel, begin quite soberly: '*Pale Fire*, a poem in heroic couplets . . . was composed by John Francis Shade (born July 5, 1898, died July 21, 1959) during the last twenty days of his life . . . The manuscript . . . consists of eighty medium-sized index cards . . .' The mention of Shade's last twenty days adds a muted note of drama, makes us think a bit about this poem *in extremis*, but the rest seems steady enough. Then the prose goes a little odd, indicating 'all those amusing birds' in Canto One, calling Canto Two 'your favorite' and Canto Three a 'shocking tour de force'. By the end of his third paragraph, having failed to be as clear as he would like to be about the difference between a Corrected Draft and a Fair Copy, Kinbote abruptly tells us 'there is a very loud amusement park right in front of my present lodgings'. (It is a camp site, he and we later learn, but the music is still loud.) Pulling himself together, he returns to a proper academic tone: 'We possess . . . a complete calendar of his work. Canto One was begun in the small hours of July 2 . . .' But then extravagant adjectives begin to appear (devastating, cataclysmic), and Kinbote is off into a literary skirmish against a group of 'professed Shadeans', by whom he means 'Prof. Hurley and his clique'. These awful enemies have argued, without seeing the manuscript (Kinbote is not about to show it to anyone), that it is incoherent and incomplete. Kinbote certainly seems to carry his point against them, and his language, although not entirely grammatical, is not without dignity:

the imputations . . . is a malicious invention on the part of those who
would wish not so much to deplore the state in which a great poet's
work was interrupted by death as to asperse the competence, and
perhaps honesty, of its present editor and commentator.

It is a prickly dignity, though, and the tone recalls that of the narrator of Borges' story 'Pierre Menard, author of *Don Quixote*':

It is as if yesterday we were gathered together before the final marble
and the fateful cypresses, and already Error is trying to tarnish his
Memory . . .

Error merely means the other side, the other claimants to Menard's
friendship and posterity. Borges' narrator seems to be reliably informed about Menard's habits, but his judgements are doubtful,
because he reveals so many of his prejudices: within a line or two
we learn that he is Catholic, anti-Protestant, snobbish and anti-
Semitic. I don't know when Nabokov read Borges – he certainly
admired him – but the homage here appears deliberate, since Shade
like Menard burned his manuscripts once he was done with them,
feeding them to 'the pale fire of the incinerator' just as Menard used
to make 'a gay bonfire' of his notebooks. Kinbote's 'marble finality
of an immaculate page' echoes 'the final marble' in the quotation
from Borges.

Kinbote bursts out in a rash of punctuation at the thought that
Prof. H (!) and Prof. C (!!) might work with him on his edition, and
his index emphatically mentions these scholars as absent: 'not in the
Index'. Not having their own entries, he means, since he can signal
their exclusion only by including them and saying they are not
there: a brilliant own goal. Other tell-tale signs mount up – but telling what? Kinbote insists boyishly and repeatedly on his 'powerful
red car', his 'powerful Kramler'; begins to flaunt his declared but
unlucky homosexuality (he notes 'two radiant lads' as they pass,
has his eye on 'a moody, delicate, rather wonderful boy', is much
disappointed in a young lodger, 'bad Bob', whose heterosexual
romp Kinbote sees as 'treason'). He describes his 'favorite photograph' of John Shade by referring almost entirely to himself: 'I am
wearing a white windbreaker . . . and a pair of lilac slacks . . . My
left hand is half raised . . . to remove my sunglasses . . .' The amusement park/camp site creeps into a line count – 'twin wings of five
hundred verses each, and damn that music' – and Kinbote may say

more than he wants to when he speaks of 'that carrousel inside and outside my head.' A misprint – or rather an instruction to the printer, as in *Lolita* – appears at the very moment he is describing his scholarly diligence, and that of the 'professional proofreader' he has employed. As with the mistranslation of Tolstoy in *Ada*, the joke is on our general sloppiness but also goes further: Kinbote can't concentrate, the bald but perturbed academic apparatus actually offers us the image of a mind in trouble, rather as Pierre Menard's bibliography is a sketch of his quirky intellect. We arrive at the pictures – of Kinbote and Menard – by joining up the dots.

Kinbote also speaks of Zembla in his foreword, and hints at his royal tale: 'Imagine a soft, clumsy giant; imagine a historical personage whose knowledge of money is limited to the abstract billions of a national debt; imagine an exiled prince who is unaware of the Golconda in his cuff links!' This is rather like our double imagining of Humbert ('Imagine me; I shall not exist if you do not imagine me'), as a character in a novel and an isolated, scribbling author within that novel, except that here the imagining is triple: 'I am imagining myself in this way, and would like you to go along with me'; 'I really am an exiled prince but need to live in your imaginations as well as in my exiled reality'; 'I am a character in a novel, and my role is to make questions of this kind as dizzying as possible'.

All these things are hints and clues in the foreword – worrying and amusing but far from conclusive – but feed into a full-blown portrait by the time we finish the book, albeit a portrait made of dots. Kinbote's commentary is also full of 'roaring' fast cars and homosexuality, sometimes found together: 'I had been kind enough to offer a young friend . . . to take him, in my powerful Kramler, all the way to his parents' estate, a little matter of two hundred miles . . .' He likes to talk about his 'temptations', his 'copious but sterile pleasures', and is fond of the notion of the manly, as in 'manlier pleasures', or 'both were in a manly state'. Proust and Gide are summoned up as friendly spirits. What are we to make of this?

The car is a little obvious as an emblem of glamour and power – as the emblem of fantasies of glamour and power – and is underlined more often than it needs to be. Nabokov may be spoofing such symbolism or deciding to give us a lift on to the first steps of his swaying ladder. The homosexuality is a more complex affair. Kinbote boasts about it so much, makes it so royally acceptable and successful in the world of Zembla that his very insistence becomes dreamlike, as if a deprived child were to keep seeing himself in a sweetshop. And then the sweetshop acquires shadows; darkness creeps even into the fantasy.

This is the unhappy reversal of Pnin's revenge, the flight into pity because only pity is left. Or rather it is the sadly foiled revenge of someone much unhappier than Pnin. The unloved person invents for himself a world of power, a picture-book monarchy and endless sexual satisfaction, but all power has to be exercised in order to be felt, and the new world must have its unloved ones, the excluded and the humiliated who will provide the fantasist with his triumph, but by the same token begin to resemble him as he is outside the fantasy. Kinbote alias Charles II needs someone who loves him and whom he haughtily cannot love, and a charming, betrayed, abandoned wife is just the answer. There is a romance of *not* loving, we can adore the very pain we cause, what Kinbote tenderly and cruelly calls 'the listless grace of ineffable grief'. Immediately after evoking this picture of grace, Nabokov borrows one of his own sharp jokes from *The Real Life of Sebastian Knight*, makes the figure Kinbote contemplates not, as he thinks, his queen in the distance, but a lady-in-waiting. Even mangled tenderness is misplaced in the world available to Kinbote.

And the beautiful Queen Disa, invented for the purposes of a consoling scenario, inconveniently becomes a source of guilt, in spite of all Kinbote's unapologetic evocations of his homosexuality. The King thinks he feels for her only 'friendly indifference and bleak respect'; no question of 'pity, of heartache'. 'But the heart of his dreaming self . . . made extraordinary amends':

> The gist, rather than the actual plot of the dream, was a constant re-
> futation of his not loving her. His dream-love for her exceeded in
> emotional tone, in spiritual passion and depth, anything he had ex-
> perienced in his surface existence. This love was like an endless
> wringing of hands, like a blundering of the soul through an infinite
> maze of hopelessness and remorse. They were, in a sense, amorous
> dreams, for they were permeated with tenderness . . . They were
> purer than his life.

Humbert, obsessed with Lolita, dreams in similar fashion of the more ordinary loves he could not entertain, of the pathetic, scorned Charlotte, the stupid, unfaithful Valeria. 'More precisely', Humbert says, Lolita became these women in his sleep. The dreams would end in a 'disorder of auctioneered Viennese bric-à-brac, pity, impotence and the brown wigs of tragic old women who had just been gassed.' Those wigs are astonishing, suggest that Humbert's confusion and guilt are the size of Germany. His dreams were right to put Lolita and his wives together, of course: the cruelty of his love for her was no less extreme than the cruelty of his indifference towards the others. It is as if Nabokov's characters regularly live in a world in which so-called normality is banished to the bottom of the unconscious, has to climb up, if it is to be seen at all, out of a far zone of repression. Sebastian Knight too, belatedly thinks he has 'overlooked . . . the obvious and the ordinary'. Kinbote possesses a loving heart but buried at depths almost beyond belief, and if Disa and his kingdom are a fantasy we are caught in a mind which needs an almost endless spiral to reach its humanity. Even then I'm not sure we leave the realm of pity: Kinbote's pity for Disa, our pity for him. We are in a kind of hell where all other emotions seem impossible. A love which appears only in dreams, and only as a wringing of hands, *is* pity. The miracle is that even this is not excluded in such a hell.

Kinbote's distress – I mean now his present distress, his condition as he writes, not the drab and unhappy life he has doubtless been peeling off for some time – is the picture the dots add up to. He speaks of 'excruciating headaches', of 'dark evenings that are destroying my brain'. 'Dear Jesus, do something', he suddenly implores; and in one of his most opaque and moving signals of pain glosses Shade's words 'two tongues' ('He suffocates and conjures in two tongues') with this manic list of paired languages:

English and Zemblan, English and Russian, English and Lettish, English and Estonian, English and Lithuanian, English and Russian, English and Ukrainian, English and Polish, English and Czech, English and Russian, English and Hungarian, English and Rumanian, English and Albanian, English and Bulgarian, English and Serbo-Croatian, English and Russian, American and European.

The list is apparently meaningless, and bears no relation to the line it is supposedly commenting on. We note that the pair *English and Russian* appears four times and all the others only once, and that the other languages mentioned, after the (in context) obvious Zemblan, circle closely around Russia until they find a release in a transcontinental shift. Someone's mind is both gibbering and haunted here, and it looks like Botkin's, the creature beneath the floor of Kinbote's double fiction.

Kinbote's Christianity is a clue rather like the red car, only subtler and deeper. He is a Protestant believer, thinks in terms of the Church calendar ('6th Sunday after Trinity'), sings hymns in the shower, talks devoutly of 'Our Lord', resists John Shade's good-natured agnosticism with an eloquent declaration, after St Augustine, of what God is not: 'He is not despair. He is not terror. He is not the earth in one's rattling throat, not the black hum in one's ears fading to nothing in nothing . . .' God is not these things but a terrible, near-demonic knowledge of them speaks even in these negatives; and Kinbote elsewhere hopes for salvation, 'despite the frozen mud and horror in my heart'. He contemplates suicide, half-hopes his God may after all find it forgivable: 'We who burrow in filth every day may be forgiven perhaps the one sin that ends all sins.' This language is almost as astonishing as the old women's wigs in Humbert's dreams. Mud, horror, burrow in filth: what has the poor fellow done? Nothing much, as far as we can see, except taking a few boys to bed and failing to love most of his neighbours; being pompous, fussy, full of self-regard. This is not nice, but it is not filth and horror.

Kinbote's belief is like his fantasy, a consolation which is also a torment. The God who may save him may damn him, and the fear escalates his small sins into nightmare. Or perhaps, to borrow a line of thought from Proust and Kafka, Kinbote's nightmare uses whatever comes to hand: Christianity, his daily life, the world he has found for his imagination. The guilt precedes everything; crimes can always be found to match it. The unhappiness here seems so deep and irremediable that even a Christian would surely find Kinbote's religion more of a symptom than a cure or a faith. Nabokov said in an interview that Kinbote 'certainly' committed suicide 'after putting the last touches to his edition of the poem'. This is authorial trespassing, and we don't have to pay attention to it. The only internal clue I can find is Kinbote's saying that he has examined the manuscript of the poem 'for the last time'; but he may only mean he will not need to consult it again. I think myself that Nabokov underrates the energy and the wit that Kinbote and his book still possess at the end; but must be right to point to the proximity of suicide to his narrator's mind. The novel is light and funny in all kinds of marvellous ways, but we shall miss everything if we miss its darkness.

Kinbote is even more distressed at Shade's one mention of Zembla than he is at the country's almost perfect absence from the poem. Absence after all can be remedied, interpreted, filled out; a sort of opportunity once you get the hang of it. A casual, heartless reference is much harder to deal with. Shade writes 'and now I plough/Old Zembla's fields', a whimsical evocation of the bumpy landscape of his face as he shaves. Kinbote, old Zembla himself, says 'I am a weary and sad commentator today'. 'So this is all treacherous old Shade could say about Zembla – my Zembla? While shaving his stubble off? Strange, strange . . .' Pope's line on Zembla, which Kinbote quotes, is scarcely more consoling: 'At Greenland, Zembla, or the Lord knows where'. Zembla, it seems, is a mere name for distance; for what is unknown, far enough away for us not to care what it is like.

In context, however, Pope's Zembla is an image not of distance but of relativity – and relativity precisely where it might seem to have little place, in matters of compass points and of vice. We cannot agree on the location of 'th'Extreme of Vice', Pope suggests, any more than we can finally settle where the North is:

> Ask where's the North? At York, 'tis on the Tweed;
> In Scotland, at the Orcades; and there,
> At Greenland, Zembla, or the Lord knows where:
> No creature owns it in the first degree,
> But thinks his neighbour farther gone than he.

The brilliant, multiplying jokes take the breath away; even Nabokov looks a very modest magician alongside this performance. 'It' is both vice and the north; 'owns' is both possession and confession; 'degree' is latitude in every sense and also grade, stage, grammatical term, social condition and what the dictionary calls a 'step in direct genealogical descent'; 'farther gone' makes sure that both geography and morality are still in play. This is part of what Pope means when he speaks of his concision, says he can express his 'principles, maxims, or precepts . . . more shortly' in verse than in prose.

Vice is elsewhere. It is so hideous that we have only to see it to hate it, Pope claims, but we then become familiar with its face, and familiarity breeds a sort of affection, or at least intimacy: 'We first endure, then pity, then embrace'. It is because we have embraced vice, Pope is suggesting, that we cannot confess its extremity in us, own up to it. And we cannot possess it, do not own it, because it owns us. Zembla then is a figure of plausible illusion. Vice is not really like the north, a matter of relative location. It is a sort of ruined or muffled absolute, our arguments are evasions, its proclaimed relativity merely the work of our hypocrisy. But then Nabokov produces *his* great trick, a swerve even Pope could not manage. He makes vice itself both judge and jury, has the lamentable, self-aggrandizing, self-accusing Kinbote, master of displacements, speak to us from the heart of the deluded moral universe Pope so ruthlessly identifies. Kinbote calls to us from a world of jittery relativity, a place composed entirely of second and third degrees. His is not th' extreme of vice, of course, but his consciousness of vice is extreme, and so is his unhappiness. The unbearable Kinbote asks us, in Pope's words, to endure him and pity him; the person not the vice, the sinner not the sin. Can we also embrace him? He scarcely dares hope it, and doesn't ask. Even if we can't, he has brought us very close to Christian charity. To the idea of charity, I mean; to what it would be if we were up to it.

(ii)

John Shade's poem is not about Zembla, and Kinbote's disappointment is crucial, along with his attempted piracy, and the cramming of his commentary with everything he thinks the poem should have contained. But if Kinbote can't find Zembla in Shade's *Pale Fire*, he does see himself in the poem's picture of Hazel, Shade's awkward, lonely, ugly daughter, whose very smile is a sign of pain: 'it is true that Hazel Shade resembled me in certain respects.' We can take his connection to the poem much further than this because the poem is, in part at least, about the objects of pity and pity's inadequacies.

Shade's ostensible subject is what he calls 'survival after death'. This is doubly his subject, because the general question has long haunted him and because his daughter Hazel committed suicide after being stood up on a date. Another world (another life) would not only allow him to see her again, it might allow her to be happy. The poem opens (and according to Kinbote was also meant to close, the missing line 1000 repeating line 1) with an image which projects the poet himself into death and beyond:

> I was the shadow of the waxwing slain
> By the false azure in the windowpane;
> I was the smudge of ashen fluff – and I
> Lived on, flew on, in the reflected sky.

Shade becomes a shadow: killed by a mistaken perception, a bird crossing into the wrong element, taking a reflected sky for an actual one – the sort of mistake would-be realists are always making in Nabokov. He is also the bird's fluff, presumably the smudge of feathers which remained on the window after the smash; mortal and immortal.

Shade's past tenses are a little strange. Does he mean to say these are among the acts of imagination he has performed in his life, the things and places he has been in his mind? Is he situating himself beyond death? Foreseeing his own death, which occurs on the day he finishes his poem? The bird's death by error would glance at the manner of Shade's own killing. This strikes me as entirely plausible but not all that interesting – the sort of thing that adepts of Nabokov's excesses of artistry admire a lot. Even more elaborate, but also more interesting, is Brian Boyd's argument that Shade is here discreetly announcing his own *fake* death, his plan to haunt his own life in the form of the imaginary Kinbote, Shade's own invention. The reflected sky would then be Kinbote's commentary, where Shade lives on in disguise, discoursing through Kinbote's craziness on the complacency of his own poem. This is a challenging theory and may well – Boyd is persuasive on this score – represent Nabokov's own secret sense of his novel, or his sense of his novel's secret. It's certainly more appealing than the reverse theory, which makes Shade an invention of Kinbote's. But both sorts of theory, to my mind, embrace Nabokov's fictions a little too eagerly, are too keen to make them seem natural, even plausible, within their own world. I can't see the interpretative need for the claim that either of these characters has invented the other. I like their unresolved difference, see the echoes between their stories as part of Nabokov's larger sense of echo, not as a sign that there is only one fictional mind at work. There is only one actual, authorial mind at work, but if Nabokov meant to duplicate himself (twice) in Shade, he probably did well to keep this secret to himself. He trusted the text, and the text is richer than his plans.

The simplest and strangest of the meanings of the past tenses leads us straight to one of the poem's main arguments. Shade can call himself the metaphorical shadow of a slain bird because he is remembering an occasion on which he literally died and did not die. Some time after Hazel's death he has a fit or heart attack, which repeats a number of incidents in his childhood ('There was a sudden sunburst in my head . . ./I felt distributed through space and time'), and recalls Pnin's seizures of heart and memory. Shade is sure he has died, spent a moment beyond the border of life, like any number of characters in Poe. He saw a tall white fountain 'dreadfully distinct/Against the dark', and cannot shake off his sense of the truth of what he has seen, his conviction that it was not a dream or a hallucination but a perception, a glimpse of a world not known to mortals. 'My vision reeked with truth. It had the tone,/The quid-dity and quaintness of its own/Reality. It *was*' ...' He seems to find confirmation of his vision in a magazine account of what a Mrs Z, brought back to life after a heart attack, experienced 'beyond the veil'. Among the angels and the muzak and other predictable kitsch, Mrs Z is said to have seen 'a tall white fountain'. Mrs Z is no great help to Shade when he visits her ('She plied me with fruit cake, turning it all/Into an idiotic social call'), but the journalist who wrote the story provides a dazzling and unexpected piece of news, which instantly ruins all Shade's hopes of 'objective' corroboration of his vision. Mrs Z didn't see a fountain.

> There's one misprint – not that it matters much:
> *Mountain*, not *fountain*. The majestic touch.

What happens now is crucial to Shade and his poem, and an essen-tial feature of Nabokov's own theology for sceptics. Shade does not retreat to his own earlier conviction of the truth of his vision, and he does not (exactly) give the vision up. He takes the misprint as the meaning, a wilder, more entertaining instance of order and design in life.

> it dawned on me that *this*
> Was the real point, the contrapuntal theme;
> Just this: not text, but texture; not the dream
> But topsy-turvical coincidence,
> Not flimsy nonsense, but a web of sense.

Life is not only a work of art but a work of elegant mischief, of eerie frivolity. It makes 'ornaments/Of accidents and possibilities'. Or rather 'they' do, whoever they are.

> It did not matter who they were. No sound,
> No furtive light came from their involute
> Abode, but there they were, aloof and mute,
> Playing a game of worlds ...

Shade, I think, is not asking us to believe in these creatures, only to imagine them, to be pleased by the thought of their 'plexed artis-try', to find in the contemplation of their elaborate game 'something of the same/Pleasure in it as they who played it found'.

are, as Tony Sharpe puts it, 'the annals of a mind which hasn't travelled very far', and Kinbote himself astutely says of a later part of the poem that Shade does not keep the grander promises he makes ('The poet like a fiery rooster seems to flap his wings in a preparatory burst of would-be inspiration, but the sun does not rise'). What the poem patiently suggests is that Shade's untravelled life allows him to concentrate on small treasures of perception. Of course, we shouldn't be too literal about this. Those small treasures are metonymies, meant to stand for much more than they name, for everything Shade is discreetly *not* saying about his love for Sybil and the way he sees the world. They are beautiful and they are precise, but even so there is a lot their tininess will not carry; they are in this sense quite unlike the indirections of Kinbote and Humbert and others of Nabokov's detail-haunted characters.

'Newlydead', however, has a darkness in its cleverness, and Shade's argument, as distinct from his claim to passion, is eloquent and moving, a declaration of love for life itself. The problem, which leads us into the heart of the poem, is that such an afterlife, one that stored all that was cherished in mortal flesh and time, would continue us as we are, unedited, unchanged, finding again all our mistakes as well as all our treasures. Hazel Shade would live again, the object of her parents' love; but also die again, the victim of their pity. Perhaps it is as well that Shade is wrong about all this, or that he dies in his untested belief.

Nabokov is almost certainly parodying a certain kind of teenage romance in the story of Hazel, a whole sentimental America of hazy glamour and smooth sorrow, but it is very hard to imagine John Shade doing this with his own daughter's death. There is a large element of bathos in Shade's poem, an overwrought shallowness where he seems to be aiming for depth. He has done parental anguish in close-up and young torment in long-shot, so that Hazel's suicide almost appears to be something that happens to him rather than to her. She becomes, as characters and events in Nabokov so often do, a realization of a person's worst fears, acts out the logic at the end of the nightmare. It's not at all clear what her own interest in this scenario is, or could be. She goes out on a blind date, her partner takes one look at her, fakes an excuse to be off, and leaves. Unable to bear this last confirmation of her ugliness, Hazel ends her life. It is a judgement on Shade and his wife, I think, that they find this flat little story so reasonable, and sufficient; terrible, but not out of line with their expectations.

They do love their daughter; but they cannot simply love her, cannot shake off the sense that she is a genetic and cultural disaster. She's fat and she squints, and she looks like her father, who in turns looks lumpy and androgynous (Kinbote says Shade's face 'reminded one of a fleshy Hogarthian tippler of indeterminate sex').

> She might have been you, me, or some quaint blend:
> Nature chose me so as to wrench and rend
> Your heart and mine.

There are all kinds of disavowals and burials here. If Hazel had been a boy, I take it, not much of this agony would have arisen – or it would not have been agony. She would have grown up clumsy and uncertain, but not doomed, and someone might have married her, as Sybil married the grateful Shade ('How could you . . ./Have let uncouth, hysterical John Shade/Blubber your face, and ear, and shoulder blade?'). Girls, the assumption is, have at least to be 'quaint'.

The agent here is 'Nature', choosing a course of action which will 'wrench and rend' the parents' hearts. Nothing is said about the child's heart, and a little later, when Shade reports on Hazel getting only the part of Mother Time in the school panto ('A bent charwoman with slop pail and broom'), he describes himself as sobbing 'like a fool' in the men's room, and doesn't mention Hazel's feelings at all. 'Like a fool' is self-congratulating rather than self-accusing: he gave in (foolishly) to what he thinks is his far from foolish emotion. Nature is a culture which has been internalized as inevitable, or rather is a curious cross between biology and manners: nature is desire *and* the way it is written and read in America in the 1950s. There is a life for the sexually unattractive, but no one wants it, not even the sexually unattractive themselves. When Sybil, through Shade, voices and opposes this prejudice, the argument is shrill and ridiculous, fails to express anything except their own complicity in the baleful myth:

> 'But this is prejudice! You should rejoice
> That she is innocent. Why overstress
> The physical? She *wants* to look a mess.
> Virgins have written some *resplendent* books.
> Lovemaking is not everything. Good looks
> Are not *that* indispensable!'

Good looks *are* indispensable if they are the only currency you recognize. Hazel doesn't want to look a mess. The bogus word *resplendent* cries out Sybil's lack of conviction. The poem continues with these amazing, beautiful, heartless lines, where Nature again is blamed for a human addiction to conventions:

> And still
> Old Pan would call from every painted hill,
> And still the demons of our pity spoke . . .

Old Pan is ancient sex and modern dating, everything Hazel is not going to get. No man will want her or lay her, or more decorously, Jerome Kernishly put, 'no lips would share the lipstick of her smoke'; 'a white-scarfed beau/Would never come for her; she'd never go,/A dream of gauze and jasmine, to that dance'.

The clichés suggest that Nabokov at least, if not Shade, knows there is something seriously wrong here. But even Shade understands that pity is demonic, a destructive, unwelcome emotion. Shade insists that Hazel was his 'darling': 'difficult, morose – /But still my darling' – and we have no reason to doubt him. What troubles us (troubles me) is Shade's and Sybil's assumption that pity in this case, however unwelcome, is unquestionably the right emotion, entirely grounded, what anyone would feel. They cannot keep their pity out of their love; keep it, their language suggests, from swamping their love. When Shade says of Hazel – these are his last words about her before he recounts the night of her suicide – 'I think she always nursed a small mad hope', the hope in question is simply, terminally, that a man will desire her. If this was all her hope, to the degree that its dashing was enough to lead her to kill herself, she was surely more a victim of the manners of her time than anyone has to be or should be. Perhaps her other small mad hope was that her parents would be able to think of something other than her sexual unattractiveness, put it out of their minds, and just love her. Both parents seem in this respect like modern, sex-ridden variants on the pushy mothers in Jane Austen.

Isn't this going too far, taking these slight figures as much more substantial and problematic than they can be, behaving as if a realist's child psychology and social concern were relevant to this fantastic and satirical novel? No doubt; and we should add that it is easy to be humane with hindsight, when the beauty-loving fifties are long enough gone. It's not that we don't (excessively) love beauty even now, but we do love other things too. It's also true that the desperate unhappiness of sexual need, or more broadly of feeling unwanted or unwantable, is a vivid reality at any time, and not only for those who are (thought to be) ugly. My suggestion is simply that Hazel's parents' pity must be part of the problem, and seems weirdly foregrounded in Shade's consciousness, and therefore in ours. This precisely is the link with Kinbote. When he says Hazel resembles him in certain respects, we catch a rare glimpse of Nabokov behind him, offering an unusually broad clue to something he is anxious his readers should not miss, what he would call a 'structural' effect: the demons of pity are at work in both realms, poem and commentary, Shade's and Kinbote's, a sign that love has been harried and dwarfed, rendered insufficient (for Hazel); become unavailable and even unthinkable (for our narrator). This is what I have called hell, where the demons are, the end of the emotional world.

Kinbote sees himself in Hazel, but he doesn't always want us to see him seeing himself in this way. Hazel's story is his story, including the rejections and the thoughts of suicide, and he gives us all the connections we need; but he also projects her as 'other', someone he himself might pity, a resemblance not an identity. At times, indeed, he sees her as a kind of enemy, too much on Shade's mind. This is another way, perhaps, of getting at the horror of Kinbote's sense of himself, the displacement and the denial, his erratic zig-zagging from indulgence to abasement.

'Hazel' here is the textual Hazel of Shade's poem, which Kinbote has read again and again, the girl who appears chiefly as a calamity that has happened to her parents; and the Hazel he has reconstructed from a conversation with Shade's former secretary, who is also the cousin of the young man who backed off from the blind date. There is a delicate irony in Kinbote's finding the poem's account of Hazel 'quite clear and complete; maybe a little too complete, architectonically, since the reader cannot help feeling that it has been expanded amd elaborated to the detriment of certain other richer and rarer matters ousted by it'. 'The reader' is the jealous Kinbote himself, finding too much Hazel and not enough Zembla in the poem. Still, the comment can be read in several ways, and we have already glanced at some of the other matters ousted by the completeness/complacency of Shade's story.

Kinbote understands that Shade is 'lacerated with pity' for Hazel – this time in connection not with her looks or her chances but with a poltergeist that assailed her when she was sixteen. But Shade's pity, again, seems to involve a kind of genetic guilt, since he wonders whether Hazel's poltergeist may not be related to his own boyhood fits, and Kinbote notes that the Shades were '*afraid of Hazel* and afraid to hurt her' (my italics). Later he invents a 'scene' with father, mother and daughter which he feels 'cannot be too far removed from the truth', and which expresses far more understanding of Hazel's anger and frustration than either parent seems to manage. The last stage direction is

> Two minutes pass. Life is hopeless, afterlife heartless. Hazel is heard quietly weeping in the dark. John Shade lights a lantern. Sybil lights a cigarette. Meeting adjourned.

What has happened is that Hazel has been seeing strange lights in an old barn, and has wanted her parents to witness them with her. They are decent enough to go along, not patient enough to watch with her for very long, and they see nothing. I don't know how much we are to gather from the fact that a little earlier, returning from one of her solitary vigils in the barn, Hazel catches sight of a 'phantastic figure' as she returns home, and lets out 'a howl of terror'. The figure is her father, in pyjamas and bathrobe, made motley by patches of darkness and pale gleams from the porch light.

Hazel then is Kinbote's rival in the poem, taking up what he thinks is his space. And she *is* him, the stranger, the exile, the unwanted, the one visited by visions. Nothing is more revealing than Kinbote's gloss on the events leading up to her suicide. In the poem, the boy takes one look at Hazel and invents his excuse: 'suddenly Pete Dean/Clutching at his brow exclaimed that he had clean forgotten an appointment with a chum/Who'd land in jail if he, Pete, did not come,/Et cetera . . .' The 'et cetera', like the clutched brow, marks Shade's disbelief. Kinbote reports, naively or deviously, Pete's cousin's assertion that the boy 'might have exaggerated a bit, but certainly did not fib' about his dramatic appointment. He is at this point more interested in the boy (he has been looking at photographs of him) than in the unfortunate Hazel, and says rather grandly, 'Such obligations are not to be treated lightly or disdainfully'. Indeed not, when they exist. Kinbote's homophilia has romanticized a shabby excuse, made a noble male romance out of it, a miniature Zembla. He is forgetting Hazel, in the way he keeps forgetting the probably imaginary Disa for his probably imaginary pleasures. And yet he forgets himself as he does this, heedlessly or desperately indulges a more flamboyant self at the expense of a sadder one, since he is himself so regularly forgotten, always outside, always too late, the person the poem does not reflect or record, and whom life (as represented by his defecting boyfriends) seems to treat much as the poem does. Can we, or anyone, reach him except through the demons of our pity?

(iii)

How does John Shade meet his death? In one sense the answer is easy. He is shot as he approaches, in Kinbote's company, the house Kinbote has rented. Kinbote's gardener hits the killer on the head, and takes his gun. The killer is arrested. Here is where the paths fork. There is a plain-seeming story; and there is Kinbote's version, fantastic, grandiose and self-admiring. We arrive at the plain story, however, by reading *across* Kinbote's; he is our only source. In Henry James, we often understand meanings the narrator would rather keep from us, guess at much that is not said. In Gogol and Nabokov we have to disbelieve the declared story, what is actually said to us, in order to arrive at a simple truth. The simple truth is a matter of interpretative labour, the wild fantasy easier to get at: a good philosophical joke.

The truth, then, seems to be that the killer is one Jack Grey, an escapee from a prison for the criminally insane, who sought to avenge himself on the judge who put him away. Shade resembles the judge; and Kinbote is living in the judge's house while the judge is away in England. Grey is in the right place, but has the wrong person. This story seeps slowly but clearly enough through Kinbote's story, partly because he denies it far too vehemently ('ridiculous stories about the terrifying shadows that Judge Goldsworth's gown threw across the underworld'), mainly because he talks about it when he doesn't need to. He is the one who says, with a sarcasm that backfires into shrillness, 'let us not forget Jack Grey!', and introduces into his Zembla the slightly compromising analogy of 'hoodlums who itch to torture the invulnerable gentleman whose testimony clapped them in prison for life' . Admittedly the analogy has plural hoodlums and concerns testimony rather than sentence, but we can be forgiven for thinking it has crept in to Kinbote's mind from the very story he wishes to deny.

Kinbote's version is that Grey is not an American criminal but a Zemblan assassin, whose target was Kinbote/Charles II, and not Shade or the judge. 'It is evil piffle', Kinbote insists, 'to assert that he aimed not at me ... but at the gray-locked gentleman behind me'. The 'truth of the tragedy' is that Kinbote is 'not a "chance witness" but the protagonist, and the main, if only potential victim'. The killer is merely 'posing as Jack Grey', the simple truth is a front, the *sort* of truth we are ready to believe. Kinbote supports this claim with a whole life-history of the assassin, whom he identifies as Jakob Gradus (also known as Jack Degree or Jacques de Gray, or James de Gray, other aliases Ravus, Ravenstone and d'Argus), and by a detailed account of his quest for the exiled king, and his travels to America. The killer himself is not going to confirm or deny either story, since as Gradus or Grey, Zemblan assassin or American killer, he is dead in prison, having cut his throat with a razor blade. Kinbote claims to have spoken to him in gaol before he died, but his vagueness doesn't inspire confidence: 'I did manage to obtain, soon after his detention, an interview, perhaps even two interviews, with the prisoner'. Earlier Kinbote speaks of his 'last interview with the jailed killer', which indicates more than one interview, but he also speaks of 'a long talk I had with the killer'. The hesitation suggests Kinbote has not quite decided which story to tell (or has forgotten which story he is telling): what sort of basis he wants to claim for his intimate knowledge of Gradus/Grey's movements.

More suspicious still, but then *so* suspicious that it throws the whole question open again, is Kinbote's claim that Gradus' movements towards Shade are synchronized with Shade's writing his poem. This suggests that Gradus is less a person than a personification in time of Shade's imminent death. Shade is writing his death, getting closer to it as he gets closer to the end of the poem. Another way of putting this would be as a kind of narrative conundrum, about how hindsight is to be used in story-telling. Since Kinbote knows Shade is killed on the day he finishes his poem, it is for Kinbote unalterably true that Shade is writing his way towards his death. In *Lolita* Humbert writes of 'precise fate' as 'that synchronizing phantom', and Kinbote has cast himself as a sort of posterior fate. He is the phantom who converts belated knowledge into imputed design, mere sequence into intricate plot.

We shall accompany Gradus in constant thought, as he makes his way from distant dim Zembla to green Appalachia, through the entire length of the poem, following the road of its rhythm, riding past in a rhyme, skidding around the corner of a run-on, breathing with the caesura, swinging down to the foot of the page from line to line as from branch to branch ... steadily marching nearer in iambic motion, crossing streets, moving up with his valise on the escalator of the pentameter, stepping off, boarding a new train of thought, entering the hall of a hotel, putting out the bedlight, while Shade blots out a word, and falling asleep as the poet lays down his pen for the night.

The extended metaphor, almost an allegory, treats the poem as landscape, a vehicle, a city, a tree, a tempo; it places Gradus in the (written) poem, and in a parallel, cross-cut sequence with the writing of it. It is fanciful and complicated and a little precarious, but it does not (need not) trouble our sense of the independent fictional reality of Gradus, any more than Fielding's narrative antics compromise the fictional agency of Tom Jones. Kinbote tells us he was tempted to fake certain things, to synchonize Gradus' departure from Zembla with the exact date of Shade's beginning his poem, that is a few minutes into July 2, 1959. Alas, Gradus left home on July 5. Again, we wonder whether an invented person could possibly travel on anything but the perfectly appropriate date, but such apparent slippages, of course, in fiction, journalism and in ordinary lying, are among the ways you make untruths feel truthful. Later Kinbote abandons all such scruples (or tricks) and synchronizes to the minute Shade's beginning his poem with Gradus' election as the king's executioner. This is not only intricately 'composed', it is distinctly eerie, since it makes Shade's poem the start of his death and ties it magically to the conspiracy against Kinbote's life: as if the poem were plotting against its editor. There is a similar suggestion in the idea that 'the force propelling' Gradus 'is the magic action of Shade's poem itself, the very mechanism and sweep of verse, the powerful iambic motor'. Gradus is not only in the poem, parallel to the poem, he is driven by the poem. Kinbote's very artistry, his endless self-congratulation in this respect, is a form of paranoia, reveals that he cannot disentangle death and writing.

At other times Kinbote's overt compositional grasp is a little less secure:

> Gradus, after a refreshing night at the summer house of our consul in Copenhagen . . . had entered . . . a clothes store in order to conform to his description in later notes . . . Migraine again worse today.

This is rather like the reporting of the Christ of the gospels as doing certain acts 'that the Scriptures might be fulfilled', or Milton saying in *Paradise Lost* that God 'in order to render man inexcusable' sends Raphael down to tell Adam the whole story of the creation and the war in heaven. A later knowledge, a secret causality, ruffles the narrative syntax, creates interference in the electrical sense; a 'now' sneaks into the 'then', and a suspicious mind will imagine extensive rewriting, perhaps inventing, is going on. With Kinbote, a great gulf seems to open between two quite different situations. Either he has reconstructed (but not invented) Gradus' movements, elegantly synchronized them with what he knows about the composition of the poem; or he has made the whole business up, Gradus and his movements, and maybe (but to what extent?) the country Gradus came from. His migraine might seem to settle the matter but doesn't. He knows something sounds wrong, but perhaps it is just an artistic slip, a hurry into hindsight, an awkward conflation of two narrative orders. Or he has given the whole game away, momentarily blown the cover of his fantasy. He probably feels he has done the second, and we do too; but it ain't necessarily, textually so.

Gradus also appears elsewhere in the text, and on the wrong (the right) side. He is – the reversed letters of his name are – Sudarg of Bokay, a Zemblan mirrormaker; 'of genius', the index says, 'life span not known'. It is not surprising perhaps that the mirror image of an assassin should be a craftsman, but the existence of *both* of them does begin to look like a mirage; done with mirrors. Where are we? At this point we can, I think, cautiously identify another sort of truth; the truth not quite of fantasy but at least of metaphor and fiction. Gradus and most of Zembla may be Kinbote's fantasies; Jack Grey and the unhappy Kinbote/Botkin the literal inhabitants of John Shade's world, of Nabokov's fictional America. But someone killed John Shade. Death came for him; and Gradus, even more than a bungling Zemblan assassin, is a grotesque portrait of encroaching, intrusive death. The metaphor acknowledges accident, let's say, but lends it a story; it is no longer an empty or solitary or unhoused accident.

What the portrait suggests is not only that we all die, but that death can be pictured, needs to be pictured as a particular sort of enemy of life: dogged, unimaginative, inefficient, levelling, laughable, infirm, at times almost pitiable but also brutal, mindless, and even in error, lethal. One of Gradus' entries in the index describes him as 'lynching the wrong people', and this is a sort of synecdoche for his career. Death in this view is not merely the end of life, it is a mockery of it, what life is not, a form of anti-life. Of course Gradus is not *only* death. There are other ways of refusing life, and in some respects Gradus is also Kinbote himself, or a grey travesty of Kinbote's worst moments. Gradus reported attempts ('several times') to castrate himself are a nightmare parody of Kinbote's 'sterile pleasures' – seeming himself to be about to make just this connection,

Kinbote curtly writes, 'I think I shall break this note here'. Gradus is also a political portrait, in large part a portrait of a Stalinist, and it is no accident, I think, that the assassination of Trotsky hovers over the plot-line of *Pale Fire*: there are points where politics and ethics do meet. Of course Nabokov, outside the text, did not make much distinction between Leninists and Stalinists, or even between Stalinists and Trotskyites. But then history is a little louder than opinion in this case: is there a more famous instance of a killer from an authoritarian state crossing the Atlantic to murder a former ruler?

> Oh, surely, Gradus is active, capable, helpful, often indispensable. At the foot of the scaffold, on a raw and gray morning, it is Gradus who sweeps the night's powder snow off the narrow steps; but his long leathery face will not be the last one that the man who must mount those steps is to see in this world. It is Gradus who buys the cheap fiber valise that a luckier guy will plant, with a time bomb inside, under the bed of a former henchman. Nobody knows better than Gradus how to set a trap by means of a fake advertisement, but the rich old widow whom it hooks is courted and slain by another.

Kinbote is demoting death by addressing death's dim assistant. Or rather, he is distinguishing between death as a project, a design on life, and death as a result, an end and a beginning. He is also, in his way, echoing Donne, whose famous sonnet Sybil Shade translates into French ('*Ne sois pas fière, Mort! Quoique certains te disent/Et puissante et terrible, ah, Mort, tu ne l'es pas*'), attracting pedantic commentary from Kinbote: 'one deplores the superfluous ejaculation in the second line'.

Again we glimpse Nabokov behind Kinbote, inviting us to reread Donne's perspective-shifting portrait of death. Death is not 'mighty and dreadful', Donne says, indeed we may even feel sorry for 'poor Death', since it is inevitably foiled by the resurrection: 'those whom thou think'st thou dost overthrow,/Die not ...' Death is 'slave to fate, chance, kings, and desperate men' – Kinbote points us to what he sees as the personal application of the last four words – and at the last judgement death itself will die. The idea of death as a slave brings us back to Gradus: death can kill, we might say, diverging from Donne, but it can't kill whomever it wants to. It can only take orders; and often, the case of Gradus suggests, will bungle their execution.

Pale Fire ends with a vision of death as a better Gradus – still only Gradus, a matter of degree, still mindlessly bent on the destruction of what he cannot understand, but more efficient, not a project but a completion, the death no one can stave off for ever:

> somebody, somewhere, will quietly set out – somebody has already set out, somebody still rather far away is buying a ticket, is boarding a bus, a ship, a plane, has landed, is walking towards a million photographers, and presently he will ring at my door – a bigger, more respectable, more competent Gradus.

This is Kinbote's voice, of course, the voice of a man deeply caught up in his old royal fantasies. But there is genuine heroism here, a virtual refusal of the very mortality which seems to be acknowledged. Or at least of the terms on which this mortality is offered to us. This Gradus, the successful one, may be more respectable and more competent, but he is still an assassin, and death itself is pictured only as an act of pointless violence, incompatible with anything human we may care about. This is one of the meanings of what Kinbote calls his 'rather anti-Darwinian aphorism': 'The one who kills is *always* his victim's inferior'; nothing to be proud of. Death is not an event in life, Wittgenstein said. Kinbote cannot contemplate it as an event in nature. This is noble, the fantasy *is* a kind of truth; and whatever Nabokov says, it's hard to believe this man is ready for suicide. It is worth noting that what I am calling Kinbote's nobility is consistent with what seems to be Nabokov's own personal myth. Death in his work is almost always seen as a rough interruption, a violent discourtesy, a surprise. Lolita dies in childbirth, Humbert in prison. Adam Krug in *Bend Sinister* dies in a burst of gunfire and madness, the author twitching him out of pain into the dimension of words. Cincinattus C. receives a similar benefaction at the moment of his beheading. Sebastian Knight's father dies as a result of wounds received in a duel, his mother from a rare disease, Sebastian himself dies young from the same disease. Luzhin in *The Defence* throws himself out of a window to his death.

This is to say, perhaps, that the voice we hear at the end of *Pale Fire* is no longer just Kinbote's. He has attracted to himself, in the last paragraph, not only the identity of Nabokov (an identity of Nabokov), but something like the braveries of fiction itself, a form of freedom no earlier character in Nabokov attains. When previous characters in Nabokov discover they are characters in a novel, they think of themselves as authored, their lives scripted, written from elsewhere. Kinbote sees himself not only as a character in a novel but as the potential author of other works of fiction. He also seems to know, as Joyce's Molly Bloom does ('Jamesy, let me up out of this'), *whose* fiction he is in. If he manages to avoid suicide ('God will help me, I trust, to rid myself of any desire to follow the example of two other characters in this work' – not people in his world, we note, but 'characters in this work', the novel that his edition of Shade's *Pale Fire* has become), he expects to 'assume other disguises, other forms':

> I may turn up yet, on another campus, as an old, happy, healthy, heterosexual Russian, a writer in exile, sans fame, sans future, sans audience, sans anything but his art . . . I may pander to the simple tastes of theatrical critics and cook up a stage play, an old-fashioned melodrama with three principles: a lunatic who intends to kill an imaginary king, another lunatic who imagines himself to be that king, and a distinguished old poet who stumbles by chance into the line of fire, and perishes in the clash between the two figments. Oh, I may do many things!

If Kinbote were to turn up in the form he describes, he would be Nabokov as Nabokov often seems to have thought of himself: the fictional creation of someone who might in turn be fictional; a man who after all needed the conclusive evidence of autobiography for himself as well as for others. But the deepest and most mischievous implication here is not personal and psychological but philosophical, or at least speculative. The echo of Jacques' speech in *As You Like It* reminds us that all the world's a stage, which in this context suggests we cannot tell the stage from the stalls, or where the acting ends. Or to put that more ambitiously, in the language of Kinbote's projected melodrama, people perish not only from the discourse of others, as Barthes says, but from the very imagination of others, caught in the clash of lurid figments. It is even possible that more people have died in such clashes than in any other, that dreams of race and tribe and religion, for example, have killed more people than all our pragmatic-looking wars.

The order of Kinbote's *dramatis personae* is important, and we recognize, with a touch of dizziness, that while his plot seems to have come from the novel we have just read, it is curiously scrambled, doesn't match our reading in any coherent fashion. There is a lunatic intending to kill an imaginary king – a Grey who somehow thought he was Gradus. There is another lunatic who imagines himself to be 'that king' – a Kinbote who would not only be clearly identified as mad but would seem to be invading someone else's lunatic fantasy. And Shade either way, as in 'reality', whatever version we take, dies because someone driven by long imaginings, of vengeance or instructions, seeks to act out in the world the tortures of the head and heart.

A character in a novel by Thomas Pynchon, a one-time student of Nabokov's at Cornell, thinks the First World War 'destroyed a kind of privacy, perhaps the privacy of dream. Committed us . . . to work out three o'clock anxieties, excesses of character, political hallucinations on a live mass, a real human population'. If all the world's a stage, there is no privacy, no security of wings or dressing rooms; no place to hide from the competing figments. And yet the figments, terrible and playful, brilliant and banal, are ours, and if Kinbote even at his lightest keeps calling up horror and darkness he also evokes possibility, the 'many things' he may do.

> History permitting, I may sail back to my recovered kingdom, and with a great sob greet the gray coastline and the gleam of a roof in the rain. I may huddle and groan in a madhouse.

He will hang on to his fantasy, or he will have to let it go. He may continue to exist, as he says, or he may submit to his thoughts of death, become his own Gradus. What matters is not what happens but what might happen, the multiple chances, the darkness confronted but not, for the moment, embraced. This is one of the more attractive meanings of 'fiction'; another life of the kind John Shade couldn't see and didn't get. Perhaps Kinbote will turn up not as Nabokov, but as someone quite different from his former self and from his author; like Pnin becoming a martinet.

9
Happy Families:
Ada

a novel in the old mood then
will occupy my gay decline

Pushkin, *Eugene Onegin*

(i)

To read *Ada* is to enter a sickly and elaborate world, a sort of hell which parades as paradise; or a genuine paradise which is so broken, threatened, haunted, gloated over that it feels like an enhancement of hell. This is a novel about a magically achieved happiness – several happinesses – but it also describes happiness as an 'ordeal' and as a 'tiger', and contrives to take it away on the swiftest and flimsiest excuses.

Ada looks – wants to look – like a gleeful, unrepentant celebration of the life of the senses, the infinitely particular details of physical pleasure, with underage sex and incest thrown in just to show how recklessly indifferent our author and fictional lovers are to the morbid conventions which hamper the rest of us. We shouldn't underestimate Nabokov's successes in this line. The twelve-year-old Ada Veen says she is 'physical, horribly physical', sounding like a popular song of the 1980s; she is even more physical than her athletic fourteen-year-old brother/lover Van Veen:

> Their craving for each other grew unbearable if within a few hours it was not satisfied several times, in sun or shade, on roof or in cellar, anywhere. Despite uncommon resources of ardor, young Van could hardly keep pace with his pale little *amorette* . . . Their immoderate exploitation of physical joy amounted to madness . . .

This sounds like an old man's fantasy about youth, with a little myth of female sexual rapacity thrown in; and no doubt it is. But detail is all, as Nabokov and his favourite characters keep telling us,

206

and what Nabokov manages to do in *Ada* is to convert the indelicate excess of recurring sex scenes into an extraordinary delicacy of detail; to evoke the separate moments of an endlessly differentiated sexual experience, rather than its clinical or moral generalities.

> After the first contact, so light, so mute, between his soft lips and her softer skin had been established – high up in that dappled tree, with only that stray ardilla daintily leavesdropping – nothing seemed changed in one sense, all was lost in another. Such contacts evolve their own texture; a tactile sensation is a blind spot; we touch in silhouette.

'Ardilla' is Spanish for squirrel, but also seems to be a little Ada, given a few extra letters and set loose in a pastoral animal kingdom. 'Leavesdropping' is Nabokov's invention: the squirrel is listening in on the lovers' mute meeting, and dropping leaves, and perhaps dropping through the leaves. This first contact is fleeting and accidental, though, and we continue for a while to see Ada through Van's unfulfilled and unmanageable desire, his still unassuaged appetite for 'her pale, voluptuous, impermissible skin'.

> Very lightly he let his parched lips travel down her warm hair and hot nape. It was the sweetest, the strongest, the most mysterious sensation that the boy had ever experienced . . .

Before long, and perhaps too easily, the children become lovers in the fullest sexual sense. Too easily for the novel's good, I mean, rather than for theirs. Ada responds to Van's blossoming desire, we are told, because 'nature is motion and growth'. That's nice to know, but nature's motion and growth isn't always so helpful.

The lovers learn each other's bodies as if they were strange countries.

> She was shaded with a mere touch of coal at the mystery point of her chalk-white body. A bad boil had left a scar between two ribs. He kissed it, and lay back on his clasped hands. She was inspecting from above his tanned body the ant caravan to the oasis of the navel; he was decidely hirsute for so young a boy. Her young round breasts were just above his face.

This – and there is 'much, much more', as the novel's last words say in a slightly larger context – is the erotic as an art of memory, for the characters, grown older. As an art of the imagination (I take it) for Nabokov and us. The imagination ('individual, magically detailed imagination') is defined elsewhere in *Ada* as 'third sight': not an evasion of reality, and not, quite, a reconstruction of it. More like divination, the scrupulous invention of what's already there. In spite of (or because of) a certain slackness in its plotting, the book is full of brilliantly imagined, intimately specified, thoroughly realized sexual acts and facts.

Van, recollecting his early love in extreme old age (ninety-seven plus when he corrects the proofs of the text we are reading) gets a little nervous at times, and writes brutally and flippantly because he is nervous. But then Ada, whose late notes are also included in our text, rebukes him for making their pure love sound like 'a dirty farce', and for resorting to 'vague anatomical terms that a psychiatrist remembers from his student days'. When Van writes of their 'freely and dirtily and delightfully' indulging in their sexual exercises, he himself remarks that he is trying to 'trivialize' his excitement with a fake 'moral corrective'. And even then, this and other trivializations seem to represent a fear of feeling, and later on a fear that the sheer weight of old happiness will break him down, rather than moral qualms of any seriousness.

It's true that Van does use the word 'seduced' when he finally speaks to his father about the affair ('I seduced your daughter', 'I seduced her in the summer of eighteen eighty-four'), but he's being gentlemanly, and he is speaking the language his father (no mean seducer himself) will understand. It's also true that the lovers describe their childhood affair as 'too early' and 'much too premature', but this is more because they like the thought that someone (their parents, the neighbours, the servants, the reader) is going to be shocked than because they feel any sort of shock themselves. And the idea of incest merely amuses them. They can see it's a problem for breeders, of humans and sheep, but they can't see how such vulgar practicalities apply to them – and in any case, as they later learn, Van is sterile, so there would be no question of these children having children. The case is closed. Taboo? What taboo?

Well, there is a certain amount of play with incest as a grand romantic theme, associated with Chateaubriand and Byron, and the word hovers in the children's Scrabble games (insect, scient, incest) and the adults' related anagrammatical jokes ('He was omniscient. Better say, omni-incest'). But none of this goes beyond faint naughtiness, a sense of what might cause a shiver in *other* people. Van and Ada are, as Ada says, the 'superimperial couple, *sverhimperatorskaya cheta*', a prodigious, exceptional pair even among 'billions of brilliant couples'. This is their life: 'to be inquired into, to be painted, to be denounced, to be put to music, or to the question and death . . .' They can do what they want, and they do. They ought to be happy, and they are.

Yet something tugs at this guilt-free world, this paradise of sex and the senses, and if it isn't guilt, what is it? We need a rather fuller grasp of the novel's plot to answer this question, and a sense of its scenes and images, its texture.

About halfway through the book Nabokov offers us a lengthy family portrait, or home movie, a full-blown intimate dinner-party, 'a family of four seated around an oval dinner table, bright with flowers and crystal'. The food and wine are good (well, pretty good), and described in great detail; the conversation is lively, although not nearly as scintillating (or as funny) as it is probably supposed to be. Father drinks a lot, mother seems vaguely out of it, the children show off: an ordinary evening in New England, if a little posher than most of us manage most nights. Yet the children feel there was something 'faintly off-key' about the whole show, and we know there is something more than faintly off-key about it, that Nabokov has set it up as an elaborately reversed *trompe l'oeil*, a picture of the truth which is supposed to look like a fake. This is the nuclear family in its basic form: the father, Dementiy Veen, the mother Marina Veen, the son Van Veen, the daughter Ada Veen. Except that these are only the biological facts, and the social facts, the visible historical arrangements, are quite different. Dementiy is (or was) married not to Marina but to Marina's sister Aqua, now dead; Marina is married to Dementiy's cousin Daniel, who should have been here tonight, but was delayed so that Nabokov could set up this complicated visual illusion. Van and Ada, as far as the world knows, are first cousins, belonging to two separate marriages: Dementiy is his acknowledged father, Marina is her acknowledged mother. Lucette, the actual daughter of Daniel and Marina, is either away from home or in bed, and her absence is signalled by two occurrences of the same question about her. 'By the way, how's Lucette?' Dementiy asks, but doesn't get a reply because dinner is served. Later he asks again, but by this time he's ready to go, and doesn't wait for an answer. Lucette's invisibility reinforces the direct biological display, just as her presence would have complicated the picture.

One more time, since this is pretty complicated: Aqua and Marina, twins, married Dementiy and Daniel, cousins; Dementiy had an affair with Marina, both before and after Marina's marriage;

Van and Ada are the children of that affair. There's a nice slippage
in the family scene when Marina says to Ada 'You know quite well
that your father disapproves of your smoking at table.' Dementiy,
relaxed, murmurs, 'Oh, it's all right', and Marina has to insist that
she had her husband in view, Ada's nominal and legal father. The
children already know – have known for four years, since they discovered all kinds of tell-tale papers in an attic – about their actual
parentage; but their parents still don't know they know.

Nabokov loves these mirror effects, these double delusions.
They're very tricky at first sight, vertigo-inducing; but they are
structured by a powerful logic, which wants us to keep seeing (at
least) two stories at once – in this case, the present, public story and
the old, sentimental one. If we can do this, we shall do better than
Dementiy, who can't find his former mistress in the new coarsened
lady, and is aggrieved by the 'complete collapse of the past'. In
Nabokov's most extravagant case in this novel, we are invited to
contemplate the story of the world of the fiction and the story of
the world outside it in reverse formation. We are happy enough
with the idea that novels depict fictional worlds. Why then – this is
how the logic goes – wouldn't characters in novels view our world
as fictional, possibly resembling their reality in some ways, but
largely fantastic and in many respects crazy.

Ada is set on a planet called Demonia, or Antiterra. Its history
and geography are ours, but scrambled in all kinds of unlikely
ways. The British annexed France after the battle of Waterloo; the
Crimean War was thirty years late. There were cars and other inventions on Demonia long before we had them, they had movies
even in the 1880s; but a terrible disaster resulted in a complete ban
on electricity, and its replacement by water as a source of power.
The Demonian population of North America is English and
Russian speaking – as if Nabokov's plight had become a nation –
and what we used to call Soviet Russia is just Tartary, a barbarous,
ignored realm on the other side of the world. There is much more
of this kind of stuff, some of it inventive and amusing, a lot of it
pretty plodding; we can see Nabokov splitting his sides, but it's not
always easy to laugh along. The ruler of France is Lord Goal,
Queen Victoria gets reversed into King Victor; Paris is Lute, Cambridge is Chose, Harvard is Aardvark; Borges appears as Osberg, T
S Eliot becomes a Jewish businessman, there are all kinds of jolly
attacks on Freud, tastelessly associated with Hitler in the name Dr
Sig Heiler. 'Marx *père*, the popular author of "historical" plays', is
a rather better gag, but in general the Nabokov of *Ada* has to work

pretty hard for his jokes, and we see the sweat and strain. For the Penguin edition of 1971 he even agreed to provide a set of notes, translating all the French phrases (Humbert, where are you now?), and heavily explaining a good number of wheezes which weren't any too lightfooted in the first place. 'Pat Rishin: a play on "patrician"... She Yawns: Chillon's.' Please.

What has happened here is that the 'idiotically sly novelist' of old has become the idiotically friendly punster; but behind both of them lurks a more interesting figure, a writer who cannot hear a word as saying only one thing if there is a chance that it can be got to say more, by whatever contortions of tongue or syntax. Of course, Nabokov is only dabbling in what was the delirious method of *Finnegans Wake*, but the spirit is the same. A commitment to puns, even to lame or laboured puns, signals a language haunted by meanings far in excess of the one in front of us. This is not exactly Benjamin's 'pure language', but there is a philosophical implication here, something like Wittgenstein's 'Whatever we see could be other than it is'. Everything we say is shadowed by a crowd of ghosts, speaking our own language or others. Language, even the most brilliant language, is a kind of shortfall of reason, a leap into graphic or phonetic chaos, the beginning of a story which loves nonsense, but not only nonsense, and (probably) has no end. Another, hyperbolic way of saying some of this would be to point, as Van/Nabokov does, to the 'curious affinity between certain aspects of Scrabble and those of planchette'. He means the way the letters on the table can seem to read or meet the minds of the players: Ada thinks the lamp needs more *kerosin* and the letters S,R,E,N,O,K,I are the ones she draws when it's her turn to play. We remember 'The Vane Sisters' too, and the spirits with a taste for acrostics, in Nabokov's own story and in Shakespeare. The Vane sisters, incidentally, appear in one of Van's dreams, but he thinks the name is just a version of his own.

Nabokov has marvellous puns in *Ada* as well as lamentable ones, but the real interest of the mirror game of fiction, the scrambled pun between worlds, is what happens to *our* world in the process. The world of *Ada* is a whimsical rendering of ours, if we take ours as primary. But from that world, ours is a lurid and unlikely dream, and there is considerable merit in seeing our world in this way, particularly if we would like to wake up and change it. The very existence of our Terra is contested on Antiterra; or rather not even contested, but assumed to be a delusion: 'deranged minds (ready to plunge into any abyss) accepted it in support and token of their own irrationality'. Thus the unfortunate Aqua actually imagines skyscrapers, refrigerators, aeroplanes, elevators, gramophones: all absent from Antiterra, and sure signs of her madness. Van, a psychologist, becomes a specialist in Terrology, and writes a 'philosophical novel' based on what his patients tell him about this fantasized other world.

> Sick minds identified the notion of a Terra planet with that of another world and this 'Other World' got confused not only with the 'Next World' but with the Real World in us and beyond us.

And that's just the sick minds. There is only one world, Nabokov is suggesting – 'this our sufficient world', as Van writes, although he writes from Demonia. We invent other worlds and next worlds, discover so-called new worlds, construct fictional and non-fictional worlds in words and on film and in other media, because we can't settle for the sufficiency of the one world we've got. Should we settle? What if one of those 'other' worlds should turn out actually to be another one, as distinct from a zone of our own or an extrapolation from it? If we exist, then the mad people of Antiterra are right, and their apparent delusions are intermittent revelations, glimpses of the real thing. Nabokov wants, as Brian Boyd and others have suggested, to keep open the possibility of a real other world, an after-life, for instance, and certainly he rails against the limitations of our cramped, one-shot, mortal, human life. But the possibility works as a warning against the impoverishment and complacency of our imagining rather than as a spiritualist wager, and Nabokov's texts are firmly sceptical, whatever his private beliefs.

What is the 'Real World in us and beyond us'? We remember the games with the word 'real' in *The Real Life of Sebastian Knight*. There is much similar mischief in *Ada*, and again, the mischief often makes brilliant sense. Physical sex, Dementiy's first encounter with Marina, then a twenty-four year old actress, seems to him a 'brief abyss of absolute reality between two bogus fulgurations of fabricated life'. This is an easily had reality, though, and a conventional one, since the lovers have linked between the acts of Marina's play. Van's stepping, during his and Ada's first summer together, into 'the green reality of the garden' is a little more complicated, although the contrast with the stage continues here. He has felt 'as if he were taking part in a play', and presumably the play includes all the inhabitants of the house, as well as the house itself as a social space. The green garden leads us straight into Marvell, which might be another story, but isn't, since Marvell's poem 'The Garden' is a recurring point of reference in *Ada*, and is also concerned with two (or more) worlds: the garden and the city, repose and ambition, the sea and the earth, the mind and material creation. There is just a chance that this 'green reality' will annihilate all that's made if we let it. And when Van finds himself 'stumbling on melons', he re-enacts Marvell's brilliant rural recreation of the fortunate fall. As if the very profusion of fruit turned paradise into a problem.

In the most often quoted discussion of 'reality' in the book, the word is said to have 'lost the quotes it wore like claws'; it becomes bare, vivid, indisputable reality, and for Van as for his father, this happens during the sexual act, except that now the whole of life, and not only a theatrical illusion, is judged by this reality; seems at best to need the old claws and at worst to be beyond the help of punctuation.

> For one spasm or two, he was safe. The new naked reality needed no tentacle or anchor; it lasted a moment, but could be repeated as often as he and she were physically able to make love. The color and fire of that instant reality depended solely on Ada's identity as perceived by him. It had nothing to do with virtue or the vanity of virtue in a large sense . . .

Instant reality. It is intense enough, and we recognize it; but it seems narcissistic in this description, saved from solipsism only by Ada's collaboration – and even then she merely provides an identity for Van to 'perceive'.

Her own sense of reality, and of 'reality' is more complex than his, and more generous, and she has a complete and playful theory to articulate it. She divides the world into '"real things" which were unfrequent and priceless, simply "things" which formed the routine stuff of life, and "ghost things", also called "fogs", such as fever, toothache, dreadful disappointments, and death.' What is notable here is that things, real things and ghost things can be material or immaterial, and that even apparently irresistible realities like toothache and death are ghostly to Ada; they can't be denied, perhaps, but they don't have to be allowed into the world as if they belong there. 'Children of her type contrive the purest philosophies', Van/Nabokov says, but I don't know what he/they mean by type. The philosophy is exactly Nabokov's own as I have tried to describe it in relation to pain and cruelty and death. Ghost things are not unreal, but they have no place in the 'Real World in us and beyond us', and neither do mere 'things'. Existence is not a qualification, any more than being alive is the same as living. Reality is an accolade for Ada, the name of an achievement or an exceptional piece of luck: breakfast on a balcony, clover honey glowing in the sun, a wasp on her plate, Van's presence.

More than half of *Ada* is dedicated to the evocation of two summers, 1884 and 1888, when Van and Ada are fourteen/twelve and eighteen/sixteen. They meet only four times, briefly, in the interval between these years; and after 1888 are separated again. They have brief seasons of happiness together in 1892 and 1905, but begin their long shared ever-after life only in 1922, when Van is fifty-two and Ada is fifty – you can always count on a chronophobe for an attention to the clock. There is a strong sense throughout the book that they are fated to love each other *and* to be sundered ('their much too premature and in many ways fatal romance'; 'she had always known that disaster would come today or tomorrow, a question of time or rather timing on the part of fate'); but fate in Nabokov is always a name for the author who's up to something, and in this case the characters are up to something too.

> 'But *this*,' exclaimed Ada, 'is certain, this is reality, this is pure fact, this forest, this moss, your hand, the ladybird on my leg, this cannot be taken away, can it? (it will, it was). *This* has all come together *here*, no matter how the paths twisted and fooled each other, and got fouled up: they inevitably met here!'

The four words in the bracket merely state what happened, with the grim conviction of hindsight: not a destiny but a report on a passionate historical and philosophical mistake. Of course the whole book cries out that Ada is not mistaken, that nothing was taken away ('nothing, nothing, nothing has changed'); an echo in fiction of the chief strategy of *Speak, Memory*. The moss and the ladybird are not gone since they are there *now*, in a multiple series of *nows*, as the late Van writes/remembers the young Ada's speech, and as we read it. But then the paradox of *Speak, Memory* also operates here: you can't deny your loss without naming it and suffering it again; without making evident that your verbal or remembered realities, however spectacular, are only verbal or remembered. Fate is ordinary time here, passing and piling up, and also something else: whatever suddenly takes cherished realities away, and whatever determines the timing of the theft. Fate is the author, fixing the plot; but the author in turn is chasing an insight, a sense of what has to go wrong, even in the blessed imagination. It's clear that Van and Ada are wonderfully happy when they are young and when they are old – well, let's say older; equally clear that they have missed, squandered, spent apart what should have been the best years of their love. The exceptional, superimperial quality of their relationship means, it seems, that they are allowed only small doses of it in their prime.

Yet what is striking about the hindrances to Van and Ada's love, once we have worked through the extraordinary detail of their being together and the fine pathos of their being apart, is not some awesome, fatal quality in the obstacles, the shadow of incest or the moral law; or a deep interdiction of the kind which structures *Tristan and Isolde* and *Romeo and Juliet*, the ban or barrier beneath the marriage or the feuding family, which may be a figure for the impossibility of love itself. It is just this impossibility that Nabokov wishes lyrically to deny: doom isn't necessary, happiness is real and available even for the star-crossed, and all happy families *are* happy in their own way. What separates Van and Ada, the series of events and considerations which separate them, is sheer contingency and convention, the very things your superimperial couples like to think they float above.

Van and Ada don't elope when they are young – as Nabokov, in *Speak, Memory*, reports himself trying to elope with the girl he calls Colette. Van meekly goes back to school and university, accepting as necessary the social structures of his time and family. In 1888 he is enraged by Ada's infidelities, and doesn't see her for four years – she is 'horribly physical', as she says, and she is also kind, she doesn't like to say no to the suffering desires of others, as we have seen with Van. Nature is motion and growth. In 1892, their father finds out about the affair, Van contemplates suicide but decides against it. Both accept their father's decree ('All right, I have bribed many officials in my wild life, but neither you nor I can bribe a whole culture, a whole country'). What happened to their amused indifference to the idea of incest, or indeed to their sense of what amounts to an additional attraction in it? When they piece together the puzzle and discover they are brother and sister – in their first summer together, 1884 – we learn that this is a 'confirmation of something both had forefelt in an obscure, amusing, bodily rather than moral way'. This seems to be a manner of saying that incest, for some people, is a magical magnet, draws them together even before they know what it is. Happy families are happy in their own special way. Ada marries a sturdy, boring fellow; she and Van steal a few delirious days together in 1905, plan to run off, but then the husband is ill, and Ada feels she must go back to him. Seventeen years later, free at last, Ada flies to Van, and after a scary, beautifully evoked moment in which they seem to each other like portly old folks in whom no trace of their childhood grace or allure remains, they find their old, unchanged love, as if they were redeemed and stately Humberts who had a real second chance with Lolita, and they live together, aging a lot and creaking a bit, but in 'a steady hum of happiness', until they ... Well, they don't quite die. They are alive at the book's end; are dead, an editor tells us, when we read it. They die '*into* the finished book' as Van hopefully puts it; they become their admirers, or if we can't admire them as much as they'd like, they become what Van calls their 'unknown dreamers', their alternately charmed and infuriated readers. They are us; they won't exist if we don't imagine them. This condition is cryptically imaged in the space between the helpful but also misleading family tree at the beginning of the book and the editorial note on the following page. In the family tree Ivan (1870-) and Adelaida (1872-) have only birth-dates; the note says that with a few minor exceptions 'all the persons mentioned by name in this book are dead. [Ed.]' Our heroes died *hors-texte*, as Derrida might say; there isn't a page it could have happened on. Well, in some editions, there is just one blank page – perhaps it happened there. The grisly little echo of *dead* and *Ed* is a prefatory bit of Nabokov signature, and a hint that language is always likely to get up and mock you.

Back to school; conventional male rage at an equally conventional female infidelity (see John Donne, Ariosto, and a line of jokes running from the Middle Ages to Marlene Dietrich); Dad's disapproval; the husband's sickness: it's hard to believe Nabokov couldn't have done better than this by way of impediments to a Great Love. At times he himself seems to mock the poverty of the impediments: 'he had to ... catch the same boat back to England – and join a circus tour which involved people he could not let down'. Sounds a bit like Pete's reason for calling off his date with Hazel in *Pale Fire*, but why would Van be making such excuses to Ada? I think we are meant to feel the lameness here, sense that Van is actually frightened of the love which is his life; but elsewhere I'm not so sure. There does seem to be a genuine failure of the imagination, or of the patience which leads to invention, at the level of the plot. Nabokov couldn't get himself, or couldn't wait, to realize adequate, or less conventional obstacles to Van and Ada's love. But then this impatience may be one of the aspects of what Edward Said, remembering Adorno, thinks of as 'lateness': a mingling of mastery and apparent ineptness, an unwillingness or an inability to work through the developments that are a crucial aspect of any mature (that is, not yet late) art. Nabokov was 70 when *Ada* was published. More immediately, the effect resembles that of an actor or an actress simulating an accident without entire success – so that we see the intention that is not supposed to be there. That is, either the supposed accident just looks intentional (I'm thinking of a moment in Buñuel's *Belle de jour*, where the script calls for Catherine Deneuve to drop some flowers involuntarily, and Deneuve, trying for this, creates a lovely image of a woman dropping flowers with evident distaste for the sender) or we see the intention to simulate an accident. At this level, it is the intention that becomes legible, becomes the text. Our text is not the series of obstacles which keep Van and Ada apart, but the manifest intention to keep them apart, even when the obstacles are not up to much. I don't mean we have to treat Nabokov's failure here as a success; only that the failure, in the context of so many successes, is revealing.

(ii)

What it reveals is the answer to our question about what it is, if not guilt, that pulls our lovers out of paradise. The answers, rather: a series of flaws or second thoughts within happiness itself. And the imagery of the novel makes richly clear what the plot indicates only in its parsimony. Nabokov, to repeat, doesn't think happiness is impossible; but he can't make it last. Why?

There is, first, a general fear of feeling, which I have already mentioned, a terror of the very happiness you seek and can't do without. There is, second, the sense, constitutive of love, surely, that either partner or both could change for no reason. This is how Van feels when he returns, aged eighteen, to see Ada after a long absence:

> the pang and panic of finding her changed, hating what he wanted, condemning it as wrong, explaining to him dreadful new circumstances – that they were both dead or existed only as extras in a house rented for a motion picture.

An incipient or smothered guilt plays a role here, of course; but the guilt is then used as fuel for uncertainty – love's own uncertainty, the uncertainty that feeds on whatever it can find. 'Whenever I start thinking of my love for a person,' Nabokov writes in *Speak, Memory*, 'I am in the habit of immediately drawing radii from my love . . . to monstrously remote points of the universe. Something impels me to measure the consciousness of my love against such un-imaginable and incalculable things as the behaviour of nebulae (whose very remoteness seems a form of insanity), the dreadful pit-falls of eternity, the unknowledgeable beyond the unknown, the helplessness, the cold, the sickening involutions and interpenetra-tions of space and time. It is a pernicious habit, but I can do nothing about it'. Sounds like referential mania, and this seems to be the sense of the remarkably oblique parable which Van attaches to the 'radiant amazement' of the start of his physical affair with Ada. 'Had it *really* happened?' he asks. 'Are we *really* free?'

> Certain caged birds, say Chinese amateurs shaking with fatman mirth, knock themselves out against the bars (and lie unconscious for a few minutes) every blessed morning, right upon awakening, in an automatic, dream-continuing, dreamlined dash – although they are, those iridescent dreamers, quite perky and docile and talkative the rest of the time.

Certain dreams, of love and freedom say, are stronger than any material fact, at least until they hit the bars. The birds' daily illusion is obviously more attractive than the Chinamen's realistic mirth, but their knocking themselves out is troubling, and their being so perky and docile and talkative is scarcely less so. The parable doesn't fit Van's case, since the cage has miraculously opened for him; but then it's striking that he should tell it. Perhaps he's think-ing of the ape in the Jardin des Plantes who drew the bars of his cage, and started Nabokov off on *Lolita*. In the midst of his amazing happiness he sketches a scenario which makes that happi-ness a forlorn dash into disappointment – as if disappointment were its ordinary habitat.

For there is, third among our flaws in happiness, the belief, en-demic to happiness, surely, not that it won't last but that it *can't*. Fate, and happiness's always imagined end, are expressions of the preciousness of the feeling: you measure it by what it would mean to lose it. 'The thrushes were sweetly whistling in the bright-green garden as the dark-green shadows drew in their claws.' Very beauti-ful, but the movement of the sentence makes claws and shadows the ordinary features of the garden, things that need to be withdrawn for the emergence of paradise; or at least it suggests that the claws and the shadows could come back as smoothly as they left. This is a way of saying, perhaps, that paradise and its loss are integral to each other. Not only that the true paradises are lost paradises, as Proust suggests, but that there is no paradise without loss, it isn't paradise if you can't lose it. Before he wrote his first novel, *Mary* (1925), Nabokov was working on but did not finish a novel called *Happiness [Schastie]*, and all his early stories turn on happiness and its loss: on loss as internal to happiness, not its end but its anticipated completion. 'It seemed to him,' we read in 'The Return of Chorb', 1925, 'that happiness itself had that smell, the smell of dead leaves'.

Van writes of the world of the book as 'Eden or Hades', and the imagery of paradise in *Ada*, once we look at it more closely, is far more ambiguous than Van's frequently gloating tone leads us to expect. In the following passage, the ostensible subject is Ada's infidelities, and we reach it through an affectionate parody of Tolstoy, helpfully named for us as such:

> We all know those old wardrobes in old hotels in the Old World subalpine zone. At first one opens them with the utmost care, very slowly, in the vain hope of hushing the excruciating creak, the growing groan that the door emits midway. Before long one discovers, however, that if it is opened or closed with celerity, in one resolute sweep, the hellish hinge is taken by surprise, and triumphant silence achieved. Van and Ada, for all the exquisite and powerful bliss that engulfed and repleted them (and we do not mean here the rose sore of Eros alone), knew that certain memories had to be left closed, lest they wrench every nerve of the soul with their monstrous moan. But if the operation is performed swiftly, if indelible evils are mentioned between two quick quips, there is a chance that the anesthetic of life itself may allay unforgettable agony in the process of swinging its door.

What's important here, I think, beyond Van's irritated vanity and the whole unequal question of male and female fidelity, is the language of pain and memory (excruciating, groan, wrench, moan, agony); the hellish hinge in the house of bliss, the oddly extreme 'indelible evils', the implication that life is an anaesthetic, that life needs an anaesthetic. It is (in part) the language of Pnin forcing himself not to remember the death of Mira Beloshkin, except that the occasion is more trivial, Van and Ada are far happier than Pnin, and they do remember what pains them, even if they have to do it in a rush. Above all, I want to suggest, the passage evokes a certain interdependence of happiness and misery. The long moan is not an accident, the echo of something that happens to happiness. It is inside happiness; when you speed it up you don't hear it, but you only seem to make it go away.

It is in this spirit, I think, that we should read a bilingual (or perhaps multilingual) pun which occurs several times in the novel, and links Ada's name phonetically with hell. 'I'll be with him in the depths *moego ada*', Ada says, translating the phrase herself as 'of my Hades'. She renders *adova dochka*, a play on a character's name in an imaginary work of literature, as 'Hell's daughter'. And twice, once from Ada, and once from Aqua, Van's supposed mother, we get the doubling of the pun which also involves the Russian word *iz*, out of. '*Teper' iz ada*', Aqua writes in her suicide note, now out of hell. And Ada in a letter offers a howl '*iz ada*'. Hell in this context is clearly unhappiness rather than disgrace or damnation; it is how you feel when you can't feel worse. But then what does the equation of Ada with this condition mean? And how does the double pun actually work, what is the eerie, almost uncanny effect it gets beyond its cleverness? *Iz ada*/is Ada. The mind construes 'out of' but the English-attuned ear receives 'is'. This *is* Ada, and Ada is Eden and Hades at once. She is Van's heaven and hell, could only be both. She is his happiness, his 'whole life', as he says; and she is also, the clash of languages suggests, the meeting which must constantly have taken place in Nabokov's mind, and which takes place in ours whenever we read this novel, unhappiness itself, the moan which awaits even the most perfect bliss, not because happiness is doomed, or because fate is unkind, but because happiness is intelligible only under threat; intelligible only as its own threat.

There is a last worry about happiness, a last clawed shadow to be looked at, and it is figured in the person of Van and Ada's half-sister Lucette. Well, it is also prefigured in the person of Aqua, gradually losing her mind and signing her last letter not only as someone 'now out of hell' but as 'my sister's sister'. Her very name disappears – there is no other signature to her letter – she is *only* a relationship, not a subject but only a foil, a mirror, an echo, the detritus of another life. Lucette, similarly, thinks of herself only as what she is not: not Ada, not part of the parading superimperial couple, not loved by Van. And she too commits suicide. It's clear that these dark strains in the novel are meant to get us to think again about all its vaunted happiness, and Bobbie Ann Mason and Brian Boyd have made this point well. But it's less clear what our thoughts are meant to be; what they can be. It's obvious, for example, that Dementiy and Marina have treated Aqua appallingly, foisting a child on her, persuading her that her own still-born baby somehow survived to become Van; but this heartless deception is evident, not even an inference, still less a meaning. We can't moralize what's already moralized.

There is a clue here, though. The temptation of all moralizers, even the most delicate, is to draft an alternative motion, to convert what they think should have happened into a moral imperative. This is to confuse behaviour which would have avoided the issue, maybe (people should have been nicer to Aqua), with the moral questions raised by the issue itself. If we can resist the should-have-been or the should-have-done – practical questions too late for practice – we can perhaps explore what Van calls 'real, or at least responsible, life' without falling into a pantomime of lessons to be learned. The case of Lucette requires all the moral agility we can muster.

She is four years younger than Ada. She has inherited her father's red hair and light fresh colouring, a contrast to Ada's dark hair and pale skin. In Van and Ada's first sex-drenched summers, Lucette is endlessly getting in the way, curious, pushed aside, learning more than she ought to but receiving less attention than she wants. Van and Ada lock her up, tie her up, leave her in the bathtub, tease her sexually. Later, when the lovers get together in Manhattan, just before their father discovers all and pronounces his edict, there is an extraordinary scene of sexual incitement *à trois*, where Van and Ada play in bed with a reluctant Lucette out of a kind of jubilation, an overflow of licence and happiness. Well, there's a touch of cruelty there too, a sense that their happiness needs a beautiful but unhappy witness, more than kin and all too kind. Van feels badly about it afterwards and apologizes for 'that shameful, though basically innocent scene'. Ada thinks this is 'pompous, puritanical rot'. The problem is that Lucette is in love with Van, and that neither Van nor Ada have any more time for her now than they had in their childhood. They are fond of her, and Ada has initiated her into all kinds of all-girl sexual activities; but when Ada says Van is breaking Lucette's heart he replies 'I cannot brood over broken hearts', and neither of them gives her another thought until much later. She is not even a speck on their happiness; she is what their happiness makes invisible.

Some years later, in 1901, Lucette and Van meet in Paris, and start to travel back to America on the same boat. Lucette has got it into her head that if she can persuade Van to sleep with her once, he will love her and stay with her, and she makes all kind of extravagant propositions. He will marry her, Ada will come and live with them, Lucette will leave them alone, they'll flourish happily ever after. At this point Nabokov produces the most marvellous writing in the book, and does several things better than he has ever done them.

He makes Lucette the most attractive of all his young women, perhaps of all his characters; she is funny, touching, gallant, physically irresistible. Like Pnin she is unfailingly polite, and even in the midst of her despair over Van shows a 'staunch courtesy' to a boring couple. When she sets about dying, she tries 'to think up something amusing, harmless, and scintillating to say in a suicide note', and the wit here is surely hers rather than Van's. Van thinks of himself as moral for not sleeping with her, but he seems just stuffy and hypocritical about his own desire, and is about to give in anyway, when he sees Ada in a film which is showing on board. This is enough to put him back on the path of notional virtue, he tells Lucette (falsely) that he has a woman with him, and so can't spend the night with her. She takes several sea-sickness pills and three stiff vodkas, and throws herself into the Atlantic. Her body is not found.

What Nabokov also does, apart from making Lucette so attractive, is develop to an extreme the mode of writing of the scenes concerning the death of David Krug in *Bend Sinister*. That is to say, he evokes a desperate bewilderment and distress through an apparent or initial alienation effect that makes much of Brecht look downright cosy. The result of this distancing is to make us scramble for closeness, claw at the obstacles to our emotion, find our own Lucette in the very language that seems to keep losing her. Her head starts to 'swim like hell' from the drugs and the drink. The idiom seems a grisly and tasteless joke until you realize it is Lucette's own. 'Swim like hell from sharks, Tobakovich!' The reference is Admiral Tobakoff, after whom the ship is named, and who is said to have saved his life by swimming around comfortably 'for hours, frightening away sharks with snatches of old songs and that sort of thing'. The language then becomes more decorous, close to pathos. Lucette can scarcely walk to the upper deck.

> While dragging herself up she had to hang on to the rail. Her twisted progress was that of a cripple. Once on the open deck she felt the solid impact of the black night, and the mobility of the accidental home she was about to leave.

This is strong, and elegant, but Nabokov now makes an extra-ordinary move. He introduces Van in the act of dictating this sombre prose, and Van's secretary in the act of mishearing it, and later not knowing how to spell it; then Van again losing his script.

> Although Lucette had never died before – no, *dived* before, Violet – from such a height, in such a disorder of shadow and snaking re-flections, she went with hardly a splash through the wave that humped to welcome her . . . Owing to the tumultuous swell and her not being sure which way to peer through the spray and the darkness and her own tentacling hair – t,a,c,l – she could not make out the lights of the liner, an easily imagined many-eyed bulk, receding in heartless triumph. Now I've lost my note.
> Got it.

When the next paragraph includes a pun on the secretary's name (Oceanus Nox/Violet Knox), you begin to think the writing has gone beserk, and there are more stumbles.

> At every slap and splash of cold wild salt, she heaved with anise-flavoured nausea and there was an increasing number, okay, or numbness, in her neck and arms. As she began losing track of her-self, she thought it proper to inform a series of receding Lucettes – telling them to pass it on and on in a trick-crystal regression – that what death amounted to was only a more complete assortment of the infinite fractions of solitude.

'Thought it proper' is perfect – Lucette is decorous even when she is drunk and dying – and the fractions of solitude are exquisite. The earlier bumbling and punning, you realize, comes from Van's own emotion, and the sight of this old man dictating a death he can scarcely bear to think about thickens and darkens the story without reducing its impact in the least. On the contrary. 'In my works, I try not to "explain" anything,' Van later says pompously in con-versation, 'I merely describe'. Earlier, he had said, more interestingly, of the family dinner party scene, that it was 'easier described than imagined'. Lucette's death is not described, and he can't really imagine it. What we see is his attempt to write it, with its combination of uncertain tone, distraction, a deep regret that is not quite guilt, and patches of spectacular verbal success. The chapter ends with a motorboat search for Lucette, and the younger Van in the water, 'who, having been propelled out of the boat when it shied from its own sudden shadow, kept bobbing and bawling the drowned girl's name in the black, foam-veined, complicated waters.' 'Complicated': the abstract word where we expected the concrete one. It makes the sound of trickery, as if the sea were the source of the absences and entanglements which consumed Lucette and her hopes of happiness.

It is at this point that we need to look at and get beyond the apparently practical moral question. What should Van and Ada have done about Lucette? Shouldn't Van have slept with her and made her happy? The very idea seems crass, and Nabokov has constructed his story to make it seem so. They could have behaved better, certainly, and they could have thought about the consequences of the sexual education they were imparting. It's true, as Ada says, that they 'did not love her enough'; not true, I think, as Ada also suggests, that they '*teased* her to death'. They could have altered their relation to her and perhaps its outcome. But they couldn't – couldn't have wanted to and couldn't have been expected to – refuse their happiness or in any way change her exclusion from it. She is like Kinbote, or Hazel, or Queen Disa in Kinbote's fantasy, closest to the last, perhaps, since she is so charming and vulnerable. But that is what happiness is; among other things, a form of brutality. It knows no charity, cannot resort to mere kindness. Van and Ada have many faults, but in regard to Lucette and her death their only fault is to love each other, and to remember their happiness, obsessively, when they have lost it; to fail to imagine, even from the shores of lost happiness, what the actual world of the unhappy looks like, or that there is such a world. 'I cannot express', Ada says after Lucette's death, 'how unhappy I am, the more so as we never learned . . . that such unhappiness could exist.' How could they learn, and why should they? What's unimaginably miserable about Lucette's death is the misery of the excluded life that led to it, the fixation on the happiness you can see but can't have. You'd have to be unhappy yourself to know that, and expect to stay unhappy. All unhappy families are alike, and happiness has no time for their sameness.

(iii)

What seem to be Van's last words – another bit of signature, recalling similar games in *Lolita* – appear just over a third of the way through the book, in the form of a note on the 'galley proofs which a bedridden old man heroically corrects'. He is shaky but unrepentant, and just as offensive as ever:

The asses who might really think that in the starlight of eternity, *my*, Van Veen's, and *her*, Ada Veen's, conjunction, somewhere in North America, in the nineteenth century represented but one trillionth of a trillionth part of a pinpoint planet's significance can bray *ailleurs, ailleurs, ailleurs* (the English word would not supply the onomato-poeic element; old Veen is kind), because the rapture of her identity, placed under the microscope of reality (which is the only reality), shows a complex system of those subtle bridges which the senses tra-verse – laughing, embraced, throwing flowers in the air – between membrane and brain, and which always was and is a form of memory, even at the moment of its perception. I am weak. I write badly. I may die tonight. My magic carpet no longer skims over crown canopies and gaping nestlings, and her rarest orchids. Insert.

The old wretch is wonderfully touching at the end of this para-graph, and *ailleurs*, elsewhere, is a nice cross-lingual joke. But the quantifying asses, even with their starlight, are far too easy a target; and as so often in Nabokov, something subtle and difficult lurks beneath the distracting bluster. We are not going to argue that the conjunction of Van and Ada doesn't matter in the long run; on the contrary, we are likely to think all human conjunctions matter, in the long and the short run. Any closely watched identity would show us the senses, happily or unhappily, traversing their subtle bridges, and it's easy to agree that the system of these bridges, in anyone, ought to be called memory. But this is not quite what Van wishes to propose. He says the rapture of Ada's identity – not just identity but the rapture of an identity, his ecstatic sense of the way she senses, and not just any identity, only Ada's – reveals to us what we need to know, and he is claiming not that everyone matters but that either he and Ada matter more than everyone, or no one mat-ters at all. It's the old game of dolts and geniuses, there is no middle position. Pnin believes in a democracy of ghosts, but Van believes, rather desperately, as the writing suggests, in an aristocracy of per-ception.

It's not easy to place Nabokov, or any of our Nabokovs, in this argument, and I suppose it's not meant to be easy. We should recall, probably, Humbert's cry towards the end of *Lolita*:

Unless it can be proven to me – to me as I am now, today, with my heart and my beard, and my putrefaction – that in the infinite run it does not matter a jot that a North American girl-child named Dolores Haze had been deprived of her childhood by a maniac, un-less this can be proven (and if it can, then life is a joke), I see nothing for the treatment of my misery but the melancholy and very local palliative of articulate art.

The 'genius' of the girl-child is no part of this proof, in success or failure, and even unrapturous childhoods have a right to continue. We may also want to think of Geoffrey Hill's magnificent lines in 'Funeral Music':

> If it is without
> Consequence when we vaunt and suffer, or
> If it is not, all echoes are the same
> In such eternity. Then tell me, love,
> How that should comfort us – or anyone
> Dragged half-unnerved out of this worldly place,
> Crying to the end 'I have not finished'.

Human difference, the incomplete human project, is asserted against the indifference of the realm where all echoes are the same. What matters is not the consequence or its absence, but the need for consequence; it is the need that makes us who we are. This isn't a comfort, any more than the argument about the echoes; but it means there is someone there, a person marked by lack, if by nothing else. Both Humbert's and Hill's implications are democratic here, in spite of the aristocratic manners and drift of much of what both have to say. What matters is the ordinary person, 'or anyone'; or rather the abolition of ordinariness, the rediscovered extravagance of who anyone is.

In one sense Nabokov, the (conservative) liberal and the American, certainly believed just this. But he would have thought it sentimental to regard any and all human differences as important, and he would have had considerable trouble in believing that difference was even a question for many people, or for most people. That's what a mob or a mass is, a set of supposed persons with only one voice or one thought, and that thought borrowed from somewhere else, some system of propaganda or long laid-down mythology. Of course, Nabokov had a mythology of his own, which precisely needed the masses, the flattened and vulgar backdrop against which his heroes, and he himself, could cut their distinguished figures; so that paradoxically his arguments about uniqueness and the rest have a slightly ready-made, off-the-peg quality: the difference, perhaps, is between a mass which thinks it

226

isn't one, and a mass which hasn't even thought about it. So Nabokov, with Van, must regard Van and Ada as very special, in ways that most other people are not; he has invented Van and Ada as embodiments, and very persuasive ones most of the time, of what being special means. Nabokov would also think, no doubt, that most of Van's detractors, actual and potential, within the fiction and without, are likely to be asses, and *Ada* is full of petulant and impatient dismissals of probable dissent. Van talks freely of his own 'genius', and regularly jumps on 'the innocents of critical appraisal, the social-scene commentators, the moralists, the idea-mongers and so forth':

> No accursed generalizer, with a half-penny mind and dry-fig heart, would be able to explain (and this is my sweetest revenge for all the detractions my lifework has met with) the individual vagaries evolved in those and similar matters [Van's 'adoration' of his father and 'indifference' to his mother]. No art and no genius would exist without such vagaries, and this is a final pronouncement, damning all clowns and clods.

These instances are – well, this last instance is – more emphatic and blinkered than Nabokov himself usually was, but the voice is very similar to the voice of the prefaces to his Russian works in English translation, and I take it he is giving Van a little extra licence rather than setting him up for serious criticism in this respect.

What we do need to see is that Van is sick and dying when he writes about the braying asses, that his own mixed stridency and tenderness is a part of his weakness; and that the stuff about the vagaries of art and genius is camouflage – real opinions used to hide real ambivalences of feeling. It's true that Van adores his raffish father, and that he doesn't care as he should for his mother. But a page or so before this outburst, he has re-created his mother's scatty speech with tremendous intimacy and sympathy ('Recollections are always a little "stylized" (*stilizovani*), as your father used to say, an irresistible and hateful man . . . I think even the shortest separation is a kind of training for the Elysian Games – who said that? I said that'), rather as Humbert is able to evoke the Lolita he himself can't see. Van's indifference to his mother is a matter of past, conscious practice, but it doesn't inform the writing; and the outburst about clowns and clods is designed to cover this discrepancy, to displace and simplify what anyone else would call guilt.

I think it's enough to see the situation here – to see Van as a situated, human, brilliant, fallible, opinionated writer with more than a passing resemblance to Nabokov. We don't have to separate Nabokov from Van in some categoric and stable, morally antiseptic way, as both Mason and Boyd do, with the best of intentions; and we don't have to assume Van *is* Nabokov, give or take a few thousand brothels and a bit of incest, as most other critics and readers do. Even David Rampton, having scrupulously identified the critical question ('I shall sometimes ascribe to Nabokov opinions that strictly speaking belong to his narrator, Van Veen' – this is better, Rampton says, than assuming that Nabokov maintains 'a controlled distance between himself and his narrator'), invites us to take Nabokov's 'non-fictional utterances as our guide' to the fictional world of *Ada*, as if there were no difficulty in doing this, and ends by seeing all Van's snobberies simply as Nabokov's own. My suggestion is that we don't need a single authorial opinion on these or any other matters, and that as far as any lively text is concerned, we can't have one anyway. We can find out what Nabokov (or several Nabokovs) thought of Van Veen by looking at the interviews collected in *Strong Opinions* ('Van Veen, the charming villain of my book', 'I loathe Van Veen', and so on). But these are only opinions, the simplifying testimony of an interested witness to a complex act. *Ada*, the novel, has no fixed opinions. Van is Nabokov; not Nabokov; the relation changes from page to page, and who is 'Nabokov' here anyway? The relation that chiefly matters in a text like this, and indeed in many texts, is not that of author to character, but of constructed character to reader. There is no reason for us to accept Van's views because they are Nabokov's, or to reject them because they are not. The question is, what do *we* think of them? What are their implications and consequences, where do they take us, or leave us? What do *we* make of the asses and the privileged perceptions of our heroes? It's easy to recognize the schemata of Van's anxious rhetoric, but if we take the democratic line about 'anyone' and the abolition of ordinariness, can we save ourselves from the temptation to refuse all distinctions, from an ideological praise of difference which may well end up as an indifference to everything, a failure of attention disguised as tolerance? Don't answer straight away.

Late in the book, craving and courting sympathy, Van describes himself as 'this strange, friendless, rather repulsive nonagenarian', hopefully adding 'cries of "no, no!" in lectorial, sororial, editorial brackets'. The difficulty with all of Van's self-accusations is that they turn into bids for our complicity. When he tells us that his young nurse went mad, as well as his mother, he thinks of Lucette's suicide too, and luridly writes 'no sooner did all the fond, all the frail, come into close contact with him . . . than they were bound to know anguish and calamity, unless strengthened by a strain of his father's blood'. He means only Ada is safe from him, safe with him, but he *is* repulsive here, a sort of Heathcliff without the excuse of passion, the Gothic hero who loves the thought of all the damage he's causing, takes it as a compliment. The damage is important, though, and we can take this thought further.

Van's response to complications in his life is always violence, sometimes ritualized by the aristocratic notion of the duel, sometimes not. When he learns that Ada has been unfaithful to him, he sets out to kill both suitors – as it happens Fate, alias Nabokov, gets there before him, arranging for one to die of tuberculosis, the other in a war. The goriest, nastiest moment in the book (if we except the scene in a brothel where Van tries out, for fun, a young boy with dysentery) involves Van's blinding of the man who spied on him and Ada in their early summers, and took photographs of them. Van makes the threat quite clearly – 'I will . . . horsewhip his eyes out' – but we think it's rhetorical. We learn that it wasn't only in a later narrative parenthesis about blackmailers: 'Kim . . . would have bothered Ada again had he not been carried out of his cottage with one eye hanging on a red thread and the other drowned in its blood'. This is bad enough, but Van's continuing contentment is worse. Ada regrets the deed, but Van doesn't. '"Amends have been made", replied fat Van with a fat man's chuckle.' He means the unfortunate Kim is in a home and has plenty of books in braille, but the chuckle is obscene, and he must know it, at least at the time of writing. He must remember too, even if we don't, his own parable of the fat Chinamen and their amusement at the error the caged birds keep making. We are not invited to like Van here, or even to dislike him. To wonder, rather, what gives him the right to be so pleased with himself, and how he can manage it.

The question is all the more urgent because he at first offers the horsewhipping of Kim and the book we are reading as alternatives: both of them forms of revenge for the snooper's photograph album, for what Van sees as an invasion and travesty of their love.

'I will either horsewhip his eyes out or redeem our childhood by making a book of it: *Ardis*, a family chronicle.'
   'Oh, do!' said Ada . . .

She means do make a book of it, but she seems to endorse both acts, or either. Banish plump Jack, and banish all the world. A page or so later Van decides he won't write the book, but we don't (I didn't, even on successive readings) fully realize what this means for poor, seedy Kim. Van used an alpenstock, apparently, rather than a horsewhip. We learn this from Ada, and her syntax, again, allows for an ambiguity. 'But, you know, there's one thing I regret: your use of an alpenstock to release a brute's fury'. This is the only time we hear about the actual weapon, so perhaps the awkwardness just comes from the passing on of 'rapid narrative information', as Ada calls it early in the book. But she does seem to say, or can be seen as saying, that she regrets the instrument rather than the deed. In any event, Van blinds the man *and* writes the book. Has he redeemed their childhood? He has immortalized it, as Humbert immortalized Lolita. But redemption in Van's sense – the rescue of their life from the eyes of others, a mode in which a book and a blinding can be seen as equivalents – is what no writer could really want to achieve, and fortunately Van doesn't achieve it. He remains pretty blind himself, morally, and I'm not sure Nabokov sees as much as he might. *Ada* is the book of paradise and also, in its way, a book of horrors. But the prose is all eyes, misses absolutely nothing, survives the death of the author and the monstrosity of the hero, and it will be best perhaps to fade out on what Van (rightly, I think), calls his purest sob, 'the purest *sanglot* in the book'. The French word sends us to Mallarmé's 'Après-midi d'un faune', with its satyr ravishing and losing two nymphs he found tangled in each other, creatures he calls the 'inhuman' one and the 'timid' one; cousins of Ada and Lucette, perhaps. His prey escapes him, he says, without pity for the drunken sob he was still caught up in, *Sans pitié pour le sanglot dont j'étais encore ivre*. Here is Van in an Italian brothel, far from Ada, and far from confident he will ever see her again:

A cauliflowered candle was messily burning in its tin cup on the window ledge next to the guitar-shaped paper-wrapped bunch of long roses for which nobody had troubled to find, or could have found, a vase. On a bed, some way off, lay a pregnant woman, smoking, looking up at the smoke mingling its volutes with the shadows on the ceiling, one knee raised, one hand dreamily scratching her brown groin. Far beyond her, a door standing ajar gave on what appeared to be a moonlit gallery but was really an abandoned, half-demolished, vast reception room with a broken outer wall, zigzag fissures in the floor, and the black ghost of a gaping grand piano, emitting, as if all by itself, spooky glissando twangs in the middle of the night. Through a great rip in the marbleized brick and plaster, the naked sea, not seen but heard as a panting space separated from time, dully boomed, dully withdrew its platter of pebbles, and, with the crumbling sounds, indolent gusts of warm wind reached the un-walled rooms, disturbing the volutes of shadow above the woman, and a bit of dirty fluff that had drifted down on to her pale belly, and even the reflection of the candle in a cracked pane of the bluish case-ment. Beneath it, on a rump-tickling coarse couch, Van reclined, pouting pensively, pensively caressing the pretty head on his chest, flooded by the black hair of a much younger sister or cousin of the wretched florinda on the tumbled bed. The child's eyes were closed, and whenever he kissed their moist convex lids the rhythmic motion of her blind breasts changed or stopped altogether, and was pre-sently resumed.

Style and signature; and a curious peace, as if time had stopped, as if the world ended in the delicate details of this misery.

Epilogue:
the History of Pain

Van Veen in *Ada*, like the Nabokov of *Speak, Memory*, affects not to believe in time; or in our time, the time that passes and is measured on clocks; that writes itself into the aging body, and never looks back. His quest is for what he variously calls true time, pure time, perceptual time, tangible time; the essence of time, the texture of time, the lining of time. 'I am also aware,' he says, 'that Time is a fluid medium for the culture of metaphors.' Worse, he is aware that virtually all these metaphors are borrowed from space, which he insists on seeing as the enemy. His project is to sever time from space ('One can be a hater of Space, and a lover of Time'), and to abolish the future as a temporal category ('The future is but a quack at the court of Chronos'). The future doesn't come after the present, in a straight line from the past, and the present isn't much of a straight line anyway. The future is always imaginary, and could always be cancelled, as it so often is in Nabokov: even John Shade's modest certainty that he will be alive tomorrow is ruined by a present event.

But then what is time, what time is left, and why is it so elusive? 'Why is it so difficult – so degradingly difficult – to bring the notion of Time into mental focus and keep it there for inspection? What an effort, what fumbling, what irritating fatigue!' The whole of *Ada*'s Part Four, a sort of essay-novella, is explicitly devoted to this problem, and much of the novel worries at it implicitly or obliquely. There are two answers to the question, I think, neither of which Van or Nabokov would much like, although they might accept the second as implicit in their own practice. The first is that the very object of inquiry is bogus, can't be focused because it doesn't exist. It is like looking for Language, or Goodness, or any other universal, rather than the thousands of shifting but identifiable things and groups of things we find in languages, behaviour and the world. There are many kinds of time: why would any of them be the only true time, an essence making all other times inessential? The second answer is that when Van says 'nowness is the only reality we know', speaks of a 'glittering "now"' as 'the only reality of Time's texture', and tries to capture the moment between moments, the

beat between the heartbeats, his quest is not for time at all but for
something like an awareness of awareness, a consciousness not of
self alone but of world *and* self in the instant of perception. Even
so, it seems like recycled Bergson, and pretty muddled; and fortunately Van the novelist keeps creeping up on Van the philosopher,
and Nabokov the novelist has never been away, and is more philosophical than either.

As Van speculates on time, he litters his language not only with
similes of space but with similes taken from motoring, from his
own journey from the Dolomites to Switzerland, in the summer of
1922, to meet Ada and live with her for the rest of their long lives.
The future he denies at this point is in one sense all there is, all he
cares about. It is the moment, yet to come, when he and Ada will
finally meet again. But of course he is right about its status: it is a
category of possibility and hope, not of time. Anything could happen, she might not be there when he arrives, she might never come;
she might be dead, he could die in an accident. The similes are
stealthy but insistent: a driving licence, reverse gear, speed and
curve, glove compartment, road map, red light, wipers, odometer,
tyres, highway symbols, blind bend. As we read, as the images
multiply and become clearer, we realize that they are not *only*
similes, that the essay is also a narrative, and Van finally drives into
Mont Roux, which I guess is what Montreux is called on Demonia,
'under garlands of heart-rending welcome' on a single day but at
several times. 'Today is Monday, July 14, 1922, five-thirteen p.m.
by my wrist watch, eleven fifty-two by my ear's built-in clock,
four-ten by all the timepieces in town.' No sight of pure time here,
although we might think all three times are right. Van has been
crossing space, taking time, dreaming his future even as he quarrels
with the familiar representations of those things. The result is to
qualify his arguments but not quite to wreck them. In part this is
because the fantasy of freedom from space and time and the future
is very powerful, and not confined to Van. Borges, alias Osberg,
has a wonderful essay called 'A New Refutation of Time', which
ends with a moving acknowledgement of the refutation's unravell-
ing:

And yet, and yet – To deny temporal succession, to deny the ego, to
deny the astronomical universe, are apparent desperations and secret
assuagements. Our destiny (unlike the hell of Swedenborg and the
hell of Tibetan mythology) is not horrible because of its unreality; it
is horrible because it is irreversible and iron-bound. Time is the sub-
stance I am made of. Time is a river that carries me away, but I am

the river; it is a tiger that mangles me, but I am the tiger; it is a fire that consumes me, but I am the fire. The world, alas, is real; I, alas, am Borges.

And Van, in any case, has another trick up his sleeve. When she arrives in Switzerland, Ada telephones him, as if she were reversing the role of Nabokov himself, in *Speak, Memory*, placing a call to a lost country. 'Now it so happened that she had never – never, at least, in adult life – spoken to him by phone; hence the phone had preserved the very essence, the bright vibration of her vocal chords, the little "leap" in her larynx, the laugh clinging to the contour of the phrase, as if afraid in girlish glee to slip off the quick words it rode. It was the timbre of their past, as if the past had put through that call, a miraculous connection . . .' Of course the call doesn't abolish time, or allow us to find its essence, in spite of Van's feeling that 'the very essence' of Ada's young voice still sounds in the fifty-year-old woman. Ada and Van have aged, and keep aging; can't, when they meet, recognize their old loves in these plump strangers. But the voice makes memory speak, and speak *now*; the past is present, time is neither lost nor found but multiplied. Nabokov is closer to Proust than he thought he was. There *are* cracks and loops in time, intermittences, they are what allow us to be time's subjects without being its slaves.

What is irrefutable about time for Nabokov, his version of Borges' river and fire and tiger, is its contribution to human pain. 'An element of pure time enters into pain', Van writes, 'into the thick, steady, solid duration of "I-can't-bear-it pain" . . .' I would gloss 'pure time', again, as awareness of awareness: the mind's attention to the body's irresistible story. As *Ada* ends, the words 'time' and 'pain' cross over. The couple is 'time-racked', they feel there is 'no pain' to finish the book, and it is 'high pain for *Ada* to be completed'. We remember Pnin and his thought that 'the history of man is the history of pain'. This is a reason for wanting to refuse or rewrite history, as Nabokov so often does. His fiction is full of forking paths, where contingency itself, the fact that things might be different, is a form of freedom. But it is also full of converging paths, flights or sketches that only confirm the existence of the prison, the zoo of words and things. Pain is the insufferable indignity, and the failure to remember or imagine it, as it brutalizes the self and others, is the unhappy privilege of solipsists and torturers. Nabokov's morality, a subtle, almost invisible, quirky, but curiously sturdy affair, is the magician's best act, a scene of refusal which is also a scene of recognition. The tricks are a glittering re-arrangement of the damage-strewn world, the pile of debris which Walter Benjamin called history; but they also represent what they rearrange, the world and its pain persist in these texts beyond all re-futation if not beyond elegant or arrogant resistance. The magician's doubts are inseparable from his successes. They *are* his successes, they sustain the magic that seems to make them vanish.

Chronology:
Works by Vladimir Nabokov
in English

(Dates of writing of Russian texts are given in brackets)

Laughter in the Dark	1938 (1931)
The Real Life of Sebastian Knight	1941
Nikolay Gogol	1944
Bend Sinister	1947
Speak, Memory	1951, 1966
Lolita	1955
Pnin	1957
Nabokov's Dozen	1958
Invitation to a Beheading	1959 (1934-1935)
Pale Fire	1962
The Gift	1963 (1936-1938)
The Defence	1964 (1929)
Eugene Onegin	1964
The Eye	1965 (1930)
Despair	1966 (1932)
The Waltz Invention	1966 (1938)
King, Queen, Knave	1968 (1928)
Ada	1969
Mary	1970 (1925)
Glory	1971 (1930)
Poems and Problems	1971
Transparent Things	1972
A Russian Beauty and other stories	1973 (1927-1940)
Strong Opinions	1973
Look at the Harlequins	1974
Tyrants Destroyed	1975 (1924-1939)
Details of a Sunset	1976 (1924-1935)
Lectures on Literature	1980

Notes

Full publication details are given on first listing of a work: thereafter short titles are used.

Preface: Tricks of Loss

3   'almost exclusively a writer': Vladimir Nabokov, *Selected Letters 1940-1977*, (Weidenfeld and Nicolson, 1990), p.382.

        simply says: Brian Boyd, *Vladimir Nabokov: the American Years*, (Chatto & Windus, 1991), p.662.

        lean lecturer: Nabokov, *Strong Opinions*, 1973: (Vintage, N.Y., 1990), p.xv.

        'Some day': Andrew Field, *VN: his life in part*, (Hamish Hamilton, 1977), p.249.

        'a terrible desire to write': Boyd, *Vladimir Nabokov: the American Years*, p.52.

        'the intensity of pain': Andrew Field, *VN: his life in part*, pp.249-250.

4   'I have lain', 'I get more and more dissatisfied', 'too old to change': Simon Karlinsky, ed, *The Nabokov-Wilson Letters 1940-1971*, (Weidenfeld and Nicolson, 1979), pp.120, 69, 44.

        'had to': Nabokov, 'On a book entitled *Lolita*', 1956: *Lolita*, (Penguin, 1980), p.315.

        'like moving': Boyd, *Vladimir Nabokov: the American Years*, p.35.

        'exceedingly painful': Nabokov, *Strong Opinions*, p.54.

5   'after fifteen years of absence': *Selected Letters*, p.149.

        'marvellous Russian language': Boyd, *Vladimir Nabokov: the American Years*, p.490.

        'Conrad knew': *Nabokov-Wilson Letters*, p.253.

6   'a profound sense of spiritual security': Elizabeth Beaujour, *Alien Tongues*, (Cornell University Press, 1989), p.84.

        'Curiosity': Nabokov, *Bend Sinister*, 1947: (Penguin, 1974), p.47.

7   as Roland Barthes says: Roland Barthes, 'Longtemps je me suis couché de bonne heure', 1978: in *Le Bruissement de la langue*, (Seuil, 1984), p. 321; *The Rustle of Language*, (Blackwell, 1986), p. 285.

8   'We think not in words': Nabokov, *Strong Opinions*, p.30.

        'I loved doing simple tricks': Nabokov, *Strong Opinions*, p.11.

Chapter 1: Deaths of the Author

9 [Epigraph] 'To write': Roland Barthes, *Critique et Verité*, (Seuil, 1966), p.34; *Criticism and Truth*, (Athlone Press, 1987), p.51.

10 'After the age of fifty': Julio Cortázar, *Un tal Lucas*, (Bruguera, 1979), pp.127-128; *A Certain Lucas*, (Knopf, 1988), p.140.'the middle of our life': Barthes, 'Longtemps je me suis couché de bonne heure', pp.320-321/284-285.

'as a kind of gradual accumulation': Nabokov, *Strong Opinions*, 1973: (Vintage, N.Y., 1990), p.10.

11 chronicled by Roland Barthes: 'La mort de l'auteur', 1968: in *Le bruissement de la langue/The Rustle of Language*, pp.61-67/49-55; and in *Image-Music-Text*, (Fontana, 1977), pp.142-148, and a number of anthologies.

'immense event': Friedrich Nietzsche, *Die fröhliche Wissenschaft ('La gaya scienza')*, 1882; in *Werke*, (Hanser, 1966), vol II, p.127; *The Portable Nietzsche*, (Penguin, 1976), p.96.

'No lyricism', 'The artist must so arrange things': Gustave Flaubert, letters of February 1 and March 27, 1852 to Louise Colet: *Correspondance*, 2e série (1847-1852), (Conard, 1926), pp.361, 380. [my translation]

'The author in his work': Flaubert, letter of December 9, 1852 to Louise Colet: *Correspondance*, 3e série (1852-1854), (Conard, 1927), pp.61-62.

12 'The artist, like the God of the creation': James Joyce, *Portrait of the Artist as a Young Man*, 1914-1915: (Penguin, 1992), p.233.

'the pure work': Stéphane Mallarmé, 'Crise de vers', 1896: in *Oeuvres complètes*, Gallimard, 1945, p.366. [my translation]

echoing absences: See especially *L'Ecriture et la différence*, (Seuil, 1967), *Writing and Difference*, (Routledge, 1978); and *La Dissémination*, (Seuil, 1972), *Dissemination*, (Athlone Press, 1981).

'The progress of an artist': T S Eliot, 'Tradition and the Individual Talent', 1919: *Selected Essays*, (Harcourt, Brace & World, 1964), pp.7, 10-11.

'the bundle of accident': W B Yeats, 'A general introduction for my work', 1937: *Essays and Introductions*, (Collier Books, 1968), p.509.

'a book is the product': Marcel Proust, 'La méthode de Sainte-Beuve', 1908: in *Contre Sainte-Beuve*, (Gallimard, 1971), pp.221-222; *Against Sainte-Beuve*, (Penguin, 1988), p.12.

like the ghostly twin: Henry James, 'The Private Life', 1892: *The Figure in the Carpet and other stories*, (Penguin, 1986), pp.189-231.

13 the American New Critics: See especially W K Wimsatt/Monroe Beardsley, 'The Intentional Fallacy', 1946: in W K Wimsatt, *The Verbal Icon*, (Methuen, 1970), p.4.

13 'search for "real life"': Aleksandr Pushkin, *Eugene Onegin*, translated from the Russian, with a Commentary, by Vladimir Nabokov, (Princeton University Press, 1975), Vol II, p.5.
  'As Pushkin's historian', 'republish a dead author's works': *Eugene Onegin*, Vol I, p.59.

14 'unless these and other mechanisms': *Eugene Onegin*, Vol I, p.7.
  'to beware of applying': Jonathan Swift, *The Battle of the Books*, 1704: *Gulliver's Travels and other writing*, (Bantam Books, 1962), p.396.

15 'Student explains': Nabokov, *Strong Opinions*, p.30.

16 'The birth of the reader': Barthes, 'La mort de l'auteur', pp.67/55/148.
  'not merely the product': Lionel Trilling, 'Freud and literature', 1947: *The Liberal Imagination*. (Anchor Books, 1953), p.49.

17 'something outside life': Boyd, *Vladimir Nabokov: the Russian Years*, (Chatto & Windus, 1990), p.192.
  'never to remember': Nabokov, *Pnin*, 1957: (Penguin, 1960), p.112.
  'austere, cold,': Dmitri Nabokov, 'Introduction', *Selected Letters*, p.xvii.

18 'and really': John Updike, dustjacket, *Selected Letters*.
  '"unpleasant" quality': Nabokov, *Selected Letters*, p.150.
  'the best part': Nabokov, *Strong Opinions*, pp.154-155.
  'Writing': Barthes, 'La mort de l'auteur', pp.61/49/142.

19 'Every piece of writing': Jacques Derrida, *De la Grammatologie*, (Editions de Minuit, 1967), p.100; *Of Grammatology*, (Johns Hopkins University Press, 1976), p.69.
  'But in the text': Roland Barthes, *Le plaisir du texte*, (Seuil, 1973), pp.45-46; *The Pleasure of the Text*, (Farrar, Straus and Giroux, 1975), p.27.
  'author function': Michel Foucault, 'Qu'est-ce qu'un auteur?', *Bulletin de la société francaise de philosophie*, 1969, p.83; 'What is an author?', in *Language, Counter-Memory, Practice*, (Blackwell, 1977), p.125.

20 'will always be impossible': Barthes, 'La mort de l'auteur', pp.61/49/142.
  Barthes himself: Roland Barthes, *S/Z*, (Seuil, 1970; Farrar, Straus and Giroux, 1974).

21 'the man who suffers': Eliot, 'Tradition and the individual talent', p.8.

22 impeccably told: Brian Boyd, *Vladimir Nabokov: the Russian Years*; *Vladimir Nabokov: the American Years*, 1990 and 1991).

23 'You shall be': Ben Jonson, *The Fortunate Isles*, in *Ben Jonson*, ed Herford and Simpson, (Clarendon Press, 1941), Vol.vii, p.712. I am grateful to Gareth Roberts for this reference.

24 'The front hall': Nabokov, *Lolita*, 1955: (Penguin, 1980), pp.36-37.

25 'What I heard': *Lolita*, p.306.
  'Gently I rolled back': *Lolita*, pp.291-292.

26   'That Friday evening': Nabokov, 'Signs and Symbols', 1948: *Nabokov's Dozen*, (Penguin, 1960), pp.53-54.

Chapter 2: Lost Souls: *The Real Life of Sebastian Knight*

29   [Epigraph] 'the martyr': Geoffrey Hill, 'Of commerce and society', in *Collected Poems* (Penguin, 1985), p.51.
       The real: Henry James, Preface to *The American*, 1907: *The Art of the Novel*, (Scribner's, 1962), p.31.

30   'Now he had caught something real': Nabokov, *The Real Life of Sebastian Knight*, 1947: (Penguin, 1964): All references are to this edition.

31   'Real' belongs: J.L. Austin, *Sense and Sensibilia*, 1959: (Oxford University Press, 1964), p.73.
       'oppressive and tender': Nabokov, *The Eye*, 1930: (Penguin, 1992), p.91.

36   Pierre Menard's version: Jorge Luis Borges, 'Pierre Menard Autor del Quijote', 1941: *Ficciones*, (Emecé, 1956), pp.45-57; *Labyrinths*, (Penguin, 1970), pp.62-71.

45   Vladimir Alexandrov sees: Vladimir Alexandrov, *Nabokov's Otherworld*, (Princeton University Press, 1991), pp.150, 154.

47   her book on strangers: Julia Kristeva, *Etrangers à nous-mêmes*, 1988: (Gallimard, 1991), p.12; *Strangers to Ourselves*, (Harvester, 1991), p.3.

48   Kristeva suggests: Kristeva, *Etrangers à nous-mêmes*, pp.55, 57/*Strangers to Ourselves*, pp.36, 38.

50   to Edmund Wilson he writes: *Nabokov-Wilson Letters*, p.44.
       Robert Alter suggests: Robert Alter, *Necessary Angels*, (Harvard University Press, 1991), pp.21, 75-76.

Chapter 3: The Cruelty of Chance

55   [Epigraph] 'No, wait a minute': Jean Stafford, 'The Philosophy Lesson', in *Collected Stories* (Hogarth Press 1986), p.369.
       'The notion of symbol': VN, *Strong Opinions*, p.304, 305. See also W W Rowe, *Nabokov's Deceptive World*, (New York University Press, 1971).

56   'A few feet away', *Nabokov's Dozen*, p.54.
       'the sound of a bath': Nabokov, *Strong Opinions*, p.305-306.

57   'So suddenly': Nabokov, *Bend Sinister*, 1947, (Penguin, 1974), p.178. All references are to this edition.

59   as Barthes says: Roland Barthes, *La chambre claire*, (Gallimard Seuil, 1980), pp.150-151; *Camera Lucida*, (Jonathan Cape, 1982), p.96.

59   'the death of a child': Richard Rorty, *Contingency, Irony, and Solidarity*, (Cambridge University Press, 1989), p.163.

64   'A German student': Nabokov, *Speak, Memory*, (Penguin, 1969), pp.213-214.

65   'an inability to put up with': Rorty, *Contingency, Irony, and Solidarity*, p.155.

66   Nabokov said: Nabokov, *Selected Letters*, p.117.

67   'the fatal error', 'some correspondence': Nabokov, *Lectures on Don Quixote* (Weidenfeld & Nicolson, 1983), pp.1, 4.
'Real life': Nabokov, *Nabokov's Dozen*, p.176.
'In these very rare cases': Nabokov, 'Signs and Symbols', 1948: in *Nabokov's Dozen*, pp.54-55. All references are to this edition.

68   'I shall have occasion to speak': Nabokov, *Gogol*, 1944: (Oxford University Press, 1989), pp.63-64.
a splendid book: *The Oxford Companion to the Mind*, ed Richard L Gregory, (Oxford University Press, 1987), pp.576-577.

71   'never *can* directly know': Henry James, Preface to *The American*, pp.31-32.

73   'beings akin to him': Nabokov, *Invitation to a Beheading*, 1935: (Penguin, 1963), p.191.
'It may all end': Nabokov, 'That in Aleppo once . . .' , 1943: *Nabokov's Dozen*, p.123.

75   'I could isolate': Nabokov, 'The Vane Sisters', 1959: in *Tyrants Destroyed and Other Stories*, (Penguin, 1981), p.219. All references are to this edition.
'I am really quite depressed', 'My difficulty': Nabokov, *Selected Letters*, p.117, 286.

76   'my difficulty': *Selected Letters*, p.284.
'this particular trick': Nabokov, note in *Tyrants Destroyed*, p.201.
'rather sniffily replied', 'the coincidence of Cynthia's spirit': *Selected Letters*, pp.118, 117.

79   Borges' story: Jorge Luis Borges, 'La loteria en Babilonia'/'The Lottery in Babylon', in *Ficciones/Labyrinths*, pp.67-75/55-61.
'no different one by one': Thomas Pynchon, *V.*, 1963: (Bantam Books, 1964), p.433.

81   Nabokov had heard,: Boyd, *Vladimir Nabokov: the American Years*, p.190.
Nabokov grumbles: Boyd, p.191.

Chapter 4: The World Without Us: *Speak, Memory*

83   [Epigraph] 'Is history not simply that time': Roland Barthes, *La*

Chambre claire, (Seuil, 1980), pp.100-1; *Camera Lucida* (Jonathan Cape, 1982), p.64.

83   'I confess I do not believe': Nabokov, *Speak, Memory*, 1966: (Penguin, 1969), p.109. All references are to this edition.

90   as Jane Grayson notes: Jane Grayson, *Nabokov Translated*, (Oxford University Press, 1977), pp.224-226.

91   brilliantly discussed: Boyd, *Vladimir Nabokov: the Russian Years*, pp.7-8.

Chapter 5: The Language of *Lolita*

103   [Epigraph] 'I only write like this': Alexander Pushkin, *Eugene Onegin*, translated by Charles Johnston, (Scolar Press, 1977), p.25.
        'a breeze from wonderland': Nabokov, *Lolita*, 1955 (Penguin, 1980), p.131. All references are to this edition.

104   'whatever it is': F. W. Dupee, 'A Preface to *Lolita*', 1955: in *The King of the Cats*, (University of Chicago Press, 1984), p.119.

105   'Writing, you know': Plato, *Phaedrus*, tr. by W C Helmhold and W G Rabinowitz (Bobbs-Merrill, 1956), pp.69-70.

106   Derrida's famous claim: Jacques Derrida, *De la Grammatologie/Of Grammatology*, pp.227/158.

107   'No, it is not *my* sense', 'I would put it differently': Nabokov, *Strong Opinions*, pp.93, 94.

110   'Colloquial baroque': Alfred Appel, '*Lolita*: the springboard of parody', in L S Dembo, *Nabokov: the man and his work*, (University of Wisconsin Press, 1967), p.136.

111   'not quite fair': *Nabokov-Wilson Letters*, p.51.
        'Easy, you know, does it, son': Nabokov, *Transparent Things*, 1972, (Penguin, 1975), p.107.
        the poet John Shade: Nabokov, *Pale Fire*, 1962: (Penguin, 1973), p.58.

112   'extremely *distrait*': Nabokov, *Strong Opinions*, p.211.

117   the ground floor: Mary McCarthy, 'A Bolt from the Blue', 1962: in *The Writing on the Wall*, (Harcourt, Brace & World, 1970), p.16.

118   As René Girard has pointed out: René Girard, '*To double business bound*', (John Hopkins University Press, 1978), pp.188-195. Girard is concerned with what he calls 'texts of mystified persecution', involving lynching, anti-semitism, all forms of scapegoating. The particular sentence I am thinking of is: 'We cannot read the text of persecution, correctly unless we become able to rehabilitate the victims, to realize that the accusations against them are groundless.'

121   'having so much imagination': Henry James, 'The Jolly Corner', 1908: in *Selected Tales*, (Everyman, 1982), p.369.

'the precursor who may already': Rorty, *Contingency, Irony, and Solidarity*, p.154.

123   as Lucy Maddox has pointed out: Lucy Maddox, *Nabokov's Novels in English*, (University of Georgia Press, 1983), p.78.

125   'some delegate of the Mann Act': The Mann Act (1910) prohibited the transporting of women across state lines for immoral purposes. If a woman was a minor the penalty could be doubled. I am grateful to Richard Maltby for these details.

127   'I was very despairing': Franz Kafka, 'Brief an den Vater', 1919: 'Letter to his Father/Brief an den Vater', (Schocken Books, 1966), pp.18-21.

128   'The manner in which all of the pieces': quoted in Walter and Miriam Schneir, *Invitation to an Inquest*, (W H Allen, 1966), p.370.

130   went into such detail: Nabokov, *Strong Opinions*, p.163.

133   'It is a brave affair': Wallace Stevens, 'Notes toward a Supreme Fiction', 1942: in *The Palm at the End of the Mind*, (Vintage, N.Y., 1972), p.229.

135   'Life's nonsense': Stevens, 'Notes toward a Supreme Fiction', p.209.

'I shall be remembered': Nabokov, *Strong Opinions*, p.106.

136   as David Rampton attractively argues: David Rampton, *Vladimir Nabokov*, (Cambridge University Press, 1984), p.114.

139   Michael Long thinks: Michael Long, *Marvell, Nabokov*, (Clarendon Press, 1984), p.150.

Appel and Rampton: Appel, '*Lolita*: the springboard of parody', p.128, Rampton, *Vladimir Nabokov*, pp.114-115.

140   'dictated by some principle of compensation', 'intricately sordid situations': Dupee, 'A preface to *Lolita*', pp.125, 112-113.

141   'I believe in my abandonment': Geoffrey Hill, 'Funeral Music', 1968: *Collected Poems*, (Penguin, 1985), p.75.

Chapter 6: The Poem of the Past: *Eugene Onegin*

143   [Epigraph] 'Then practice losing farther': Elizabeth Bishop, 'One Art', in *Geography III*, (Farrar, Straus & Giroux, 1776), p.40.

'stopped by a similar stutter': Nabokov, *Invitation to a Beheading*, p.7.

'Languages are not strangers': Walter Benjamin, 'Die Aufgabe des Übersetzers', 1923: *Schriften*, IV.1, (Suhrkamp, 1972), p.12. *Illuminations*, (Schocken Books, 1969), pp.72.

144   'Ce beau jardin': Nabokov, *Ada, or Ardor: a family chronicle*, 1969: (Penguin, 1971), p.76.

144   by Raymond Queneau: Raymond Queneau, *Exercices de style*, (Gallimard, 1947); *Exercises in Style*, (John Calder, 1979); *Zazie dans le métro*, (Gallimard, 1959), *Zazie in the Metro*, (John Calder, 1982). Nabokov read both books, and described the former as 'a thrilling masterpiece' [*Strong Opinions*, p.173].

          'Central reciprocal relationship': Benjamin, *Schriften*, IV.1, p.12; *Illuminations*, p.72.

          'that elaborately choice French': Leo Tolstoy, *War and Peace*, 1869: translated by Constance Garnett (Heinemann, 1911), p.1.

          'an incomplete, feeble translation': Pushkin, *Eugene Onegin*, 1831: translated by Nabokov (Princeton University Press, 1964), Vol.I, p.164. All references are to this edition.

145   translates and transliterates: Nabokov, *The Real Life of Sebastian Knight*, pp.156-157.

146   'and everything': Nabokov, *Lolita*, p.182.

          Van Veen, after seeking: Nabokov, *Ada*, p.237.

          'I shall be remembered', 'Flaubert speaks': Nabokov, *Strong Opinions*, pp.106, 77.

147   Alexander Gerschenkron: Alexander Gerschenkron, 'A Magnificent Monument?', *Modern Philology*, 63 (1966), quoted in John Johnston, 'Translation as Simulacrum', in Lawrence Venuti, ed, *Rethinking Translation*, (Routledge, 1992), p.45. Gerschenkron's article, by another sort of translation, appears in the bibliography of Brian Boyd's *Vladimir Nabokov: the American Years* (p.751), as 'A Manufactured Moment?', same journal, same date. The journal itself, I have to report, has neither of the above but 'A Manufactured Monument?'

          Charles Johnston's excellent 1977 version: Alexander Pushkin, *Eugene Onegin*, translated by Charles Johnston, (Scolar Press, 1977).

148   'You always came too late': Douglas Robinson, *The Translator's Turn*, (John Hopkins University Press, 1991), p.243.

149   anathema: See Venuti, *Rethinking Translation*, especially Venuti's introduction, pp.1-17, and Lori Chamberlain, 'Gender and the Metaphorics of Translation,' pp.57-74.

150   the hallowed concepts: Walter Benjamin, 'Das Kunstwerk im Zeitalter seiner technischen Reproduzierbarkeit', 1936: *Schriften*, I, 2, p.431; 'The work of art in the age of mechanical reproduction', *Illuminations*, p.218.

          What we have: cf. Andrew Benjamin, 'Translating Origins', in Venuti, p.33: 'A translation does not unify a complex event, thereby rendering it singular or self-identical. Translation is only possible because of the complexity.'

          'hope's deceptive dinner', 'a monotonous breed': Pushkin, *Eugene Onegin* [Johnston], pp.46, 132.

151   'but now the mansion is forsaken': Pushkin, *Eugene Onegin* [Johnston], p.155.

153   'greatest happiness': Nabokov, *Strong Opinions*, p.69.

154   'He who is not in some measure': The reference is to Hazlitt's 'On Pedantry', 1817.

155   author of a commentary: *Evgenij Onegin*, edited with an introduction and commentary by Dmitry Cizevsky, (Harvard University Press, 1953).

156   'least of all a clown': Nabokov, *Selected Letters*, p.178.

Chapter 7: Pnin's Revenge

157   [Epigraph] 'I have discovered': Nikolai Gogal, *Diary of a Madman and Other Stories*, translated by Ronald Wilks, (Penguin, 1972), p.38.
    '"My name is so-and-so"': Nabokov, *The Real Life of Sebastian Knight*, p.118.

158   'the elderly passenger': Nabokov, *Pnin*, 1957: (Penguin, 1960), p.7. All references are to this edition.

166   as Paul de Man has shown: Paul de Man, *Allegories of Reading* (Yale University Press, 1979), pp.278-301.

170   a very interesting essay: Alex de Jonge, 'Nabokov's uses of pattern', in Peter Quennell, ed, *Nabokov: a tribute*, (Weidenfeld & Nicolson, 1979), p.65.
    'All Nature is but Art': Alexander Pope, *Essay on Man*, 1733-1734: in *Poems*, (Yale University Press, 1963), p.515.
    'Only as an aesthetic phenomenon': Friedrich Nietzsche, *Die Geburt der Tragödie*, 1872: *Werke*, Vol.I, p.40; *The Birth of Tragedy* (Vintage, N.Y., 1967), p.52.
    as Michael Silk and Peter Stern suggest: M S Silk and J P Stern, *Nietzsche on Tragedy*, (Cambridge University Press, 1981), p.295.

171   'To be quite candid': Nabokov, *Strong Opinions*, p.45.
    'James Joyce's mistake': *Strong Opinions*, p.30.

Chapter 8: The Demons of our Pity: *Pale Fire*

173   [Epigraph] 'I have been too unhappy': Jean Rhys, *Wide Sargasso Sea*, (Penguin, 1968), p.92.
    'baldheaded suntanned professor': Nabokov, *Pale Fire*, 1962: (Penguin, 1973), p.221. All references are to this edition.

174   'Pnin saw himself': Nabokov, *Pnin*, p.91.

175 'the boy ... and Pnin': Nabokov, *Strong Opinions*, p.84.

Brian Boyd suggests: Brian Boyd, *Vladimir Nabokov: the American Years*, p.274: 'Nabokov did not think up *Pale Fire* until two years after writing this chapter of *Pnin*, and did not begin writing the novel for another three years after that'.

'An Italian film': Nabokov, *Pnin*, pp.71-72.

176 and Zembla appears: Pope, *An Essay on Man, Poems*, p.523.

177 'A Jack-in-the-box': Mary McCarthy, *The Writing on the Wall*, p.15.

178 as Lucy Maddox does: Lucy Maddox, *Nabokov's Novels in English*, p.21.

182 'It is as if yesterday': Borges, 'Pierre Menard', in *Ficciones/Labyrinths*, pp.62/45.

184 'disorder of auctioneered Viennese bric-à-brac': Nabokov, *Lolita*, p.252.

186 'after putting the last touches': Nabokov, *Strong Opinions*, p.74.

187 'Ask where's the North': Pope, *An Essay on Man, Poems*, p.523.

part of what Pope means: Pope, *Poems*, p.502.

189 Boyd is persuasive: Brian Boyd, *Vladimir Nabokov: the American Years*, p.445.

191 behind Robert Frost: Robert Frost, 'Design', in *Poems*, (Washington Square Press, 1971), p.212:

> What had that flower to do with being white,
> The wayside blue and innocent heal-all?
> What brought the kindred spider to that height,
> Then steered the white moth thither in the night?
> What but design of darkness to appall? –
> If design govern in a thing so small.

192 Nabokov in a letter: Nabokov, *Selected Letters*, p.57.

193 'the annals of a mind': Tony Sharpe, *Vladimir Nabokov*, (Edward Arnold, 1991), p.85.

203 Death is not an event in life: Ludwig Wittgenstein, *Tractatus Logico-Philosophicus*, (Routledge & Kegan Paul, 1961), p.72.

204 as Barthes says: Roland Barthes, *S/Z*, pp.190/184.

205 'destroyed a kind of privacy': Thomas Pynchon, *V*, p.230.

Chapter 9: Happy Families: *Ada*

206 [Epigraph] 'a novel in the old mood': Alexander Pushkin, *Eugene Onegin*, translated by Nabokov, (Princeton Unversity Press, 1981), p.155.

'Their craving for each other': Nabokov, *Ada*, 1969: (Penguin, 1971), p.112. All references are to this edition.

211   'pure language': Benjamin, *Schriften*, IV.1, pp.14, 17, 18/*Illuminations*, pp.74, 77, 79.
'Whatever we see': Wittgenstein, *Tractatus*, p.58.

212   Brian Boyd and others: Vladimir Alexandrov, *Nabokov's Otherworld*, 1991; Brian Boyd, *Nabokov's Ada: the place of consciousness*, (Ardis, 1985); W W Rowe, *Nabokov's Spectral Dimension*, (Ardis, 1981).

217   remembering Adorno: Edward Said, 'Adorno as lateness itself', unpublished lecture given in London, 1993 and in Exeter, 1994.

218   'Whenever I start thinking': Nabokov, *Speak, Memory*, p.227.

219   'It seemed to him': Nabokov, 'The Return of Chorb', 1925: *Details of a Sunset*, (Weidenfeld & Nicolson, 1976), p.65.

220   have made this point well: Bobbie Ann Mason, *Nabokov's Garden: a guide to Ada*, (Ardis, 1974), Brian Boyd, *Nabokov's Ada*, 1985.

225   'Unless it can be proven': Nabokov, *Lolita*, p.281.

226   'If it is without': Geoffrey Hill, *Collected Poems*, p.77.

228   even David Rampton: David Rampton, *Vladimir Nabokov*, p.122.
looking at the interviews: Nabokov, *Strong Opinions*, pp.120, 143.

Epilogue

233   recycled Bergson: for example, from Henri Bergson, *Essai sur les données immédiates de la conscience*, 1889; *Matière et mémoire*, 1896; *La Pensée et le mouvement*, 1934.
'And yet, and yet': Jorge Luis Borges, *Otras inquisiciones*, (Emecé, 1960), p.256; *Other Inquisitions*, (Washington Square Press, 1966), p.197.

235   which Walter Benjamin called history: Walter Benjamin, 'Über den Begriff der Geschichte', 1940: *Schriften*, I,2, p.697; 'Theses on the philosophy of history', *Illuminations*, p.257.

Index